Red Book Plus:
Family Court Essential Materials
2015–2016

Red Book Plus:
Family Court Essential Materials
2015–2016

JORDAN PUBLISHING

PRACTICE PLUS

Published by Family Law
a publishing imprint of
Jordan Publishing Limited
21 St Thomas Street
Bristol BS1 6JS

British Library Cataloguing-in-Publication Data

A catalogue record for this book is available from the British Library.

ISBN 978 1 78473 164 9

Typeset by Letterpart Limited, Caterham on the Hill, Surrey CR3 5XL

Printed in Great Britain by CPI Group (UK) Ltd, Croydon, CR0 4YY

Foreword to the First Edition

I am delighted to have been asked to introduce this work, a companion to *The Family Court Practice* ('the Red Book') and a guide to the more common applications in the Family Court. Helpful cross-references appear in the opening sentences of each section, both to the Red Book and to Jordan Publishing's *PracticePlus*, with innovative flowcharts to assist the practitioner at various stages of the application.

This is a refreshing and informative guide which outlines the steps to be taken from start to finish, accompanying those steps with reminders and tips, alerting the practitioner to common pitfalls faced in the legal process and the frequent hurdles placed in the way of the client. Common errors, additional powers of the court, and practical advice which even the more experienced practitioner will find immensely useful (from attending court with copy documents to draft letters of instruction, communication with professionals and lay parties) are presented to the reader clearly and succinctly. One of the many skills which the family lawyer must call upon is the ability to communicate with the court, colleagues and clients and state agencies in a helpful and informed manner, and these tips are innovative and valuable. Assistance of this nature is not found in the major procedural works – there is no room for such matters – and it is enormously valuable, to have such a practical aide memoire at one's elbow.

The opening contents pages are an accessible route to the step-by-step guides which populate this work, referring the practitioner across to the authoritative source material, found within the Red Book, via the now familiar procedural guides.

The fifty pages of annexed guides to applicable tax rates, fostering allowances, 'passport' benefits and the RPI, to name but a few, will be of considerable help to those advising on financial remedies and even child care, as will the narratives on common problems and pitfalls which ensnare unsuspecting applicants.

Dry and impersonal this companion work is not, and I anticipate that it will sit comfortably with the Red Book on the shelves of all family practitioners, just as it will slip easily into the advocate's briefcase on the way to court!

His Honour Judge Anthony Cleary
November 2014

CONTENTS

PART II

KEY LEGISLATION

PART III

LEADING CASES

PART I

PRACTICE NOTES AND FLOWCHARTS

UNDEFENDED DIVORCE/CIVIL PARTNERSHIP DISSOLUTION

FLOWCHART

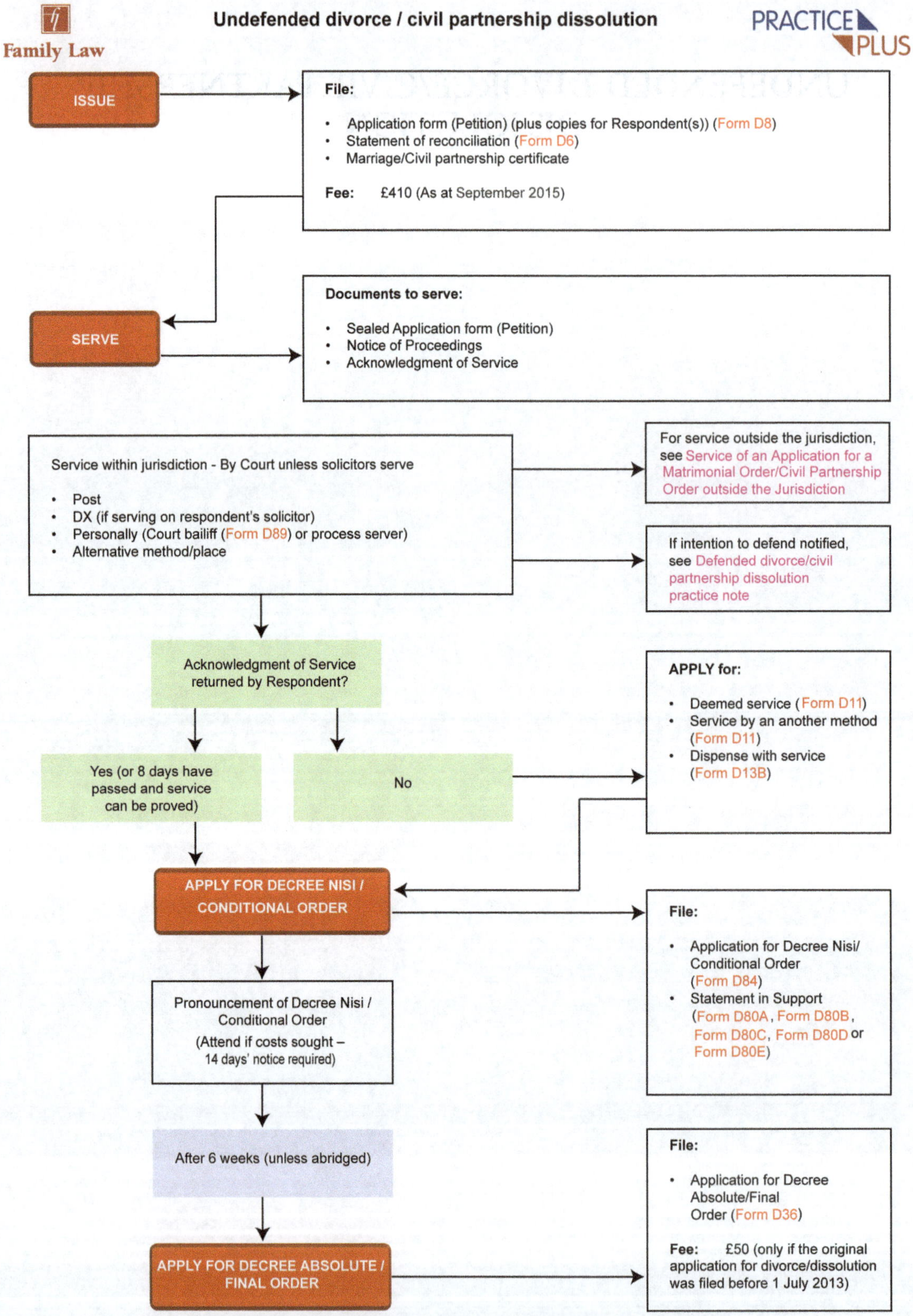
Family Law
Undefended divorce / civil partnership dissolution
PRACTICE PLUS
ISSUE
File:
• Application form (Petition) (plus copies for Respondent(s)) (Form D8)
• Statement of reconciliation (Form D6)
• Marriage/Civil partnership certificate
Fee: £410 (As at September 2015)
SERVE
Documents to serve:
• Sealed Application form (Petition)
• Notice of Proceedings
• Acknowledgment of Service
Service within jurisdiction - By Court unless solicitors serve
• Post
• DX (if serving on respondent's solicitor)
• Personally (Court bailiff (Form D89) or process server)
• Alternative method/place
For service outside the jurisdiction, see Service of an Application for a Matrimonial Order/Civil Partnership Order outside the Jurisdiction
If intention to defend notified, see Defended divorce/civil partnership dissolution practice note
Acknowledgment of Service returned by Respondent?
Yes (or 8 days have passed and service can be proved)
No
APPLY for:
• Deemed service (Form D11)
• Service by an another method (Form D11)
• Dispense with service (Form D13B)
APPLY FOR DECREE NISI / CONDITIONAL ORDER
File:
• Application for Decree Nisi/ Conditional Order (Form D84)
• Statement in Support (Form D80A, Form D80B, Form D80C, Form D80D or Form D80E)
Pronouncement of Decree Nisi / Conditional Order
(Attend if costs sought – 14 days' notice required)
After 6 weeks (unless abridged)
APPLY FOR DECREE ABSOLUTE / FINAL ORDER
File:
• Application for Decree Absolute/Final Order (Form D36)
Fee: £50 (only if the original application for divorce/dissolution was filed before 1 July 2013)

PRACTICE NOTE

See also Procedural Guide (PG) B2 in *The Red Book (Family Court Practice)*.

Issue

A marriage or civil partnership may be dissolved on the ground that it has broken down irretrievably (MCA 1973, s 1(1); CPA 2004, s 44(1)). Application is made to the Family Court (by application form, formerly by petition) for a matrimonial or civil partnership order. The parties must have been married/in a civil partnership for more than a year (MCA 1973, s 3(1); CPA 2004, s 41(1)) before an application is made. For more information about whether the court has jurisdiction to hear the divorce/dissolution see the guidance in *Family Court Practice* (*the Red Book*) at Article 3, Brussels II Revised (Council Regulation (EC) No 2201/2003).

Guidance on the divorce/dissolution process is set out in leaflets D183 and D184 (available at http://hmctsformfinder.justice.gov.uk/HMCTS/FormFinder.do).

For details regarding the centralisation of the divorce process (View from the President's Chambers: the process of reform: an update [2014] Fam Law 1259) and which court centre proceedings should be sent to, see http://www.familylaw.co.uk/news_and_comment/changes-to-the-divorce-process-in-england-and-wales-q-a and http://www.familylaw.co.uk/news_and_comment/resolution-meets-with-hmcts-regarding-new-centres-for-divorce and be alert to communications from the courts when issuing applications.

Documents

The application form (formerly the petition) (Form D8)

To prove that the marriage or civil partnership has broken down irretrievably, the applicant (petitioner) must prove one or more of five facts set out in MCA 1973, s 1(2) or, in the case of a civil partnership, four facts in CPA 2004, s 44(5).

The five facts are:

- Adultery (MCA 1973, s 1(2)(a)) (not available for civil partnership dissolution) (only conduct with a person of the opposite sex may constitute adultery – MCA 1973, s 1(6)).
- Behaviour (MCA 1973, s 1(2)(b); CPA 2004, s 44(5)(a)).
- Desertion (MCA 1973, s 1(2)(c); CPA 2004, s 44(5)(d)).
- Two years' separation and consent (MCA 1973, s 1(2)(d); CPA 2004, s 44(5)(b)).
- Five years' separation (MCA 1973, s 1(2)(e); CPA 2004, s 44(5)(c)).

Useful guidance on completing the application form is set out at *Supporting notes for guidance on completing a divorce/dissolution/(judicial) separation petition* (Form D8 (Notes)). At Part 10, section 3(a) it is usual to tick all of the financial remedies even if it is anticipated that not all of them will be required.

Also see the notes to precedents A1, A2, A3, A4 and A5 (*Family Law Precedents Service*) and Procedural Guide B2 (PG) (*Family Court Practice*) (*the Red Book*). Members of Resolution should ensure that they refer to the Resolution Code of Conduct when drafting the petition.

A co-respondent should not normally be named (see further FPR 2010, PD 7A, para 2.1).

Statement of reconciliation (Form D6)

This should only be completed if the applicant is legally represented. See the notes to precedent A8 (*Family Law Precedents Service*).

Marriage certificate/civil partnership certificate

If the original marriage/civil partnership certificate has been lost a certified copy can be ordered from the General Register Office (http://www.gro.gov.uk/gro/content/certificates/default.asp). If the application is urgent it is sometimes possible to attend the Local Register Office in person to obtain a certified copy. It is also possible to make an application without the marriage certificate in urgent cases (see further FPR 2010, PD 7A, paras 3.2 – 3.4). See precedent A5A (*Family Law Precedents Service*).

If the marriage/civil partnership certificate is not in English a notarised translation must also be filed (FPR 2010, PD 7A, para 3.1(b)).

Tips:

- Remember to include enough copies of the application form (petition) (normally three – one for the applicant, one for the court and one for the respondent).
- Do not forget to check the court fee (£410 as at September 2015) and include a cheque or postal order payable to 'HM Courts and Tribunals Service' or 'HMCTS'. The fee can also be paid in cash or by debit/credit card.
- If service is to be carried out by the applicant's solicitor remember to ask the court for 'solicitor service' at the time of filing the documents at court.
- If timing is an issue (eg a jurisdiction race) make a note of exactly when the application is filed.
- If you think you will be serving the petition outside England and Wales it is worth contacting the Foreign Process Section before filing the petition, to check if there are any special requirements for the petition to enable it to be served successfully. The foreign process section's email address is foreignprocess.rcj@hmcts.gsi.gov.uk and their telephone number is 0207 947 6691/7786/6488/6327/1741.

Serve

The following documents are required to be served on the respondent and any co-respondent (FPR 2010, r 7.8):

(1) the sealed application form (petition);

(2) the notice of proceedings; and

(3) the acknowledgment of service.

FPR 2010, Part 6, Chapter 2 governs the service of an application for a matrimonial order or civil partnership order within the jurisdiction (rr 6.3 – 6.22). Also see PD 6A.

The court will serve the documents on the respondent (and any co-respondent) unless 'solicitor service' is requested at the time of filing the documents at court.

See precedents B64 and B65 (*Family Law Precedents Service*) for an example letter to send to the respondent (or his or her solicitor) enclosing the documents for service. Members of Resolution should also refer to Resolution Guides to Good Practice on Correspondence and Service of Documents.

The application for divorce/dissolution can be withdrawn at any time before it is served by giving the court written notice (FPR 2010, r 7.9). See precedent B41 (*Family Law Precedents Service*).

Methods of service

- *Service by post* (FPR 2010, r 6.4(b))
  Service must be by first class post (or other service which provides for delivery on the next business day).
  The respondent must be served at his usual or last known address (FPR 2010, r 6.13) (unless the respondent has given another address to be served at (FPR 2010, r 6.12) or the respondent's solicitor is to accept service on the respondent's behalf in accordance with FPR 2010, r 6.11). If the usual or last known address is not known reasonable enquiries must be made (FPR 2010, r 6.13(3)). If, following reasonable enquiries, the respondent's usual or last known address cannot be ascertained the applicant can make an application to court to authorise service by an alternative method or at an alternative place (FPR 2010, r 6.19). See further 2010, PD 6A, paras 6.1 – 6.4.
- *Service by DX* (FPR 2010, r 6.4(c))
  Only where the respondent's solicitor has notified the applicant in writing that they are instructed to accept service on behalf of the respondent (FPR 2010, r 6.11).
- *Personal service* (FPR 2010, r 6.7)
  Personal service can be effected by a bailiff (FPR 2010, r 6.9) or by a process server. The petitioner may not effect personal service (FPR 2010, r 6.5(3)). A request must be made to the court for service by a bailiff in accordance with PD 6A, paras 11.1 – 12.2. The request must be made on Form D89.
  If a process server effects personal service and no acknowledgment of service is filed a certificate of service stating the date and time of personal service must be filed (FPR 2010, r 6.17) (Form FP6). Also see precedent B45 (*Family Law Precedents Service*) for an example affidavit of service in more complicated cases.

If acting for the respondent the acknowledgment of service must be completed and filed at court within 7 working days (FPR 2010, rr 7.12 and 2.9(4)). The 7 day rule applies only to cases in which the application was served within the jurisdiction – see FPR 2010, Part 6, Chapter 4, FPR 2010, r 6.42 and FPR 2010, PD 6B for cases where the application was served outside the jurisdiction (also see Service of an Application for a Matrimonial Order/Civil Partnership Order outside the Jurisdiction practice note).

If no acknowledgment of service is returned the following options are available to the applicant:

- ***Application for deemed service*** (FPR 2010, rr 6.15, 6.16) (Form D11)
  See precedent B46 (*Family Law Precedents Service*) and Part 18 practice note.
- ***Application for service by another method*** (FPR 2010, r 6.19) (Form D11)
  See above. See precedent B47 (*Family Law Precedents Service*) and Part 18 practice note.
- ***Application to dispense with service*** (FPR 2010, r 6.20)
  This must be made on Form D13B and requires supporting evidence. See precedent B51 (*Family Law Precedents Service*).
  It must be verified by a statement of truth.

Tips:

- If instructing a process server remember to provide them with a photograph of the respondent if possible as the process server will be required to show his or her means of knowledge of the identity of the person served (FPR 2010, r 6.17(3)).
- It is a good idea to take a copy of the documents to be served by the process server so that they can be exhibited to the process server's affidavit of service (if necessary).

Apply for decree nisi/conditional order

The first decree is called a decree nisi or conditional order (MCA 1973, s 1(5); CPA 2004, s 38).

In an undefended case an application for decree nisi/conditional order can be made (FPR 2010, r 7.20) once either:

- the acknowledgment of service has been returned; or
- 8 days have passed since service of the application and the applicant can prove service; or
- an order for deemed/dispense of service has been made.

Documents

Application for decree nisi/conditional order (Form D84)

This can be signed by the applicant's solicitor. It must be accompanied by a statement in support (see below).

Statement in support (Forms D80A-D80E)

There are different statements in support depending on which facts are relied upon in the application (petition) to prove irretrievable breakdown of the marriage/civil partnership:

- Form D80A – Adultery (not civil partnership);
- Form D80B – Behaviour;
- Form D80C – Desertion;
- Form D80D – 2 years and consent;
- Form D80E – 5 years.

The statement in support must be verified by a statement of truth. It should exhibit a copy of the signed acknowledgment of service.

Useful guidance is also set out in leaflet D186 (available at http://hmctsformfinder.justice.gov.uk/HMCTS/FormFinder.do).

Certificate

If the court is satisfied with the application for decree nisi/conditional order it will issue a certificate (FPR 2010, r 7.20(2)) (D84A (Certificate of Entitlement to a Decree) or D584A (Certificate of Entitlement to a Conditional Order)). It will give a date for the pronouncement of decree nisi/conditional order.

Costs

The court may deal with costs when dealing with a FPR 2010, r 7.20(2) certificate. If a party wishes to be heard on costs claimed against them written notice should be served on every party 14 days before the hearing for pronouncement of decree nisi/conditional order (FPR 2010, r 7.21(2) as amended by the Family Procedure (Amendment) Rules 2015).

Useful guidance on children and divorce/dissolution is set out in leaflet D185 (available at http://hmctsformfinder.justice.gov.uk/HMCTS/FormFinder.do).

Withdrawal of the application after service

If the application form has been served an application for an order to dismiss it must be made on Form D11 under the Part 18 procedure (see Part 18 practice note). The application can be made by consent. If opposed it must be made on notice. See precedent B43 (*Family Law Precedents Service*). See *Chai v Peng (No 2)* [2015] 1 FLR 637.

Apply for decree absolute/final order

Normal application for decree absolute/final order by the petitioner

An application for decree absolute/final order may be made (by the petitioner only) 6 weeks and one day after the pronouncement of decree nisi/conditional order (MCA 1973, s 1(5); CPA 2004, s 38(1); FPR 2010, r 7.32). The application should be made on Form D36. If the original application for divorce/dissolution was filed before 1 July 2013 there is a fee of £50.

Expedited application to apply for decree absolute/final order

An application to court to make a special order to fix a shorter time for applying for decree absolute/final order can be made (MCA 1973, s 1(5); CPA 2004, s 38(4)). The application should be made on Form D11, see precedent B40 (*Family Law Precedents Service*) and Part 18 practice note. Also see FPR 2010, PD 7A, paras 8.1 – 8.4.

Application for decree absolute/final order more than 12 months after decree nisi/conditional order

If the application for decree absolute/final order is made more than 12 months after the pronouncement of decree nisi/conditional order FPR 2010, r 7.32(3) requires that a document (1) explaining the delay; (2) stating whether the parties lived together since decree nisi; and (3) stating whether another child has been born to the couple and (if so) whether it is a child of the family is filed with the application for decree absolute/final order. This can be in the form of a letter or an affidavit (or statement verified by a statement of truth), see precedent B39 (*Family Law Precedents Service*).

Application on notice by respondent to apply for decree absolute/final order

The respondent may apply on notice for decree absolute/final order three months after the first date upon which the petitioner may have applied for decree absolute/final order (MCA 1973, s 9(2); CPA 2004, s 40(2); FPR 2010, r 7.33). The application should be made on Form D11. See precedent B37 (*Family Law Precedents Service*) and Part 18 practice note.

Useful guidance is also set out in leaflet D187 (available at http://hmctsformfinder.justice.gov.uk/HMCTS/FormFinder.do).

AMENDING AN APPLICATION FOR DIVORCE/DISSOLUTION (FORMERLY A PETITION)

FLOWCHART

Family Law

PRACTICE PLUS

Amending an application for divorce/dissolution (formerly a petition)

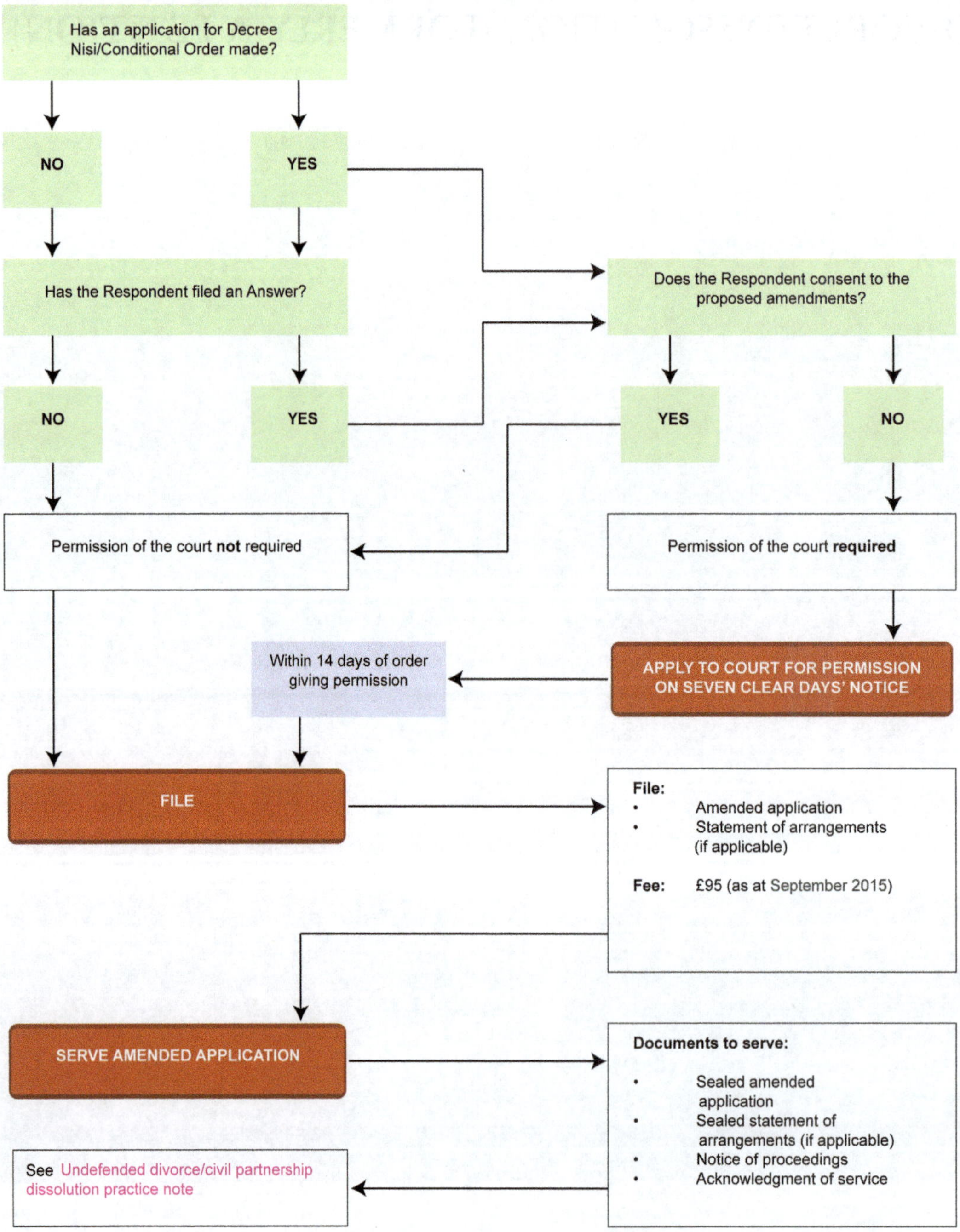

PRACTICE NOTE

See also Procedural Guide (PG) B2 in *The Red Book (Family Court Practice)*.

Apply to court for permission on seven clear days' notice

Amending an application for divorce/dissolution (petition) and making a supplemental application are governed by FPR 2010, r 7.13, which is supplemented by FPR 2010, PD 7A, paras 5.1 – 5.4.

You do **not** need permission from court to file an amended or a supplemental application for divorce/dissolution (petition) if:

- the respondent has not filed an answer and no application for decree nisi/a conditional order has been made (FPR 2010, r 7.13(1)(a), r 7.13(2)(a) and r 7.13(2)(b)); or
- the respondent(s) give written consent to the proposed amendments (FPR 2010, r 7.13(5)(a)).

You need permission if:

- the respondent has filed an answer **and** does not consent to the proposed amendments (FPR 2010, r 7.13(1)(c) and r 7.13(5)(a));
- an application for decree nisi/conditional order has been made **and** the respondent does not consent to the proposed amendments (FPR 2010, r 7.13(3) and r 7.13(6)(a)).

Application for permission

An application for permission is made under the Part 18 procedure (see further Part 18 practice note).

Documents

Application form (Form D11)

See precedent B1 (*Family Law Precedents Service*).

Statement (can be included in box 10 of the Form D11)

Set out the basis upon which the application is made (FPR 2010, r 18.7(1)). Must be verified by a statement of truth (FPR 2010, r 17.3).

Draft order

FPR 2010, r 18.7(2) requires that a draft order is attached to the application. See precedent B4 (*Family Law Precedents Service*).

Draft amended application

A copy of the proposed amended petition should accompany the application (FPR 2010, r 18.7(2), Practice Direction 7A, para 5.2(b)). See below and precedent B2 (*Family Law Precedents Service*).

Timing

7 days' notice to be given (FPR 2010, PD 18A, para 6.1).

Service

Normal service rules apply (see Service (not of an application for a matrimonial/civil partnership order) practice note).

Hearing of the application for permission

FPR 2010, PD 7A, para 5.1 states that an application for permission to amend an application for a matrimonial or civil partnership order or answer may be dealt with at a hearing.

Tips:

- When filing the application at court remember to include enough copies of the application form and supporting documents (normally three – one for the applicant, one for the court and one for the respondent).
- Do not forget to check the court fee (£50 for applications without notice or £155 for applications on notice as at September 2015) and include a cheque or postal order payable to 'HM Courts and Tribunals Service' or 'HMCTS'. The fee can also be paid in cash or by debit/credit card.

File amended application

Documents

Amended application

- Use a copy of the original application (Form D8) as a base.
- Ensure the amended application is headed 'Amended' in red and underlined.
- Type/write all amendments clearly in red and underline them in red.
- Strike through any deletions to the original application with a red line.
- The application will need to be re-dated and re-signed (below the original date and signature).
- The application should state in the margin either 'Amended without permission pursuant to FPR 2010, r 7.13(2).' or 'Amended pursuant to permission granted [*date*].'

Also see precedent B2 (*Family Law Precedents Service*).

If the application is by consent the amended application should state on the face of it – '[I/We] consent to an order in the terms of this application'- and should be signed below by the respondent or his solicitor (if on the record) (this is because the respondent's consent has to be written (FPR 2010, r 7.13(5)(a))).

The amendments to the application should either:

- be formal amendments (eg addresses); or
- if they are amendments to the particulars, be ones that relate to events occurring before the issue of the original application.

If the amendments deal with events that have occurred after the original application was filed, a supplemental application can be filed as opposed to an amended application (see precedents B7–B9 (*Family Law Precedents Service*)). Following the case of *Kim v Morris* [2013] 2 FLR 1197 the position was that a supplemental application could not be filed. This was on the basis they were omitted from the Family Procedure Rules 2010.

The Family Procedure (Amendment No 4) Rules 2014, however, took effect from 1 April 2015 to include in FPR 2010, r 7.13 supplemental applications along with the provisions about amendments of applications and answers.

If the amendments relate to a ground that was unavailable at the time the original application was issued a further application, as opposed to an amended application, should be filed (see precedents B10 and B11 (*Family Law Precedents Service*)).

A supplemental application should be drafted in Form D8.

Form D11 (only if the amendments are made by consent)

If the parties both consent to the amendments they should apply in a Form D11 to amend the application at the same time as filing the amended application. See precedent B3 (*Family Law Precedents Service*). The application should attach a draft consent order (FPR 2010, r 18.7(2)). See precedent B4 (*Family Law Precedents Service*).

The court will not list a hearing and will deal with the Form D11 and amended application on paper.

Timing

If the amended application is being filed subsequent to obtaining the court's permission, it must be filed within **14 days** of the date of the order giving permission (or other time period as the court directs) (FPR 2010, PD 7A, para 5.3).

Where permission is not required there is no time limit for filing an amended application, save that the applicant should bear in mind that the amended application should be filed prior to an answer being filed (otherwise the court's permission will be needed – unless the respondent consents to the amendments).

Tips:

- When filing the amended application at court remember to include enough copies of the application form and supporting documents (normally three – one for the applicant, one for the court and one for the respondent).
- It is a good idea to file a covering letter at court with the documents. If the amendments are by consent the letter should briefly explain the circumstances of the agreement and refer to FPR 2010, r 7.13(5)(a). If the amendments are made following an order of the court giving permission to file an amended application reference should be made to that order and a copy enclosed.
- Do not forget to check the court fee (£95 as at September 2015) and include a cheque or postal order payable to 'HM Courts and Tribunals Service' or 'HMCTS'. The fee can also be paid in cash or by debit/credit card.

Serve amended application

Documents to be served:

(1) Sealed amended application.

(2) Notice of proceedings.

(3) Acknowledgment of service.

When to serve

If an order for permission has been granted the court may have given directions as to the time period for serving the amended application (FPR 2010, r 7.13(7)(a)), otherwise the FPR 2010 does not state whether there are any time limits for serving an amended application.

Who to serve

Again, if an order for permission has been granted the court may have given directions as to who should be served (for example if the court has directed the joining of a party (FPR 2010, r 7.13(7)(b)) or that a party should cease to be a party (FPR 2010, r 7.13(8)).

If an order for permission has not been obtained the respondent(s) should be served as usual (see Undefended divorce/civil partnership dissolution practice note).

If, as a consequence of the amendments, there is a new co-respondent, he or she should be served (FPR 2010, r 7.13(4)(c)).

Method of service

The rules regarding service of an amended application are the same for service of the original application (see Undefended divorce/civil partnership dissolution practice note) save if the court has directed otherwise.

APPLICATION FOR A FINANCIAL ORDER (NOT AN INTERIM ORDER) UNDER MCA 1973 OR CPA 2004 PRE-PROCEEDINGS TO FIRST APPOINTMENT

FLOWCHART

Family Law

Applications for a financial order (not an interim order) under MCA 1973 or CPA 2004 Pre-proceedings to First Appointment

PRACTICE PLUS

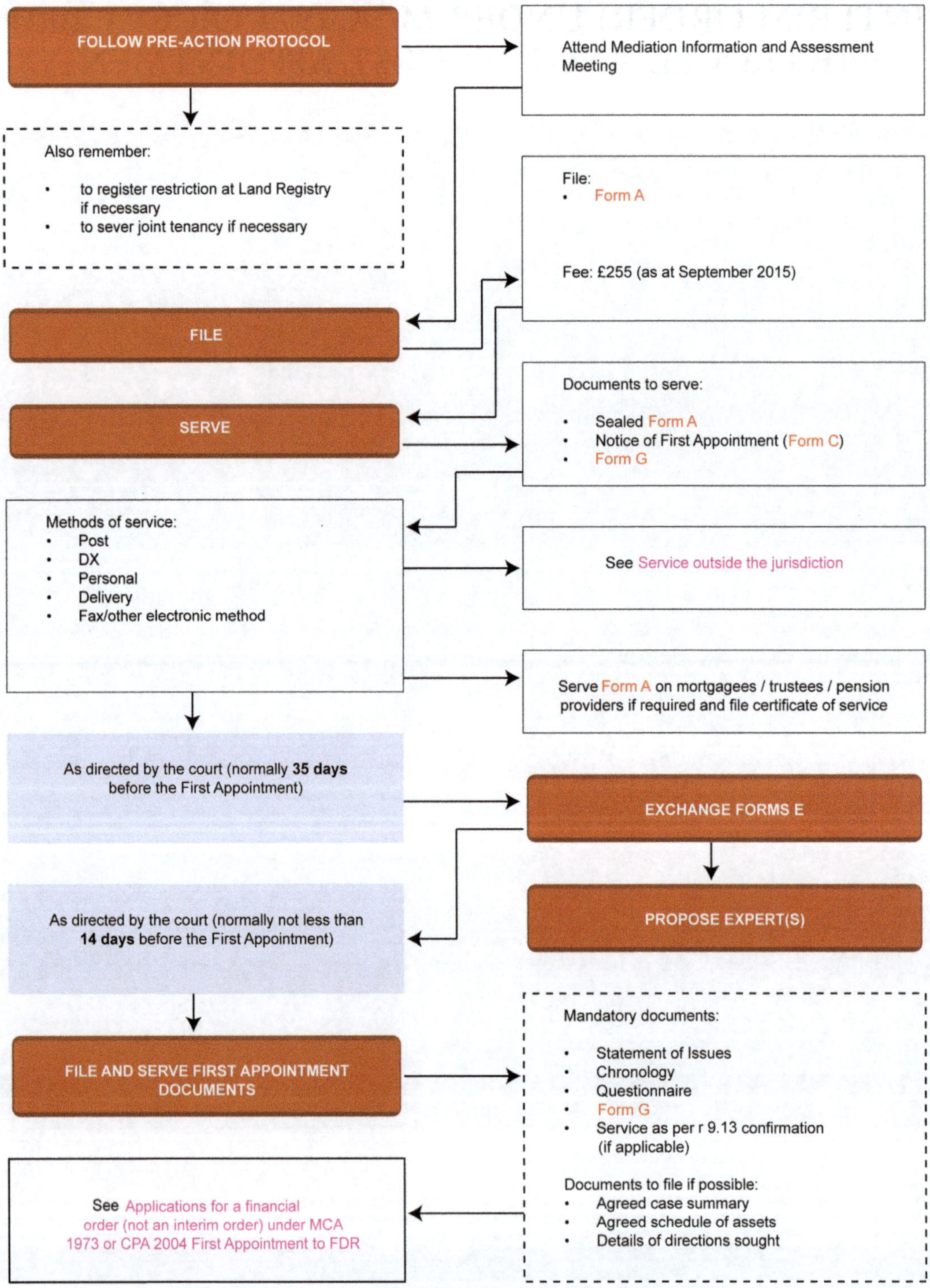

PRACTICE NOTE

See also Procedural Guide (PG) B5 in *The Red Book (Family Court Practice)*.

Follow pre-action protocol

FPR 2010, PD 9A annexes the pre-application protocol.

Paragraphs 1 – 4 outline the scope of the protocol. It is intended to apply to all applications for a financial remedy as defined by rule 2.3.

First letter

The first letter to the respondent:

- should be approved by the client in advance (FPR 2010, PD 9A, Annex, para 5);
- must focus on the clarification of claims and identification of issues and their resolution (FPR 2010, PD 9A, Annex, para 13); and
- must not raise irrelevant issues or those which might cause the other party to adopt an entrenched, polarised or hostile position (FPR 2010, PD 9A, Annex, para 14).

Solicitors writing to an unrepresented party should always recommend that he or she seeks independent legal advice and enclose a second copy of the letter to be passed to any solicitor instructed. A reasonable time limit for an answer may be 14 days (FPR 2010, PD 9A, Annex, para 5). The impact of any correspondence upon the reader and in particular the parties must always be considered.

Pre-application disclosure and negotiation

Parties are encouraged to negotiate and reach a settlement before an application to court is made although the protocol warns that excessive or disproportionate costs should not be incurred (FPR 2010, PD 9A, Annex, para 12).

Voluntary disclosure is commonly provided in Form E, which is condoned by FPR 2010, PD 9A, Annex, para 12, although not mandatory.

An application should not be issued where settlement is a reasonable prospect following pre-application disclosure and negotiation (FPR 2010, PD 9A, Annex, para 6).

Mediation Information and Assessment Meeting

Before filing an application for a financial remedy the applicant is required to attend a Mediation Information and Assessment Meeting ('**MIAM**') (FPR 2010, r 3.6). Any application for proceedings for a financial remedy (specified in FPR 2010, PD 3A, para 13) must be accompanied by a form containing either (a) a confirmation from an authorised family mediator that the prospective applicant has attended a MIAM; (b) a claim by the prospective applicant that one of the MIAM exemptions applies; or (c) a confirmation from an authorised family mediator that a mediator's exemption applies.

MIAM exemptions:

Domestic violence

- There is evidence of domestic violence, as specified in PD 3A, para 20 (FPR 2010, r 3.8(1)(a)).

Child protection concerns

- A child would be the subject of the application; and that child or another child of the family who is living with that child is currently the subject of enquiries by a local authority under section 47 of the 1989 Act or the subject of a child protection plan put in place by a local authority (FPR 2010, r 3.8(1)(b)).

Urgency

- The application must be made urgently because (FPR 2010, r 3.8(1)(c)):
  - there is risk to the life, liberty or physical safety of the prospective applicant or his or her family or his or her home or any delay caused by attending a MIAM would cause a risk of harm to a child; a risk of unlawful removal of a child from the United Kingdom, or a risk of unlawful retention of a child who is currently outside England and Wales; a significant risk of a miscarriage of justice; unreasonable hardship to the prospective applicant; or irretrievable problems in dealing with the dispute (including the irretrievable loss of significant evidence); or
  - there is a significant risk that in the period necessary to schedule and attend a MIAM, proceedings relating to the dispute will be brought in another state in which a valid claim to jurisdiction may exist, such that a court in that other State would be seised of the dispute before a court in England and Wales.

Previous MIAM attendance or MIAM exemption

- In the 4 months prior to making the application, the person attended a MIAM or participated in another form of non-court dispute resolution relating to the same or substantially the same dispute or at the time of making the application, the person is participating in another form of non-court dispute resolution relating to the same or substantially the same dispute (FPR 2010, r 3.8(1)(d)).
- In the 4 months prior to making the application, the person filed a relevant family application confirming that a MIAM exemption applied and that application related to the same or substantially the same dispute (FPR 2010, r 3.8(1)(e)).
- The application would be made in existing proceedings which are continuing and the prospective applicant attended a MIAM before initiating those proceedings (FPR 2010, r 3.8(1)(f)).
- The application would be made in existing proceedings which are continuing and a MIAM exemption applied to the application for those proceedings (FPR 2010, r 3.8(1)(g)).

Other

- There is evidence that the prospective applicant is bankrupt, as specified in FPR 2010, PD 3A, para 21 and the proceedings would be for a financial remedy (FPR 2010, r 3.8(1)(h)).
- The prospective applicant does not have sufficient contact details for any of the prospective respondents to enable a family mediator to contact any of the prospective respondents for the purpose of scheduling the MIAM (FPR 2010, r 3.8(1)(i)).
- The application would be made without notice (see further FPR 2010, PD 18A, para 5.1) (FPR 2010, r 3.8(1)(j)).

- The prospective applicant is or all of the prospective respondents are subject to a disability or other inability that would prevent attendance at a MIAM unless appropriate facilities can be offered by an authorised mediator; the prospective applicant has contacted as many authorised family mediators as have an office within fifteen miles of his or her home (or three of them if there are three or more), and all have stated that they are unable to provide such facilities; and the names, postal addresses and telephone numbers or e-mail addresses for such authorised family mediators, and the dates of contact, can be provided to the court if requested (FPR 2010, r 3.8(1)(k)).
- The prospective applicant or all of the prospective respondents cannot attend a MIAM because he or she is, or they are, as the case may be:
  - in prison or any other institution in which he or she is or they are required to be detained;
  - subject to conditions of bail that prevent contact with the other person; or
  - subject to a licence with a prohibited contact requirement in relation to the other person (FPR 2010, r 3.8(1)(l)).
- The prospective applicant or all of the prospective respondents are not habitually resident in England and Wales (FPR 2010, r 3.8(1)(m)).
- A child is one of the prospective parties by virtue of FPR 2010, r 12.3(1) (FPR 2010, r 3.8(1)(n)).
- The prospective applicant has contacted as many authorised family mediators as have an office within fifteen miles of his or her home (or three of them if there are three or more), and all of them have stated that they are not available to conduct a MIAM within fifteen business days of the date of contact; and the names, postal addresses and telephone numbers or e-mail addresses for such authorised family mediators, and the dates of contact, can be provided to the court if requested (FPR 2010, r 3.8(1)(o)).
- There is no authorised family mediator with an office within fifteen miles of the prospective applicant's home (FPR 2010, r 3.8(1)(p)).

Mediator's exemptions

An authorised family mediator confirms in the relevant form that he or she is satisfied that:

- mediation is not suitable as a means of resolving the dispute because none of the respondents is willing to attend a MIAM (FPR 2010, r 3.8(2)(a));
- mediation is not suitable as a means of resolving the dispute because all of the respondents failed without good reason to attend a MIAM appointment (FPR 2010, r 3.8(2)(b));
- mediation is otherwise not suitable as a means of resolving the dispute (FPR 2010, r 3.8(2)(c)).

Only an authorised family mediator may conduct a MIAM. FPR 2010, r 3.9(2) sets out what a mediator must do at a MIAM (for example, provide information and assess suitability, the risk of domestic violence and the risk of harm to a child).

If the party making the application uses one of the MIAM exemptions listed above the court can inquire into whether the exemption was validly claimed (FPR 2010, r 3.10(1)). If the court finds it was not validly claimed the court can adjourn proceedings and direct the parties to attend a MIAM (FPR 2010, r 3.10(2)). In deciding whether to adjourn for a MIAM the court will have regard to the factors listed at FPR 2010, r 3.10(3).

FPR 2010, PD 3A supplements FPR 2010, Part 3 and should be referred to directly. In particular it provides useful information about:

- what evidence can be used for the domestic violence MIAM exemption and the bankruptcy MIAM exemption;

- how to find an authorised family mediator;
- how to fund a MIAM (Legal Aid is available for MIAMs).

The Form A now contains MIAM provisions. A mediator should complete part 4 of the form if a MIAM has been attended or to confirm a Mediator's exemption.

Tips:

- Proportionality and case management are key, as seen in *B v B* [2013] EWHC 1232 (Fam). Consider all forms of dispute resolution, for example arbitration (see ifla.org.uk) and collaborative law, as well as mediation. See also www.resolution.org.uk/alternatives_to_court.
- See the *Family Law Directory* and www.familymediationcouncil.org.uk for help finding a local mediator.

File

An application for a financial order can be made during or after a divorce/dissolution/nullity/(judicial) separation. The financial orders available are:

- **Periodical payments** and/or secured periodical payments for spouse and/or children (MCA 1973, s 23(1)(a), (b),(d),(e) and CPA 2004, Sch 5, para 2(1) (a), (b), (d) and (e)).
- **Lump sum** for spouse and/or children (plus interest) (MCA 1973, s 23(1)(c),(f) and (6) and CPA 2004, Sch 5, paras 2(1) (c) and (f) and para 3).
- **Property adjustment order** (MCA 1973, s 24 and CPA 2004, Sch 5, paras 6 – 9).
- **Order for sale of property** (where order also made for secured periodical payments, lump sum or property adjustment) (MCA 1973, s 24A and CPA 2004, Sch 5, paras 10 – 14).
- **Pension (or pension protection fund) sharing order** (divorce/dissolution or nullity only) (MCA 1973, ss 21A – C, 24B – G, 25G and CPA 2004, Sch 5, paras 15 – 19F).
- **Pension (or pension protection fund) attachment order** (MCA 1973, ss 25B – D, 21C, 25F, 26G and CPA 2004, Sch 5, Parts 6 and 7).
- **Clean break** (divorce/dissolution or nullity only) (MCA 1973, s 25A and CPA 2004, Sch 5, para 23).

Guidance on the process of obtaining a financial order is set out in leaflet D190 (also available at http://hmctsformfinder.justice.gov.uk/HMCTS/FormFinder.do).

Also consider whether to apply for a legal services order under s 22ZA and s 22ZB MCA 1973, (or CPA 2004, Sch 5, paras 38A and 38B). A legal services order allows the court to order payments between the parties to enable the receiving party to obtain legal services for the purpose of proceedings (similar to an old style '*A v A*' order). Applications for a legal services order are covered here: Interim financial orders practice note.

The court may, in certain circumstances of grossly unreasonable behaviour in litigation, consider awarding a sum payable by one party, for retention as a 'fighting fund' to meet the other party's future legal costs in respect of subsequent litigation. See for example *Thiry v Thiry* [2014] EWHC 4046 (Fam).

Documents

Notice of [intention to proceed with] an application for a financial order (Form A)

See the notes to precedents C1 and C2 (*Family Law Precedents Service*) and Procedural Guide B5 (PG) in *Family Court Practice* (*the Red Book*).

The Form A should be signed by the applicant (or his or her solicitor) and a mediator if a MIAM has been attended or to confirm a Mediator's exemption.

The applicant does not have to be the applicant in the divorce/dissolution/nullity/(judicial) separation (the '**main suit**'); the respondent to the main suit can be the applicant in the financial proceedings.

The documents below should be filed: if there are proceedings for a matrimonial order or a civil partnership order in the Family Court, in that court, or if they are in the High Court, in that registry (FPR 2010, r 9.5).

Tips:

- Remember to include enough copies of the Form A (normally three – one for the applicant, one for the court and one for the respondent).
- Do not forget to check the court fee (£255 as at September 2015) and include a cheque or postal order payable to 'HM Courts and Tribunals Service' or 'HMCTS'. The fee can also be paid in cash or by debit/credit card.
- If service is to be carried out by the applicant's solicitor remember to ask the court for 'solicitor service' at the time of filing the documents at court.
- If the case is complex, consider whether it should be issued in the Financial Remedies Unit of the Central Family Court. See www.familylaw.co.uk/news_and_comment/how-to-refer-cases-to-the-financial-remedies-unit.

Matrimonial home rights

At the earliest opportunity, if the matrimonial home is in the respondent's name only, practitioners should consider whether the applicant ought to register a notice at the Land Registry to protect his or her home rights (otherwise known as a 'home rights notice'). A Form HR1 should be used (for registered land) (available at http://www.landregistry.gov.uk/_media/downloads/forms/HR1.pdf). Useful Guidance can be found at http://www.landregistry.gov.uk/public/guides/public-guide-4.

Sever joint tenancy

Where the applicant holds property as joint tenants with the respondent the practitioner should consider with the client whether a notice of severance of the joint tenancy ought to be served. See precedents C92 and C93 (*Family Law Precedents Service*).

Serve

The following documents are required to be served on the respondent:

(1) the sealed Form A;

(2) Notice of First Appointment (Form C) (this is produced by the court);

(3) Form G (Notice of response to First Appointment) (as to whether the First Appointment can be an FDR – it is served blank at this stage).

Methods of service

- *Service by Post/DX* (FPR 2010, r 6.23(b)).
- *Personal service* (FPR 2010, r 6.23(a)).
- *Delivery* (FPR 2010, r 6.23(c)).
- *Fax or other means of electronic communication* (FPR 2010, r 6.23(d)).

See Service (not of an application for a matrimonial/civil partnership order) practice note for further guidance.

Timing

If the court is serving the Form A, Notice of First Appointment and Form G, they must be served on the respondent **within 4 days** of the Form A being filed at court (FPR 2010, r 9.12(1)(b)).

If the applicant is serving the Form A, Notice of First Appointment and Form G, they must be served on the respondent **within 4 days** of them being received from the court (FPR 2010, r 9.12(2)(c)(i)).

Service on a mortagee

A copy of the Form A must be served by the applicant (nb the court will not serve it) on any mortgagee of land of which particulars are given in the Form A (FPR 2010, r 9.13(3)). An example letter to the mortgagee serving the application can be found at precedent C16 (*Family Law Precedents Service*). The mortgagee can make a request to court within 14 days of being served with the application for a copy of applicant's Form E (FPR 2010, r 9.13(4)). See precedent C17 (*Family Law Precedents Service*) for an example letter serving the Form E. Upon receipt of the requested copy Form E the mortgagee can, within 14 days, file an answer (FPR 2010, r 9.13(5)).

Service on a trustee / settlor

If the Form A includes an application for an order for a variation of settlement the Form A must be served by the applicant (nb the court will not serve it) (FPR 2010, r 9.13(1)):

- the trustees of the settlement;
- the settlor if living; and
- such other persons as the court directs.

The trustee/settlor/other person can make a request to court within 14 days of being served with the application for a copy of applicant's Form E (or relevant part of the Form E) (FPR 2010, r 9.13(4)). See precedent C17 (*Family Law Precedents Service*) for an example letter serving the Form E which can be adapted accordingly. Upon receipt of the requested copy Form E the trustee/settlor/other person can, within 14 days, file an answer (FPR 2010, r 9.13(5)).

Service in the case of a disposition

In the case of an application for an avoidance of disposition order, the applicant must serve copies of the application on the person in whose favour the disposition is alleged to have been made (FPR

2010, r 9.13(2)). The individual served can make a request to court within 14 days of being served with the application for a copy of applicant's Form E (or relevant part of the Form E) (FPR 2010, r 9.13(4)). See precedent C17 (*Family Law Precedents Service*) for an example letter serving the Form E which can be adapted accordingly.

Upon receipt of the requested copy Form E the person served can, within 14 days, file an answer (FPR 2010, r 9.13(5)).

Service on a pension provider

Where the Form A includes an application for a pension sharing or attachment order the Form A must be served by the applicant on the person responsible for the pension arrangement (FPR 2010, r 9.31 and 9.33). See Pensions on divorce/dissolution/nullity/(judicial) separation – Part 1 (to First Appointment) practice note for further guidance.

See precedent C18 (*Family Law Precedents Service*) for an example letter.

Important – a party with a pension is required within **7 days** of receiving the Notice of the First Appointment to request that their pension arrangement provides a 'relevant valuation' (unless the party already has a relevant valuation that is less than 12 months old).

Exchange Forms E

The court will set a date for the parties to exchange Forms E. This will not be less than **35 days before** the First Appointment (FPR 2010, r 9.14(1)).

Form E

The Form E must:

- be verified by a statement of truth (FPR 2010, r 9.14(2)(a));
- be accompanied by the following documents only:
  - any documents required by the financial statement (the Form E contains a checklist of the documents on the back page) (FPR 2010, r 9.14(2)(b)(i));
  - any other documents necessary to explain or clarify any of the information contained in the financial statement (FPR 2010, r 9.14(2)(b)(ii));
  - any documents provided to the party producing the financial statement by a person responsible for a pension arrangement, either following a request under FPR 2010, r 9.30 or as part of a relevant valuation (FPR 2010, r 9.14(2)(b)(iii); and
  - any notification or other document referred to in FPR 2010, r 9.37(2), (4) or (5) which has been received by the party producing the financial statement (FPR 2010, r 9.14(2)(b)(iv));
- comply with the requirements of PD 22A (Written Evidence) and in particular paragraphs 11.1 to 11.3 and 13.1 to 13.4 of that Direction (FPR 2010, PD 9A, para 5.1) (these paragraphs provide guidance on using photocopies and the format of the exhibited documents, for example pagination).

Guidance on completing the Form E is set out in leaflet *Form E Notes* (available at http://hmctsformfinder.justice.gov.uk/HMCTS/FormFinder.do).

Please also see the notes to precedent C19 (*Family Law Precedents Service*).

As stated above, the Form E will need to be verified by a statement of truth and so it is essential that it is accurate and that it provides full and frank disclosure. The client should have an opportunity to review a draft of the Form E and should be reminded of his or her disclosure obligations. See precedent C21 (*Family Law Precedents Service*) for an example letter to the client. Precedent C30 (*Family Law Precedents Service*) is an example letter to a client suspected not to have provided full and frank disclosure.

Filing at court

The Form E must also be filed at court by the deadline given in the Notice of First Appointment (Form C). Check with the court whether they require the accompanying documentation to be filed at court as well, particularly if the enclosures are voluminous. Commonly the court will request that only the Form E is filed. Paragraph 5.1 of FPR 2010, PD 9A specifically states that if the enclosures are bulky and it is impracticable to retain them on the court file after the First Appointment the court may give directions as to their custody pending further hearings.

Tips:

- Compiling the Form E is time consuming. Therefore it is a good idea to start gathering information for the Form E as soon as possible. See precedent C4 (*Family Law Precedents Service*) which is an initial letter to the client requesting that they complete a confidential client questionnaire (precedent C5 (*Family Law Precedents Service*)) and a schedule of outgoings (precedent C6 (*Family Law Precedents Service*)).
- A common reason for delay in completing a Form E is that a third party (for example a bank/insurance company) is slow in providing the required information/documentation (eg 12 months' worth of bank statements/valuations). Therefore it is advisable to make requests for documentation/information from third parties as soon as possible after filing the Form A and to keep on track of chasing the third party for a response. Precedent C20 (*Family Law Precedents Service*) sets out a letter to the client informing them of the enclosures that are required. If the solicitor instead of the client is to contact the third party it may be necessary to obtain a letter of authority from the client. An example letter to an insurance company requesting information and enclosing a letter of authority can be found at precedent C13 (*Family Law Precedents Service*) (see precedent C14 (*Family Law Precedents Service*) for the letter of authority) and it can be adapted for other third parties. If the requested documentation/information is not available at the time of exchange the Form E should contain a note explaining the reason for the delay and indicating when the information/documentation will be available. Once received the information/documentation should be served and filed at the earliest opportunity (FPR 2010, r 9.14(3)).
- In completing Section 3.1 (income needs) the client may find it useful to complete a template as an aide mémoire. An example schedule of outgoings can be found at precedent C6 (*Family Law Precedents Service*).
- In filling out the narrative sections of the Form E (Sections 4.2 – 4.6) regard should be had to the MCA 1973 s 25 factors (CPA 2004, Sch 5, para 23) and the answers drafted accordingly.
- Remember that at Section 2.20 the figure for D – Liabilities – should be a minus number.

Propose expert(s)

Permission from court must be obtained to file an expert's report (FPR 2010, r 25.4(2) and FPR 2010, PD 25B, para 5.1). An application for permission should be made using the Part 18 procedure (see Part 18 practice note) (FPR 2010, r 25.7(1)). However, a formal application is not normally needed as in general the matter of expert evidence is dealt with at the First Appointment and the First Appointment order will contain directions in this regard. The latest point at which an application for permission should be made is the First Appointment (FPR 2010, r 25.6(d) and FPR 2010, PD 25D, para 3.9) although the court can decide to extend the time for applying for permission where there is a good reason (FPR 2010 PD 25D, para 3.9 and 3.10).

Note that expert evidence will be restricted to that which is 'necessary' to resolve the proceedings (FPR 2010, r 25.4(3)) (see *Re H-L* [2013] 2 FLR 1434) and the court will have regard to the overriding objective (FPR 2010, r 1.1) and its case management powers under Part 4, FPR 2010 when using its discretion to direct that expert evidence is filed. There is a list of factors the court will have regard to in particular when deciding whether to give permission at FPR 2010, r 25.5(2). See also FPR 2010, PD 25D, paras 3.1 and 3.2.

The Law Society provides useful pro-forma templates dealing with instructing an expert at http://www.lawsociety.org.uk/advice/family-expert-templates/.

Single joint expert

The court may direct that a single joint expert is instructed ('SJE') (FPR 2010, r 25.11).

PD 25D states that wherever possible a single joint expert should be instructed (FPR 2010, PD 25D, para 2.1).

To that end, well in advance of the First Appointment (e.g. shortly after exchange of Forms E):

- a party wishing to instruct an expert should first give the other party a list of the names of one or more proposed suitable experts (FPR 2010, PD 25D, para 2.1);
- within 10 business days after receipt of the list of proposed experts, the other party should indicate any objection to one or more of the named experts and, if so, supply the name(s) of one or more experts whom they consider suitable (FPR 2010, PD 25D, para 2.2);
- each party should disclose whether they have already consulted any of the proposed experts about the issue(s) in question (FPR 2010, PD 25D, para 2.3); and
- if there is agreement to instruct an SJE, **before applying to the court for permission to put the expert evidence before it and directions for the use of an SJE** the parties should so far as appropriate:
  - — comply with the guidance in paragraphs FPR 2010, PD 25D, para 3.3 (Preliminary inquiries of the expert), 3.11 (the application), 3.12 (the draft order) (FPR 2010, PD 25D, para 2.6(a));
  - — have received the expert's confirmation in response to the preliminary enquiries referred to in FPR 2010, PD 25B, para 8.1 (FPR 2010, PD 25D, para 2.6(b) and 3.4); and
  - — have agreed in what proportion the SJE's fee is to be shared between them (at least in the first instance) and when it is to be paid (and if applicable, have obtained agreement for public funding) (FPR 2010, PD 25D, para 2.6(c) and (d))

(See further precedents J6, J7 and J8 (*Family Law Precedents Service*).

If the parties cannot agree who should be the SJE the court can select the expert from a list compiled by the parties or direct that the expert be selected by another method (FPR 2010, r 25.11(2)). Commonly the court will direct that one party put forward the names of, say, three potential experts, and that the other party choose one from that list. The parties should have made preliminary enquiries and obtained confirmations for all of the experts on the list (FPR 2010, PD 25D, para 3.5).

Separate experts

If the parties agree to instruct separate experts they should agree in advance that the reports will be disclosed and should make preliminary enquiries, obtain confirmations, and draft an application for permission attaching a draft order as set out in FPR 2010, PD 25D, paras 3.3 – 3.4, 3.11 and 3.12 (see above under Single joint expert).

Nb. See the *Family Law Directory* for help in identifying an expert.

Tip:

- When drafting proposed directions for the First Appointment, include provision for forward-looking directions such as questions to the expert(s), a timetable for answers, discussion between the experts if applicable. This may avoid the need for a further hearing. See further FPR 2010, r 25.7 which sets out what should be included in an application for permission to adduce expert evidence and FPR 2010, PD 25D, para 3.11. Note that a draft order should be attached – see further FPR 2010, PD 25D, para 3.12.

File and serve First Appointment documents

The court will set a date for the parties to file and serve First Appointment documents. This will not be less than **14 days before** the First Appointment (FPR 2010, r 9.14(5) and (6)).

Documents

Statement of Issues

The statement of issues should be a concise summary of the issues between the parties (FPR 2010, r 9.14(5)(a)). See notes to precedent C25 (*Family Law Precedents Service*).

Chronology

(FPR 2010, r 9.14(5)(b)). The chronology should set out key dates in the matter (eg dates of birth, date of marriage, date of separation etc.). See precedent C25 (*Family Law Precedents Service*).

Questionnaire

The questionnaire must, by reference to the concise statement of issues, set out any further information and documentation requested from the other party or a statement that no information is required (FPR 2010, r 9.14(5)(c)). See precedent C26 (*Family Law Precedents Service*).

Form G

A Form G is a notice stating whether that party will be in a position at the First Appointment to proceed on that occasion to a FDR appointment (FPR 2010, r 9.14(5)(d)). See precedent C24 (*Family Law Precedents Service*). The court has the power to treat all or part of the First Appointment as an FDR (FPR 2010, r 9.15(7)(b)).

Confirmation of the names of all persons served in accordance with r 9.13 (see above) and certificate of service

The applicant must file with the court and serve on the respondent confirmation of the names of all persons served in accordance with r 9.13(1) to (3) and that there are no other persons who must be served in accordance with those paragraphs (FPR 2010, r 9.14(6)). The applicant must also file a certificate of service (Form FP6) at or before the First Appointment (FPR 2010, r 9.13(6)).

Documents to file if possible (FPR 2010, PD 9A, para 4.1):

- Agreed case summary
- Agreed schedule of assets
- Details of directions sought including, where appropriate, the name of any expert they wish to be appointed (see above 'Propose Expert(s)'). Examples of the types of directions that can be sought are at precedent C27 (*Family Law Precedents Service*). Where a party is prevented from sending details of the directions sought and/or the name(s) of experts the party should make that information available at the First Appointment (FPR 2010, PD 9A, para 4.2).

Tip:

- Take early instructions from the client on the questionnaire posed by the other party. It may be possible to agree the contents of the questionnaires prior to the First Appointment hearing.

APPLICATIONS FOR A FINANCIAL ORDER (NOT AN INTERIM ORDER) UNDER MCA 1973 OR CPA 2004 FIRST APPOINTMENT TO FDR

FLOWCHART

Family Law

Applications for a financial order (not an interim order) under MCA 1973 or CPA 2004 First Appointment to FDR

PRACTICE PLUS

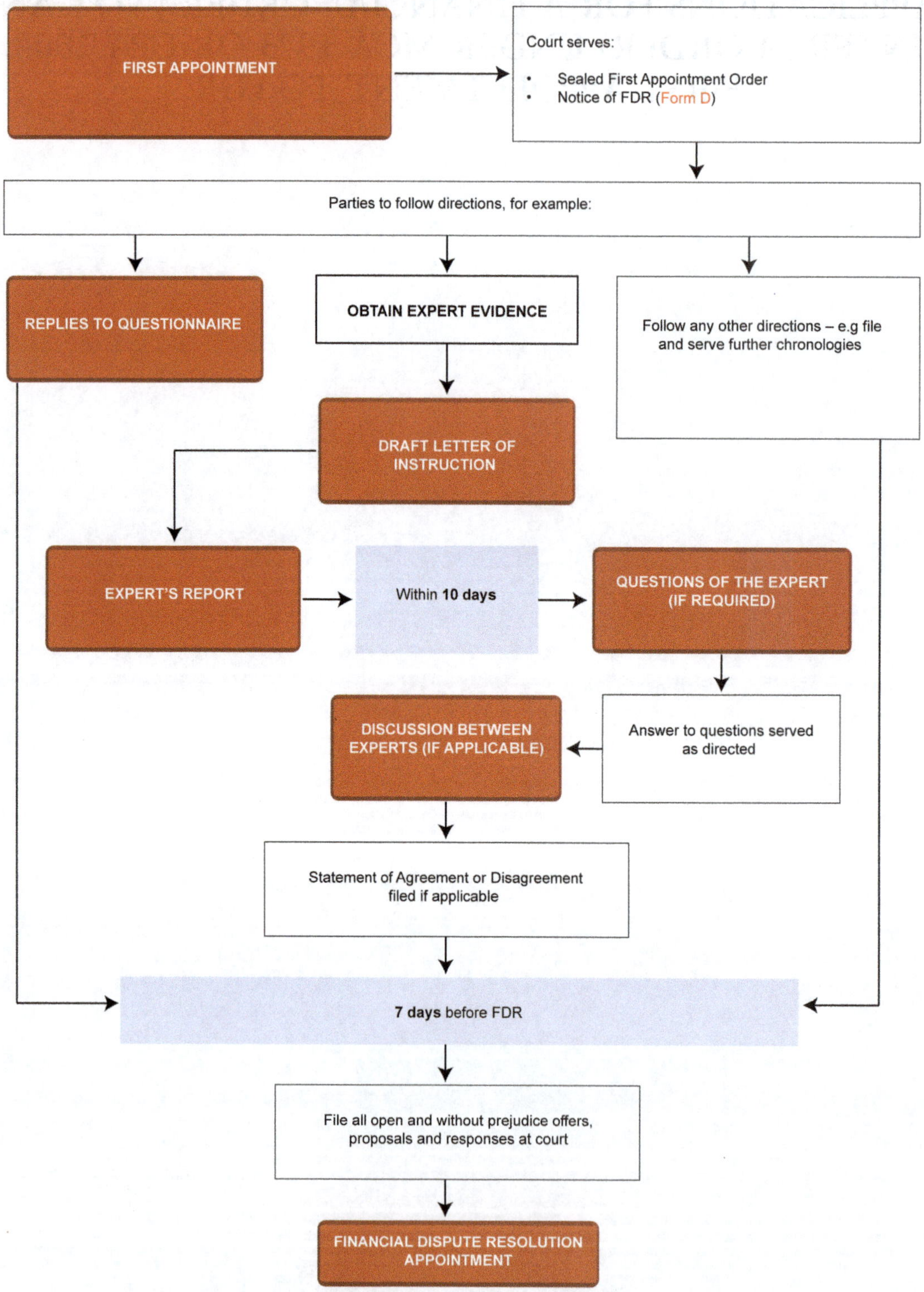

PRACTICE NOTE

See also Procedural Guide (PG) B5 in *The Red Book (Family Court Practice)*.

First Appointment

Bundles and preliminary documents

Practice Direction 27A requires a bundle to be filed in all hearings before a judge sitting in the Family Division of the High Court wherever the court may be sitting and all hearings in the Family Court (FPR 2010, PD 27A, para 2.1). The bundle should be lodged not less than 2 working days before the hearing. The Practice Direction sets out very precise rules regarding the preparation of bundles and should be referred to directly. FPR 2010, PD 27A also sets out requirements for filing preliminary documents at 11 am the day before the hearing. For further details see the Preliminary Documents box of the Applications for a financial order (not an interim order) under MCA 1973 or CPA 2004 FDR to Final Hearing practice note. See also *Re L (Procedure: Bundles: Translation)* [2015] 1 FLR 1417 for further guidance particularly on the court's stance on adherence to PD 27A.

Form H

Each party must prepare an estimate of costs (Form H) (FPR 2010, r 9.27(1)) which they should make available to the court and to the other party at the First Appointment. See precedent C36 (*Family Law Precedents Service*).

Publicity

The proceedings will be held in private (FPR 2010, r 27.10). This means that members of the public are not allowed access to the court room. However accredited members of the press are entitled to be in court (FPR 2010, r 27.11(2)(f)) unless the court directs that they shall not be allowed access (FPR 2010, r 27.11(3)). See *Family Court Practice* (*the Red Book*) notes to r 27.11 and FPR 2010, PD 27B for further information.

Also see *Emergency Remedies in the Family Courts*, para G[1.1] to para G[1.9].

Transparency in the Family Court continues to be high on the agenda. Following the Practice Guidance in February [2014] Fam Law 222 and various views (see *12th View from the President's Chambers: The process of reform: next steps* in July [2014] Fam Law 978) the President released a consultation paper *Transparency – The Next Steps: A Consultation Paper issued by the President of the Family Division* in September [2014] Fam Law 1331. Also see *Re J (A Child)* [2014] 1 FLR 523 and *Re P (Enforced Caesarean: Reporting Restrictions)* [2014] 2 FLR 410.

Attendance

Both parties must personally attend unless the court directs otherwise (FPR 2010, r 9.15(8)).

Order

The First Appointment is a 'housekeeping' hearing and must be conducted with the objective of defining the issues and saving costs (FPR 2010, r 9.15(1)).

The court:

- must determine which of the questions contained in the questionnaires must be answered and to what extent and give directions as to which of the requested documents must be produced (sometimes the court will modify the questions, for example, to narrow the time period for requested documents from 5 years to 2 years) (FPR 2010, r 9.15(2)(a) and (b));
- where appropriate must give directions for the valuation of assets (including the joint instruction of joint experts) (FPR 2010, r 9.15(3)(a));
- if required and where appropriate must give directions about obtaining and exchanging expert evidence, including giving a date for the expert to provide their written report (FPR 2010, r 9.15(3)(b) and 25.8(1)(b)) (note the need to balance the needs of the court and those of the expert – see FPR 2010, PD 25B, para 7.1);
- where appropriate must give directions as to the evidence to be adduced by each party (FPR 2010, r 9.15(3)(c));
- where appropriate must give directions as to further chronologies or schedules to be filed by each party (FPR 2010, r 9.15(3)(d));
- either must refer the case to an FDR appointment or, if it does not consider an FDR appropriate give directions:
  - that a further directions appointment be fixed;
  - that an appointment be fixed for the making of an interim order;
  - that the case be fixed for a final hearing and, where that direction is given, the court must determine the judicial level at which the case should be heard (FPR 2010, r 9.15(4) and (5));
- where appropriate, in a case where a pension sharing order or a pension attachment order is requested, direct any party with pension rights to file and serve a Pension Inquiry Form (Form P), completed in full or in part as the court may direct (FPR 2010, r 9.15(7)(c)); and
- where appropriate in a case where a pension compensation sharing order or a pension compensation attachment order is requested, direct any party with PPF compensation rights to file and serve a Pension Protection Fund Inquiry Form (Form PPF), completed in full or in part as the court may direct (FPR 2010, r 9.15(7)(d)). (See Pensions on divorce/dissolution/nullity/(judicial) separation – Part 2 (First Appointment to implementation) practice note for further guidance.)

The court may also make an interim order if an application for an interim order has been listed to be considered at the First Appointment (FPR 2010, r 9.15(7)(a)).

Costs

The court will consider whether each party has complied with the requirement to send documents with the Form E and the explanation given for any failure to comply when considering whether to make a costs order under r 28.3(5) (FPR 2010, r 9.15(6)).

Tips:

- As well as copies of the Form H, ensure you have spare copies of the First Appointment documents and Form E, in case these have not reached the court file.
- If you are proposing to instruct an expert it may be a good idea to take a draft letter of instruction to the First Appointment and try to agree it with the other side (see further 'Letter of Instruction' below).

Replies to questionnaire

At the First Appointment the court will have directed which of the questions in the questionnaire should be answered and which documents should be produced. The court will have given a deadline by which the Replies should be served.

The format of the Replies to Questionnaire document should be as follows:

Question 1

XXXXXXXXXXXXXXXXXXX

Reply 1

XXXXXXXXXXXXXXXXXXX

Question 2

XXXXXXXXXXXXXXXXXXX

Reply 2

XXXXXXXXXXXXXXXXXXX

and so on.

Replies to Questionnaire should be verified by a statement of truth (FPR 2010, PD 9A, para 5.2).

The Replies to Questionnaire should be served on the other party but should not be filed at court (unless otherwise directed) (FPR 2010, PD 9A, para 5.2).

Tip:

- There is no specific rule in the FPR 2010 which governs the issue of privilege. The general rule is that parties are required, after the preliminary exchange of documents, to make such disclosure as may be required by the court. If a party wishes to assert privilege over documents requested in the questionnaire (or in response to any other request for disclosure) the party should follow the practice as set out in the CPR 1998 (see further *Tchenguiz-Imerman v Imerman* [2014] 1 FLR 232).

Letter of instruction

The letter of instruction should be prepared, filed and served within **5 business days** after the hearing (FPR 2010, PD 25D, para 4.1).

The Law Society provides useful pro-forma templates dealing with instructing an expert at http://www.lawsociety.org.uk/advice/family-expert-templates/.

To an expert (not an SJE)

The letter of instruction should comply with paragraphs 4.1 – 6.1 of PD 25D (FPR 2010, PD 25D, para 2.5(b)). Note the enclosures, including a copy of the guidance in PDs 25B, 25D, 25E and, where appropriate, 15B.

For an example letter of instruction see precedent J13 (*Family Law Precedents Service*).

The instructions to the expert are **not** privileged against disclosure (FPR 2010, r 25.14(3)).

To a single joint expert

The instructions to a SJE should be in an agreed joint letter (FPR 2010, r 25.12(1)). If the letter cannot be agreed the letter of instruction can be determined by the court (FPR 2010, r 25.12(2)). If the court directs that the instructions to the expert can be in separate letters the parties must copy each other when sending the letter to the expert (FPR 2010, r 25.12(3)).

The letter of instruction should comply with paragraphs 4.1 – 6.1 of PD 25D (FPR 2010, PD 25D, para 2.7). Note the enclosures, including a copy of the guidance in PDs 25B (as updated), 25D, 25E and, where appropriate, 15B.

For example letters of instruction see precedents J11, J12, J13 and J14 (*Family Law Precedents Service*).

Unless the court directs otherwise, the relevant parties are jointly and severally liable for the payment of the expert's fees and expenses (FPR 2010, r 25.12(6)).

The instructions to the expert are **not** privileged against disclosure (FPR 2010, r 25.14(3)).

Expert's report

FPR 2010, r 25.14 states that an expert's report must comply with the requirements set out in PD 25B (as updated). Paragraph 9.1 of the Practice Direction sets out the requirements and should be consulted directly.

At the end of an expert's report there must be a statement that the expert understands and has complied with their duty to the court FPR 2010, r 25.14(2) and PD 25B, para 9.1. It is the expert's overriding duty to help the court on matters within their expertise (FPR 2010, r 25.3 and PD 25B, para 3.1). The duties of the expert are listed at FPR 2010, PD 25B, para 4.1.

Any party can use a disclosed expert's report as evidence at any hearing where an issue to which the report relates is being considered (FPR 2010, r 25.15).

Questions of the expert

Within **10 days** beginning on the date on which the expert's report was served a party may put written questions to the expert (FPR 2010, r 25.10(2)(c)). The questions must also be served on the other party at the same time (FPR 2010, r 25.10(2)(e)). The questions must be proportionate and for the purpose only of clarification of the report (FPR 2010, r 25.10(2)(a) and (d)). The questions can only be put once (FPR 2010, r 25.10(2)(b)).

These requirements apply unless the court directs otherwise or a Practice Direction provides otherwise (FPR 2010, r 25.10(2)).

The court will set out a timetable for answering the questions (normally in the First Appointment order) (FPR 2010, r 25.10(3)(a)).

The expert's answers are treated as part of the expert's report (FPR 2010, r 25.10(3)(b)).

If the expert does not answer a question the court can order that the party may not rely on the evidence of that expert and/or that the party may not recover the fees and expenses of that expert from any other party (FPR 2010, r 25.10(4)).

If a party is dissatisfied with a SJE's report, even after receiving answers to questions put, the party can put forward a '*Daniels v Walker (Practice Note)* [2000] 1 WLR 1382' argument to apply for the court to order that another expert report be filed. As a last resort both experts will be cross examined.

Discussions between experts

The court can direct that there be a discussion between experts for the purpose of identifying and discussing the expert issues in the proceedings; and where possible, reaching an agreed opinion on those issues (FPR 2010, r 25.16(1)).

The court may specify which issues the experts should discuss and may direct that the experts prepare a joint statement summarising which issues they agree and which they do not (a 'Statement of Agreement and Disagreement') (FPR 2010, r 25.16(2) and (3)).

See FPR 2010, PD 25E for the specific requirements of setting up a discussion between experts. In summary:

- within **15 business days** after the experts' reports have been filed and copied to the parties the 'nominated professional' (see FPR 2010, PD 25E, para 3.1) should make arrangements for the experts to meet/communicate;
- **5 business days** before the discussion/meeting the nominated professional should formulate an agenda for the meeting (normally a list of questions);
- the agenda should be sent to the experts no later than **2 business days** before the discussion/meeting;
- if a Statement of Agreement and Disagreement is required by the court it should be served and filed not later **than 5 business days** after the discussion/meeting.

Financial dispute resolution appointment (FDR)

See FPR 2010, PD 9A, paras 6.1 – 6.6 for further guidance. Also see the Family Justice Council Best Practice Guidance on Financial Dispute Resolution Appointments (available here http://www.familylaw.co.uk/system/uploads/attachments/0006/3603/JCO_Documents_FJC_Publications_fjc_financial_dispute_resolution.pdf).

Offers

The applicant must file at court details of all offers and proposals, and responses to them, not less than **7 days before** the FDR appointment (FPR 2010, r 9.17(3)). This includes all without prejudice offers as well as open offers (FPR 2010, r 9.17(4)).

Filing the without prejudice offers and responses does not make the material admissible as evidence if it would otherwise not be admissible (FPR 2010, r 9.17(4)). The applicant should request that the without prejudice papers filed are returned at the end of the FDR and not retained on the court file (FPR 2010, r 9.17(5)).

Bundles and preliminary documents

In accordance with PD 27A a bundle should be produced in readiness for the FDR. Normally an FDR bundle contains:

- skeleton arguments;
- asset schedules;
- written offers and responses; and
- Forms E without their attached documentation.

Practice Direction 27A can be referred to for guidance. FPR 2010, PD 27A also sets out requirements for filing preliminary documents at 11 am the day before the hearing. For further details see the Preliminary Documents box of the Applications for a financial order (not an interim order) under MCA 1973 or CPA 2004 FDR to Final Hearing practice note. Note that PD 27A *must* be complied with – see *Re W (Strict Compliance with Court Orders)* [2014] EWHC 22; *J v J* [2014] EWHC 3654 (Fam) and *Seagrove v Sullivan* [2015] 2 FLR 602. See also *Re L (Procedure: Bundles: Translation)* [2015] 1 FLR 1417 for further guidance, particularly on the court's stance on adherence to PD 27A.

Form H

Each party must prepare an estimate of costs (Form H) (FPR 2010, r 9.27(1)) which they should make available to the court and to the other party at the FDR. See precedent C36 (*Family Law Precedents Service*).

Publicity

The proceedings will be held in private (FPR 2010, r 27.10). This means that members of the public are not allowed access to the court room. In contrast to First Appointments, directions hearings and Final Hearings, accredited members of the press are **not** entitled to access FDRs (FPR 2010, r 27.11(1)(a)).

Attendance

Both parties must personally attend unless the court directs otherwise (FPR 2010, r 9.17(10)). The parties should arrive at least an hour early in order for there to be opportunity for negotiations to take place prior to the hearing. It is possible to adjourn the FDR (from time to time) (FPR 2010, r 9.17(7)).

Order

The FDR can be described as a court-led opportunity for negotiation. It is treated as a meeting held for the purposes of discussion and negotiation (FPR 2010, r 9.17(1)). The rules specifically state that both parties must use their best endeavours to reach agreement on matters in issue between them (FPR 2010, r 9.17(6)). The judge will consider the papers and the parties' submissions and will provide advice and an indication of the likely outcome if the case were to go to a final hearing.

At the end of the FDR the court can either:

- make an appropriate consent order (FPR 2010, r 9.17(8)); or
- give directions for the future course of the proceedings including, where appropriate
  - — the filing of evidence, including up to date information; and

— fixing a final hearing date (FPR 2010, r 9.17(9)).

The judge at the FDR cannot hear the Final Hearing or any other hearings (save for further FDRs) as he or she will review without prejudice material during the course of conducting the FDR (FPR 2010, r 9.17(2)). Also see *Currey v Currey (No 2)* [2007] 1 FLR 946, and *Myerson v Myerson* [2009] 1 FLR 826, CA. However, once the issues are determined and the order is made, a FDR judge may hear an application for variation of that order: *G v G (Role of FDR Judge)* [2007] 1 FLR 237.

Tips:

- It is a good idea to take several copies of a draft consent order to the FDR. The copies of the draft consent order can be used as a basis for negotiations and can help focus the parties on narrowing the issues between them. In the event that an agreement is reached, if possible the draft consent order (with manuscript amends if necessary) should be signed by both parties and their legal representatives and handed to the judge so that the order may be made and sealed immediately. Alternatively, if an agreement is reached but the specific drafting is not agreed the draft consent order can be used to form the basis of a Heads of Agreement which again should be signed by both parties and their legal representatives and handed to the judge. Obtaining the agreement on paper and ensuring it is signed is good evidence of a consensus and helpful if one of the parties attempts to resile from the agreement before an order is made. For further guidance about negotiated agreements and what to do if the other side seek to resile from an agreement see *Rose v Rose* [2002] 1 FLR 978, *Edgar v Edgar* (1981) 2 FLR 19, CA, *Xydhias v Xydhias* [1999] 1 FLR 683, CA, *DN v HN* [2014] EWHC 3435 (Fam), *Smith v McInerney* [1994] 2 FLR 1077; *X v X (Y and Z intervening)* [2002] 1 FLR 508 and *Rothwell v Rothwell* [2009] 2 FLR 96.
- Another option, if agreement is reached but a written consent order not finalised, is for the court to list a 5 minute mention in 2-4 weeks. The parties can then agree and sign a consent order and, when it is lodged with the court, can ask for the mention to be vacated. If the parties cannot agree the final form of the consent order before the mention the court can then give directions.

APPLICATIONS FOR A FINANCIAL ORDER (NOT AN INTERIM ORDER) UNDER MCA 1973 OR CPA 2004 FDR TO FINAL HEARING

FLOWCHART

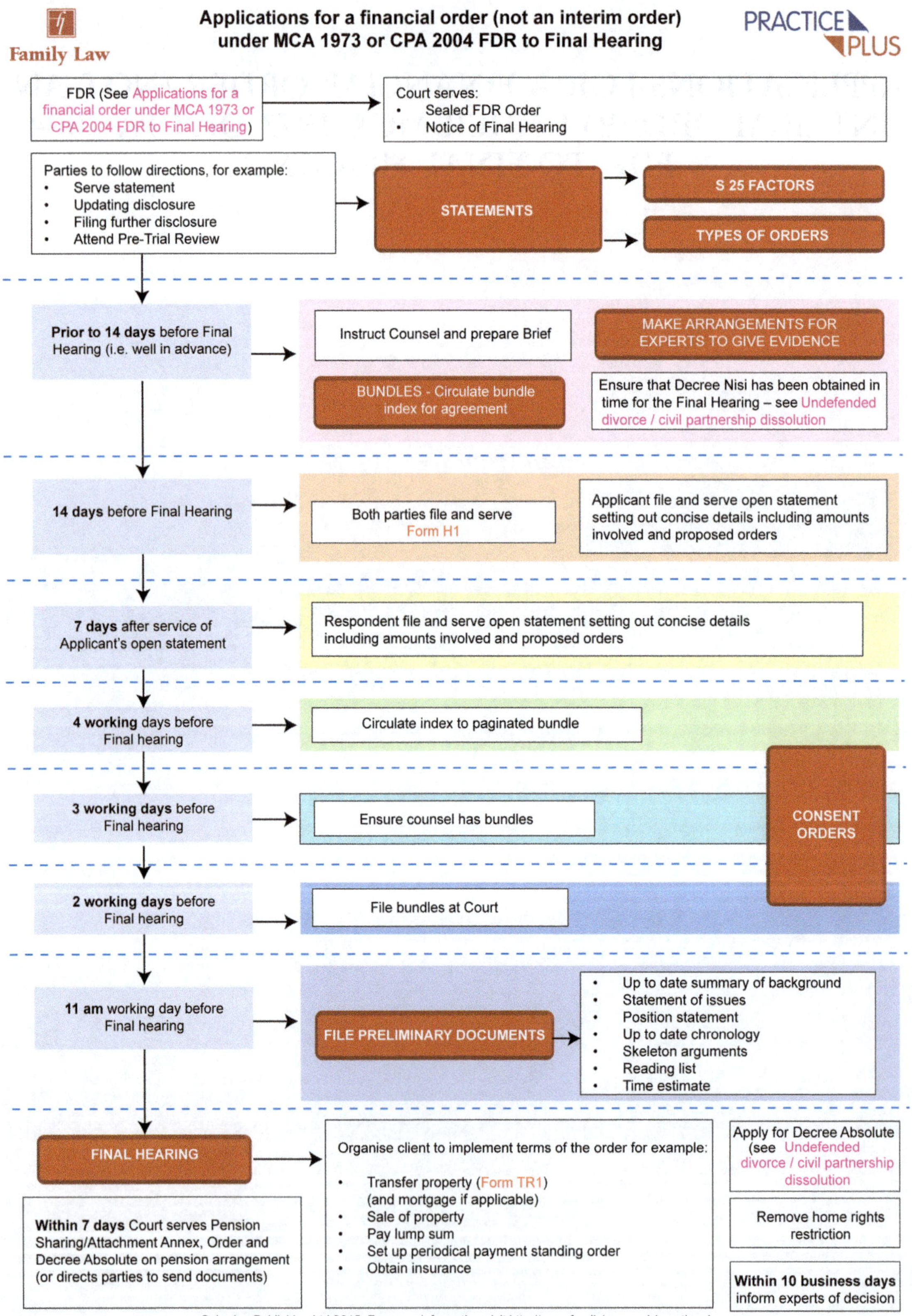
Family Law
Applications for a financial order (not an interim order) under MCA 1973 or CPA 2004 FDR to Final Hearing
PRACTICE PLUS
FDR (See Applications for a financial order under MCA 1973 or CPA 2004 FDR to Final Hearing)
Court serves:
• Sealed FDR Order
• Notice of Final Hearing
Parties to follow directions, for example:
• Serve statement
• Updating disclosure
• Filing further disclosure
• Attend Pre-Trial Review
STATEMENTS
S 25 FACTORS
TYPES OF ORDERS
Prior to 14 days before Final Hearing (i.e. well in advance)
Instruct Counsel and prepare Brief
MAKE ARRANGEMENTS FOR EXPERTS TO GIVE EVIDENCE
BUNDLES - Circulate bundle index for agreement
Ensure that Decree Nisi has been obtained in time for the Final Hearing – see Undefended divorce / civil partnership dissolution
14 days before Final Hearing
Both parties file and serve Form H1
Applicant file and serve open statement setting out concise details including amounts involved and proposed orders
7 days after service of Applicant's open statement
Respondent file and serve open statement setting out concise details including amounts involved and proposed orders
4 working days before Final hearing
Circulate index to paginated bundle
CONSENT ORDERS
3 working days before Final hearing
Ensure counsel has bundles
2 working days before Final hearing
File bundles at Court
11 am working day before Final hearing
FILE PRELIMINARY DOCUMENTS
• Up to date summary of background
• Statement of issues
• Position statement
• Up to date chronology
• Skeleton arguments
• Reading list
• Time estimate
FINAL HEARING
Organise client to implement terms of the order for example:
• Transfer property (Form TR1) (and mortgage if applicable)
• Sale of property
• Pay lump sum
• Set up periodical payment standing order
• Obtain insurance
Apply for Decree Absolute (see Undefended divorce / civil partnership dissolution
Remove home rights restriction
Within 10 business days inform experts of decision
Within 7 days Court serves Pension Sharing/Attachment Annex, Order and Decree Absolute on pension arrangement (or directs parties to send documents)

PRACTICE NOTE

See also Procedural Guide (PG) B5 in *The Red Book (Family Court Practice)*.

Statements

The court will sometimes direct that the parties produce and serve statements outlining their case in further detail. The court may direct that the statement address a specific issue (for example, contributions) or the whole of the party's case.

FPR 2010, PD 22A sets out the requirements as to the format and contents of a witness statement and should be referred to directly.

When drafting the statement practitioners should have regard to the 's 25 factors' (MCA 1973, s 25). For civil partnerships the factors are found at CPA 2004, Sch 5, para 21 and they mirror those in s 25 MCA 1973. For ease the factors shall be called the 's 25 factors' in this practice note. See 's 25 factors' below.

In drafting the statement regard should also be had to the relevant case law. See commentary to MCA 1973, s 25 and CPA 2004, Sch 5, para 21 in *Family Court Practice* (*the Red Book*). The case law identifies three main principles:

- **Needs**
- **Compensation** (See further *Lauder v Lauder* [2007] 2 FLR 802 and *H v H* [2014] EWCA Civ 1523. However see criticisms of the compensation principle – *RP v RP* [2007] 1 FLR 2105; *Hvorostovsky v Hvorostovsky* [2009] 2 FLR 1574)
- **Sharing**

See the case of *White v White* [2000] 2 FLR 981. The following specific areas may be in issue and may need to be covered in the statement:

- pre-marital/inherited wealth (see further *Smith v Smith* [2007] 2 FLR 1103; *Jones v Jones* [2011] 1 FLR 1723; *Robson v Robson* [2011] 1 FLR 751; *K v L (Non-Matrimonial Property: Special Contribution)* [2011] 2 FLR 980; *AR v AR (Treatment of Inherited Wealth)* [2012] 2 FLR 1; *Abbott v Abbott* [2008] 1 FLR 1451; *S v S (Ancillary Relief: Importance of FDR)* [2008] 1 FLR 944; *C v C* [2009] 1 FLR 8; *N v F (Financial Orders: Pre-Aquired Wealth)* [2011] 2 FLR 533, *JL v SL* [2015] EWHC 360 (Fam));
- trusts (see further *C v C (Ancillary Relief: Trust Fund)* [2010] 1 FLR 337; *B v B (Ancillary Relief)* [2010] 2 FLR 887; *Whaley v Whaley* [2012] 1 FLR 735; *Thomas v Thomas* [1995] 2 FLR 668, CA; *A v A* [2007] 2 FLR 467; *TL v ML (Ancillary Relief: Claim against Assets of Extended Family)* [2006] 1 FLR 1263; *De Bruyne v De Bruyne* [2010] 2 FLR 1240; *SR v CR (Ancillary Relief: Family Trusts)* [2009] 2 FLR 1083; *G v B* [2014] 2 FLR 292); *Quan v Bray* [2014] EWHC 3340 (Fam); *P v P* [2015] EWCA Civ 447;
- family business (see further *Re C (Divorce: Financial relief)* [2008] 1 FLR 625; *P v P (Financial Relief: Illiquid Assets)* [2005] 1 FLR 548; *H v H* [2008] 2 FLR 2092; *Re Bird Precision Bellows Ltd* [1984] 1 Ch 419, CA; *G v G (Financial Provision: Equal Division)* [2002] 2 FLR 1143; *Irvine v Irvine* [2006] 4 All ER 102 Ch; *Charman v Charman (No 2)* [2007] 1 FLR 593; *NA v MA* [2007] 1 FLR 1760; *A v A* [2006] 2 FLR 115; *R v R (Financial Relief: Company Valuation)* [2005] 2 FLR 365; *V v V (Financial Relief)* [2005] 2 FLR 697; *Ben Hashem v Al Shayif* [2009] 1 FLR 115; *Prest v Petrodel Resources Ltd & Others* [2013] 2 FLR 732; *M v M and Others* [2013] EWHC 2534 (Fam));
- marital agreements (see further *Radmacher v Granatino* [2010] 2 FLR 1900; *Z v Z (No 2) (Financial Remedy: Marriage Contract)* [2012] 1 FLR 1100; *V v V (Pre-Nuptial Agreement)*

[2012] 1 FLR 1315; *F v F (Pre-nuptial Agreement)* [2010] 1 FLR 1743; *AH v PH (Scandanavian Marriage Settlement)* [2014] 2 FLR 251; *Luckwell v Limata* [2014] 2 FLR 1252);

- *liquid v illiquid* assets (see further *Wells v Wells* [2002] 2 FLR 97, CA; *P v P (Financial Relief: Illiquid Assets)* [2005] 1 FLR 548);
- post-separation accruals (see further *H v H* [2007] 2 FLR 548; *P v P (Post-separation Accruals and Earning Capacity)* [2008] 2 FLR 1135; *H v H (Financial Provision)* [2009] 2 FLR 795; *CR v CR* [2007] 2 FLR 548; *SK v WL (Ancillary Relief: Post-Separation Accrual)* [2011] 1 FLR 1471; *Gordon (formerly Stefanou) v Stefanou* [2011] 1 FLR 1582; *S v S (Ancillary Relief after Lengthy Separation)* [2007] 1 FLR 2120; *B v B (Ancillary Relief: Post-Separation Income)* [2010] 2 FLR 1214; *H v H* [2010] 1 FLR 1864; *Jenifer E v Mark E* [2013] 2 FLR 999; *H v W (Cap on Wife's Share of Bonus Payments)* [2015] 1 FLR 75; *Cooper-Hohn v Hohn* [2015] 1 FLR 745; *JL v SL* [2015] EWHC 360 (Fam));
- 'add backs' (see further *Norris v Norris* [2003] 1 FLR 1142; *McCartney v Mills McCartney* [2008] 1 FLR 1508; *Vaughan v Vaughan* [2008] 1 FLR 1108); *US v SR* [2014] EWFC 24;
- adverse inferences where disclosure is deficient (see further *Young v Young* [2014] 2 FLR 786);
- personal injury awards (see further *Daubney v Daubney* [1976] Fam 267; *Pritchard v Cobden Ltd and Another (No 1)* [1987] 2 FLR 30, CA; *Wagstaff v Wagstaff* [1992] 1 FLR 333, CA; and *Mansfield v Mansfield* [2012] 1 FLR 117);
- pensions (see further *Vaughan v Vaughan* [2008] 1 FLR 1108, CA; *Behzadi v Behzadi* [2009] 2 FLR 649);
- cohabitation (see further *Grey v Grey* [2010] 1 FLR 1764, CA. See notes to MCA 1973, s 31 for commentary on cohabitation cases).

The statement should set out the orders sought and explain why, with reference to the s 25 factors such orders are suitable. See 'Types of Orders' below.

The application of the s 25 factors, the various types of orders and the related case-law are large and complex areas of law. This practice note sets out only a very brief summary and reference should be made to further detailed commentary which can be found in:

- *Family Court Practice (the Red Book)* (in particular see commentary to MCA 1973, s 25); and
- *Duckworth's Matrimonial Property and Finance*, para B3[33A] onwards in particular.

's 25 Factors'

The 's 25 factors' are those to which the court will have regard when exercising its discretion in making a final order. The court must have regard to all the circumstances of the case with **the first consideration being given to the welfare while a minor of any child of the family who has not attained the age of 18** (MCA 1973, s 25(1) and CPA 2004, Sch 5, para 20).

The court shall in particular have regard to the following matters:

- the **income, earning capacity, property** and **other financial resources** which each of the parties to the marriage/civil partnership has or is likely to have in the foreseeable future, including in the case of earning capacity any increase in that capacity which it would in the opinion of the court be reasonable to expect a party to the marriage/civil partnership to take steps to acquire (MCA 1973, s 25(2)(a) and CPA 2004, Sch 5, para 21(2)(a));
- the **financial needs, obligations** and **responsibilities** which each of the parties to the marriage/civil partnership has or is likely to have in the foreseeable future (MCA 1973, s 25(2)(b) and CPA 2004, Sch 5, para 21(2)(b));

- the **standard of living** enjoyed by the family before the breakdown of the marriage/civil partnership (MCA 1973, s 25(2)(c) and CPA 2004, Sch 5, para 21(2)(c)) (see further *S v S* [2008] 2 FLR 113; *G v G (Financial Remedies: Short Marriage: Trust Assets)* [2012] 2 FLR 48);
- the **age** of each party to the marriage/civil partnership and the **duration of the marriage/civil partnership** (MCA 1973, s 25(2)(d) and CPA 2004, Sch 5, para 21(2)(d)) (see further *GW v RW (Financial Provision: Departure from Equality)* [2003] 2 FLR 108; *CO v CO (Ancillary Relief: Pre-marriage cohabitation)* [2004] 1 FLR 1095; *Foster v Foster* [2003] 2 FLR 299; *Robson v Robson* [2011] 1 FLR 751; *Rossi v Rossi* [2007] 1 FLR 790; *G v G* [2012] 2 FLR 48; *Miller v Miller; McFarlane v McFarlane* [2006] 1 FLR 1186; *Fallon v Fallon* [2010] 1 FLR 910);
- any **physical or mental disability** of either of the parties to the marriage/civil partnership (MCA 1973, s 25(2)(e) and CPA 2004, Sch 5, para 21(2)(e));
- the **contributions** which each of the parties has made or is likely in the foreseeable future to make to the welfare of the family, including any contribution by looking after the home or caring for the family (MCA 1973, s 25(2)(f) and CPA 2004, Sch 5, para 21(2)(f)) (see further *Sorrell v Sorrell* [2006] 1 FLR 497; *Charman v Charman (No 4)* [2007] 1 FLR 1246, CA; *G v G (Financial Provision: Equal Division)* [2002] 2 FLR 1143; *H v H* [2010] 1 FLR 1864; *Cooper-Hohn v Hohn* [2015] 1 FLR 745;
- the **conduct** of each of the parties, if that conduct is such that it would in the opinion of the court be inequitable to disregard it (MCA 1973, s 25(2)(g) and CPA 2004, Sch 5, para 21(2)(g)) (see further *G v G (Financial Provision: Separation Agreement)* [2004] 1 FLR 1011, disapproved of in *Miller v Miller; McFarlane v McFarlane* [2006] 1 FLR 1186; *W v N* [2007] EWHC 3050 (Fam); *M v M (Third Party Subpoena: Financial Conduct)* [2006] 2 FLR 1253; *S v S (Non-matrimonial Property: Conduct)* [2007] 1 FLR 1496; *H v H (Financial Relief: Attempted Murder as Conduct)* [2006] 1 FLR 990; *Atkinson v Atkinson* [1988] 2 FLR 353; *FZ v SZ and Others (Ancillary Relief: Conduct: Valuations)* [2011] 1 FLR 64);
- in the case of proceedings for divorce/dissolution or nullity, **the value to each of the parties to the marriage/civil partnership of any benefit which, by reason of the dissolution or annulment of the marriage/civil partnership, that party will lose the chance of acquiring** (MCA 1973, s 25(2)(h) and CPA 2004, Sch 5, para 21(2)(h)).

In exercising its powers in relation to a child of the family, the court shall in particular have regard to the following matters:

- the financial needs of the child (MCA 1973, s 25(3)(a) and CPA 2004, Sch 5, para 22(2)(a));
- the income, earning capacity (if any), property and other financial resources of the child (MCA 1973, s 25(3)(b) and CPA 2004, Sch 5, para 22(2)(b));
- any physical or mental disability of the child (MCA 1973, s 25(3)(c) and CPA 2004, Sch 5, para 22(2)(c));
- the manner in which he was being and in which the parties to the marriage/civil partnership expected him to be educated or trained (MCA 1973, s 25(3)(d) and CPA 2004, Sch 5, para 22(2)(d));
- the considerations mentioned in relation to the parties to the marriage/civil partnership in paragraphs (*a*), (*b*), (*c*) and (*e*) of subsection MCA 1973 s 25(2) or CPA 2004, Sch 5, para 21(2) above (MCA 1973, s 25(3)(e) and CPA 2004, Sch 5, para 22(2)(e)).

If the child of the family is not a child of that party the court shall also have regard:

- to whether that party assumed any responsibility for the child's maintenance, and, if so, to the extent to which, and the basis upon which, that party assumed such responsibility and to the length of time for which that party discharged such responsibility (MCA 1973, s 25(4)(a) and CPA 2004, Sch 5, para 22(3)(a) and (b));

- to whether in assuming and discharging such responsibility that party did so knowing that the child was not his or her own (MCA 1973, s 25(4)(b) and CPA 2004, Sch 5, para 22(3)(c));
- to the liability of any other person to maintain the child (MCA 1973, s 25(4)(c) and CPA 2004, Sch 5, para 22(3)(d)).

Clean break (divorce/dissolution or nullity only) (MCA 1973, s 25A and CPA 2004, Sch 5, para 23).

The court is also under a duty to consider ordering a 'clean break' – 'it shall be the duty of the court to consider whether it would be appropriate so to exercise those powers that the financial obligations of each party towards the other will be terminated as soon after the grant of the decree as the court considers just and reasonable'.

Types of orders

The financial orders available are:

- **Periodical payments** and/or secured periodical payments for spouse and/or children (MCA 1973, s 23(1)(a), (b),(d),(e) and CPA 2004, Sch 5, para 2(1) (a), (b), (d) and (e))
  - **Spousal**
    Periodical payments can be for a fixed amount of time ('a term order') or until the death of either party, the remarriage or cohabitation for more than a stated period of the receiving party, or further order ('joint lives'). The term order may be for a fixed period of time (for example 5 years) or until a defined event, for example the youngest child completing tertiary education. A party can apply to extend the duration of a term order under MCA 1973, s 31 (CPA 2004, Sch 5, para 51) unless there is a s 28(1A) bar (CPA 2004, Sch 5, para 47(5)) preventing the party from doing so. If there is to be no periodical payments the court can order a clean break, meaning that the party cannot apply to court in the future for periodical payments. Alternatively, if the possibility of a future income claim is to be kept alive the court can order nominal periodical payments (eg £1 per year).
    See further *G v G* [2012] 2 FLR 48; *Flavell v Flavell* [1997] 1 FLR 353; *C v C (Financial Relief: Short Marriage)* [1997] 2 FLR 26; *Miller v Miller; McFarlane v McFarlane* [2006] 1 FLR 1186 HL; *Murphy v Murphy* [2014] EWHC 2263 (Fam); *SS v NS* [2014] EWHC 4183 (Fam).
  - **Secured**
    A party can make any number of applications for a secured periodical payments order in the absence of a direction under s 25A(3) (CPA 2004, Sch 5, para 23(4)). The earliest date on which a secured periodical payments order can commence is the date when the claim is made but, by s 28(1)(b) (CPA 2004, Sch 5, para 47(3)(a)), it can be defined to continue beyond the death of the payer.
  - **Child**
    Note that the courts do not have jurisdiction to order child maintenance if the Child Support Agency/Child Maintenance Service has jurisdiction (CSA 1991, s 8). As a general rule the Child Support Agency/Child Maintenance Service will have jurisdiction in most cases if the non-resident parent resides in the UK and the court will therefore not have jurisdiction. However the CSA 1991 legislation should be referred to directly. There are exceptions to this rule:
    - Applications for top up orders (See further CSA 1991, s 8(5)–(10); *Re P (Child: Financial Provision)* [2003] 2 FLR 865, CA; and *Dickson v Rennie* [2014] EWHC 4306 (Fam)).
    - Variations of existing periodical payments orders (s 8(3A)) (see *V v V (Child Maintenance)* [2001] 2 FLR 799).
    - *'Segal'* orders (See *Dorney-Kingdom v Dorney-Kingdom* [2000] 2 FLR 855, CA).

- Lump sums for children (see *Askew-Page v Page* [2001] Fam Law 794, *V v V (Child Maintenance)* [2001] 2 FLR 799).
- Costs (See *MT v OT (Financial provision: costs)* [2008] 2 FLR 1311).
- Consent orders.

Periodical payment orders are variable under MCA 1973, s 31 (CPA 2004, Sch 5, para 51).

- **Lump sum** for spouse and/or children (plus interest) (MCA 1973, s 23(1)(c),(f) and (6) and CPA 2004, Sch 5, paras 2(1) (c) and (f) and para 3)
  There can only be one lump sum order for the spouse/civil partner (see *Coleman v Coleman* [1973] Fam 10; *Banyard v Banyard* [1984] FLR 643). There can be more than one lump sum for children. Lump sums cannot be varied (although if a lump sum is payable in instalments the timing and amount of those instalments may be varied on application by either party (see further MCA 1973, s 31 or CPA 2004, Sch 5, para 51, *Hamilton v Hamilton* [2014] 1 FLR 55, *Dickson v Rennie* [2014] EWHC 4306 (Fam) and *Lump sum, Lump sums and Instalments: a brief history* July [2013] Fam Law 856. Also see Variation of a financial order practice note).
  The court may, in certain circumstances of grossly unreasonable behaviour in litigation, consider awarding a sum payable by one party, for retention as a 'fighting fund' to meet the other party's future legal costs in respect of subsequent litigation. See for example *Thiry v Thiry* [2014] EWHC 4046 (Fam).
- **Property adjustment order** (MCA 1973, s 24 and CPA 2004, Sch 5, paras 6 – 9)
  A property adjustment order will not take effect until Decree Absolute/Final Order. More than one property adjustment order may be made although on the subsequent application the court will consider whether the earlier order was intended to be a final and conclusive settlement, and if so the later application will be refused (see *Carson v Carson* (1981) 2 FLR 352; *Dinch v Dinch* [1987] 2 FLR 162; *Sandford v Sandford* [1986] 1 FLR 412).
- **Order for sale of property** (where order also made for secured periodical payments, lump sum or property adjustment) (MCA 1973, s 24A and CPA 2004, Sch 5, paras 10 – 14). The court can only make an order for sale of a property if it also orders a lump sum, property adjustment or secured periodical payments order. The order for sale can only take effect upon Decree Absolute/Final Order (MCA 1973, s 24A(3) and CPA 2004, Sch 5, paras 12(3)).
- **Pension (or pension protection fund) sharing order** (divorce/dissolution or nullity only) (MCA 1973, ss 21A – C, 24B – G, 25G and CPA 2004, Sch 5, paras 15 – 19F)
  There can only be one sharing order per pension (or pension protection fund) scheme (not including sharing orders from a previous divorce/dissolution). Therefore the court can make a later pension sharing order if it applies to a different pension scheme (providing the applicant's claims have not previously been dismissed). A pension sharing order does not take effect until the later of the date of Decree Absolute/Final Order (s 24B(2) or CPA 2004, Sch 5, para 19(1)) or 7 days after the time for appealing the order (Divorce etc (Pensions) Regulations 2000, reg 9). A pension (or pension protection fund) sharing order is not available for judicial separation. A pension (or pension protection fund) sharing order must be expressed as a percentage (ie not a figure). See Pensions on divorce/dissolution/nullity/(judicial) separation – Part 1 (to First Appointment) practice note for further guidance.)
- **Pension (or pension protection fund) attachment order** (MCA 1973, ss 25B – D, 21C, 25F, 26G and CPA 2004, Sch 5, Parts 6 and 7)
  A pension (or pension protection fund) attachment order is a species of financial provision order. Pension (or pension protection fund) attachment periodical payment orders, therefore, end on remarriage and can be varied at any time. A pension (or pension protection fund) attachment lump sum order can be varied (even as to amount) before either party's death. A pension (or pension protection fund) attachment order is not available if the pension arrangement is or has been subject to pension (or pension protection fund) sharing between parties to the marriage/civil partnership. See Pensions on divorce/dissolution/nullity/(judicial) separation – Part 2 (First Appointment to implementation) practice note for further guidance.)

In continuation of the family law reforms, further draft standard orders have been released by the President's family orders project team. All the draft orders can be found at http://www.jordanpublishing.co.uk/l/family-orders and whilst they await implementation, it is prudent to become familiar with and adopt their contents. The interim report of the Financial Remedies Working Group considered a number of improvements to financial proceedings, some of which would necessitate changes to the FPR 2010. Further to the first batch of draft orders released in November 2013, the report also includes within the Annexes, draft directions and final orders in financial proceedings, September [2014] Fam Law 1311. The final report (February [2015] Fam Law 196) maintains these recommendations.

Bundles

Bundles

Practice Direction 27A must be followed (see *Re W (Strict Compliance with Court Orders)* [2014] EWHC 22; *J v J* [2014] EWHC 3654 (Fam); and *Seagrove v Sullivan* [2015] 2 FLR 602) for the preparation of court bundles (FPR 2010, r 27.6). The Practice Direction sets out very precise rules regarding the preparation of bundles and should be referred to directly. It applies to all hearings before a judge sitting in the Family Division of the High Court wherever the court may be sitting, and all hearings in the Family Court save for hearings of any urgent application if and to the extent it would be impossible to comply with the Practice Direction (PD 27A, paras 2.1 and 2.4). See also *Re L (Procedure: Bundles: Translation)* [2015] 1 FLR 1417 for further guidance particularly on the court's stance on adherence to PD 27A.

In summary:

- a bundle must be provided by the party in the position of applicant (or, if there are cross-applications, by the party whose application was first in time) or, if that person is a litigant in person, by the first listed respondent who is not a litigant in person (PD 27A, para 3.1);
- PD 27A, para 4.1 sets out the content of the bundle and paras 5.1 and 5.2 set out the format of the bundle;
- if possible the content of the bundle should be agreed between the parties (FPR 2010, PD 27A, para 3.2);
- the index to the bundle should be circulated to all parties **4 working days** before the hearing (FPR 2010, PD 27A, para 6.1);
- the paginated bundle should be sent to counsel by the person instructing them **3 working days** before the hearing (FPR 2010, PD 27A, para 6.2); and
- the bundle should be lodged at the appropriate court office **2 working days** before the hearing (FPR 2010, PD 27A, para 6.3). It is advisable to obtain a receipt if possible or to seek confirmation from the court that the bundle has arrived if sent by post/DX. In the case of a hearing listed before a bench of magistrates four copies of the bundle should be lodged with the court.

Number of sets of bundles:

- Applicant
- Counsel
- Court
- Witness
- Respondent – The applicant should request an undertaking that the respondent will pay for reasonable copying charges before producing the respondent's bundle. The applicant should also enquire whether the respondent's counsel will need a copy and, if so, whether the

respondent would like it delivered straight to chambers. The respondent should meet the copying charges for his or her counsel's bundle.

Arranging for experts to give evidence

The court can direct that an expert should give evidence at the final hearing. The court will only direct that an expert should attend court if it is necessary to do so in the interests of justice (FPR 2010, r 25.9(2)) – often only the expert's written report will be required and their attendance at court will not be necessary. Where the court has directed that the expert should attend court the party who is responsible for the instruction of the expert must, by a date specified by the court prior to the hearing at which the expert is to give oral evidence, ensure that:

- a date and time (if possible, convenient to the expert) are fixed for the court to hear the expert's evidence, substantially in advance of the hearing at which the expert is to give oral evidence and no later than a specified date prior to that hearing (FPR 2010, PD 25B, para 10.1(a));
- if the expert's oral evidence is not required, the expert is notified as soon as possible (FPR 2010, PD 25B, para 10.1(b));
- the witness template accurately indicates how long the expert is likely to be giving evidence, in order to avoid the inconvenience of the expert being delayed at court (FPR 2010, PD 25B, para 10.1(c));
- consideration is given in each case to whether some or all of the experts participate by telephone conference or video link, or submit their evidence in writing, to ensure that minimum disruption is caused to professional schedules and that costs are minimised (FPR 2010, PD 25B, para 10.1(d)).

All parties shall ensure that:

- the parties' advocates have identified (whether at an advocates' meeting or by other means) the issues which the experts are to address (FPR 2010, PD 25B, para 10.2(a));
- wherever possible, a logical sequence to the evidence is arranged, with experts of the same discipline giving evidence on the same day (FPR 2010, PD 25B, para 10.2(b));
- the court is informed of any circumstance where all experts agree but a party nevertheless does not accept the agreed opinion, so that directions can be given for the proper consideration of the experts' evidence and opinion and of the party's reasons for not accepting the agreed opinion (FPR 2010, PD 25B, para 10.2(c));
- in the exceptional case the court is informed of the need for a witness summons (FPR 2010, PD 25B, para 10.2(d), see Form FP25).

Preliminary documents

Preliminary documents

PD 27A, para 4.3 sets out the preliminary documents that should be prepared and lodged by **11 am the day before the hearing** (FPR 2010, PD 27A, para 6.4):

- an up to date summary of the background to the hearing confined to those matters which are relevant to the hearing and the management of the case and limited, if practicable, to four A4 pages (FPR 2010, PD 27A, para 4.3(a));
- a statement of the issue or issues to be determined at that hearing and at the final hearing (FPR 2010, PD 27A, para 4.3(b));
- a position statement by each party including a summary of the order or directions sought by that party at the final hearing (FPR 2010, PD 27A, para 4.3(c));

- an up to date chronology if it is a final hearing or if the summary of the background is insufficient (FPR 2010, PD 27A, para 4.3(d));
- skeleton arguments, if appropriate (FPR 2010, PD 27A, para 4.3(e));
- a list of essential reading for the hearing (FPR 2010, PD 27A, para 4.3(f)); and
- the time estimate (FPR 2010, PD 27A, para 4.3(g)).

The preliminary documents should be as short and succinct as possible and should state on the front page immediately below the heading the date when it was prepared and the date of the hearing for which it was prepared (FPR 2010, PD 27A, para 4.4). The preliminary documents should be cross referenced to the relevant pages of the bundle (FPR 2010, PD 27A, para 4.5). If possible there should only be one set of preliminary documents, agreed between the parties (FPR 2010, PD 27A, para 4.6). If agreement is not possible the fact of the parties' disagreement and their differing contentions should be set out at the appropriate places in the document.

Copies of all authorities relied on must be contained in a separate composite bundle agreed between the advocates and must be lodged in hard copy (FPR 2010, PD 27A, para 6.4).

Tip:

- Take extra copies of the preliminary documents to court on the day of the final hearing, in case they have not made their way onto the court file.

Consent orders

If the parties reach an agreement at any point prior to the court determining a final order they should make an application for a consent order under FPR 2010, r 9.26.

Documents to file at court:

Original signed draft consent order (FPR 2010, r 9.26(1)(a))

The consent order can be signed by the parties' legal representatives but, if the consent order contains undertakings, it must be signed by the party giving the undertaking as well (FPR 2010, PD 9A, para 7.1). The parties must have capacity to enter into the consent order; see *MAP v RAP* [2015] 2 FLR 67.

A consent order that contains undertakings for the payment of money must include the wording set out at FPR 2010, PD 33A, paras 2.2 and 2.3 and a statement signed by the person giving the undertaking confirming that he or she understands its terms and the consequences of failing to comply. An undertaking other than for the payment of money must contain the wording in paragraphs FPR 2010, PD 37A, para 2.2.

Do not forget to attach any required annexes/schedules, for example, a pension sharing/attachment annex (Form P1 or Form P2 – see precedents C67 and C68 (*Family Law Precedents Service*)) or schedule outlining the division of the contents of the matrimonial home.

See precedents C42 – C72, C77, C78 and C79 (*Family Law Precedents Service*) and *Duckworth's Matrimonial Property and Finance*, para D2[1] – D2[7] for example consent order wording and guidance.

Copies of the draft consent order

FPR 2010, r 9.26(1)(a) requires that at least one copy of the draft order, in addition to the signed document, is filed at court. In practice it is useful to provide the court with three copies of the order ready for sealing, formatted in a way that allows the court to seal the document if approved, without the need for the court to re-type the document.

Do not forget to attach any required annexes/schedules to the copies.

Statement of Information (Form D81) (FPR 2010, r 9.26(1)(b))

- Joint Form D81
  Where each party's statement of information is contained in one form, it must be signed by both the applicant and respondent to certify that they have read the contents of the other party's statement (FPR 2010, r 9.26(2)).
- Separate Forms D81
  Where each party's statement of information is in a separate form, the form of each party must be signed by the other party to certify that they have read the contents of the statement contained in that form (FPR 2010, r 9.26(3)).

See precedent C75 (*Family Law Precedents Service*).

Respondent's Form A (marked 'for dismissal purposes only')

If there is to be a capital or income clean break the respondent's claims will need to be dismissed. If the respondent to the financial proceedings is also the respondent to the divorce/dissolution/judicial separation/nullity proceedings he or she will never have applied for financial claims (in either a Form A or a petition – unless he or she cross-petitioned) and therefore, technically, there are no claims in existence to dismiss. For this reason, commonly in such circumstances a respondent files a Form A for dismissal purposes. 'For Dismissal Purposes Only' should be marked clearly on the form so that the court does not issue it.

Note however that the report of the Financial Remedies Working Group February [2015] Fam Law 196 recommended changes so that filing a Form A for dismissal purposes would no longer be necessary.

Rule 9.34 statement (pension attachment only)

If the draft consent order includes a pension attachment order (not a pension sharing order) the draft will need to be served on the pension arrangement in advance of the draft being filed at court as FPR 2010, r 9.34 requires that a statement be filed at court confirming that the trustees or managers have been served with a copy of the application, a draft of the proposed order and certain prescribed information and have not made any objection to the proposed consent order within 21 days from service. See further notes to precedent C76 (*Family Law Precedents Service*). See Pensions on divorce/dissolution/nullity/(judicial) separation – Part 2 (First Appointment to implementation) practice note for further guidance.

The court will not act as a rubber stamp and can approve or reject a consent order. For guidance on the approval of consent orders agreed during arbitration see *S v S (Financial Remedies: Arbitral Award)* [2014] 1 FLR 1257.

Tip:

- It is a good idea to file a covering letter with the consent order setting out a check list of the documents enclosed and giving an explanation of any unusual terms.

Final hearing

Form H1

Each party should file at court and serve on the other party a Form H1 **not less than 14 days** before the final hearing (FPR 2010, r 9.27(2)). The court can take into account each party's liability for costs when considering what overall final order to make.

Open statements

The applicant should file at court and serve on the respondent an open statement which sets out concise details, including the amounts involved, of the orders which the respondent proposes to ask the court to make **not less than 14 days** before the final hearing (FPR 2010, r 9.28(1)).

The respondent should file at court and serve on the applicant an open statement which sets out concise details, including the amounts involved, of the orders which the respondent proposes to ask the court to make **not less than 7 days** after service of the applicant's open statement (FPR 2010, r 9.28(2)).

Publicity

The proceedings will be held in private (FPR 2010, r 27.10). This means that members of the public are not allowed access to the court room. However accredited members of the press are entitled to be in court (FPR 2010, r 27.11(2)(f)) unless the court directs that they shall not be allowed access (FPR 2010, r 27.11(3)). See *Family Court Practice (the Red Book)* notes to r 27.11 and FPR 2010, PD 27B for further information. Also see *Emergency Remedies in the Family Courts*, para G[1.1] to para G[1.9].

Transparency in the family court continues to be high on the agenda. Following the Practice Guidance in February [2014] Fam Law 222 and various views (see *12th View from the President's Chambers: The process of reform: next steps* in July [2014] Fam Law 978) the President released a consultation paper *Transparency – The Next Steps: A Consultation Paper issued by the President of the Family Division* in September [2014] Fam Law 1331. Also see *Re J (A Child)* [2014] 1 FLR 523 and *Re P (Enforced Caesarean: Reporting Restrictions)* [2014] 2 FLR 410.

Attendance

Both parties must personally attend unless the court directs otherwise (FPR 2010, r 27.3)). The parties will normally be required to give oral evidence.

Order

See 'Types of Orders' above.

The court will have regard to the 's 25 factors' when exercising its discretion (see 's 25 factors' above).

Implementation of the order

The final order should be read carefully and a checklist of the client's obligations drawn up. Key dates should be noted. Tasks which may be included are:

- transfer property (Form TR1) (and mortgage if applicable);
- organise sale of property;
- pay lump sum;
- set up periodical payment standing order;
- obtain insurance;
- execute trust documentation;
- transfer vehicles;
- share transfers;
- policy transfers (often requires a form from the particular institution);
- transfer/close bank accounts;
- arrange chattel collection/delivery.

Apply for Decree Absolute/Final Order

See Undefended divorce/civil partnership dissolution practice note.

Pensions

Within 7 days the court serves the Pension Sharing/Attachment Annex, Order and Decree Absolute/Final Order (or (Judicial) Separation – attachment only, sharing not available) on the pension arrangement (or directs a party to send the documents) (FPR 2010, r 9.36(2), (4) and (5)). Even if not directed to, it is a good idea to send the documents to the pension provider in any event, in case of court delays.

Inform experts

If an expert has been instructed, **within 10 business days after the Final Hearing** the solicitor instructing the expert shall inform the expert in writing of the outcome of the case and of the use made by the court of the expert's opinion (FPR 2010, r 25.19 (1)). Unless the court directs otherwise the final order and transcript must be sent to the expert (within 10 days of the order and transcript being received) (FPR 2010, r 25.19 (2)).

Remove home rights notice

A Form HR4 is required – available at http://www.landregistry.gov.uk/_media/downloads/forms/HR4.pdf. For guidance see http://www.landregistry.gov.uk/public/guides/public-guide-4.

CONTESTED APPLICATIONS UNDER TRUSTS OF LAND AND APPOINTMENT OF TRUSTEES ACT 1996, S 14, UNDER CPR 1998 PART 7

FLOWCHART

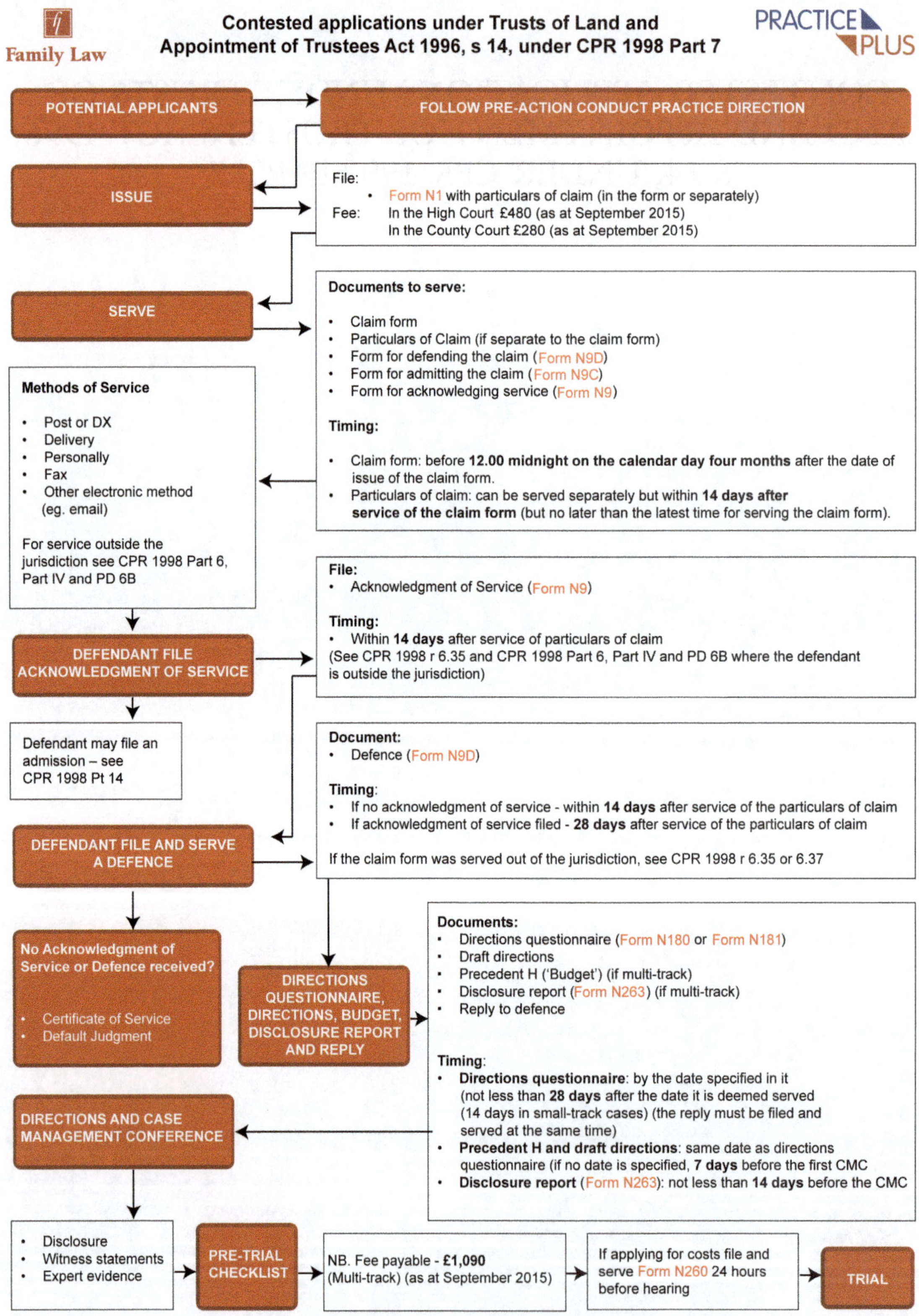
Family Law
Contested applications under Trusts of Land and Appointment of Trustees Act 1996, s 14, under CPR 1998 Part 7
PRACTICE PLUS
POTENTIAL APPLICANTS
FOLLOW PRE-ACTION CONDUCT PRACTICE DIRECTION
ISSUE
File:
• Form N1 with particulars of claim (in the form or separately)
Fee: In the High Court £480 (as at September 2015)
In the County Court £280 (as at September 2015)
SERVE
Documents to serve:
• Claim form
• Particulars of Claim (if separate to the claim form)
• Form for defending the claim (Form N9D)
• Form for admitting the claim (Form N9C)
• Form for acknowledging service (Form N9)
Timing:
• Claim form: before 12.00 midnight on the calendar day four months after the date of issue of the claim form.
• Particulars of claim: can be served separately but within 14 days after service of the claim form (but no later than the latest time for serving the claim form).
Methods of Service
• Post or DX
• Delivery
• Personally
• Fax
• Other electronic method (eg. email)
For service outside the jurisdiction see CPR 1998 Part 6, Part IV and PD 6B
DEFENDANT FILE ACKNOWLEDGMENT OF SERVICE
File:
• Acknowledgment of Service (Form N9)
Timing:
• Within 14 days after service of particulars of claim
(See CPR 1998 r 6.35 and CPR 1998 Part 6, Part IV and PD 6B where the defendant is outside the jurisdiction)
Defendant may file an admission – see CPR 1998 Pt 14
DEFENDANT FILE AND SERVE A DEFENCE
Document:
• Defence (Form N9D)
Timing:
• If no acknowledgment of service - within 14 days after service of the particulars of claim
• If acknowledgment of service filed - 28 days after service of the particulars of claim
If the claim form was served out of the jurisdiction, see CPR 1998 r 6.35 or 6.37
No Acknowledgment of Service or Defence received?
• Certificate of Service
• Default Judgment
DIRECTIONS QUESTIONNAIRE, DIRECTIONS, BUDGET, DISCLOSURE REPORT AND REPLY
Documents:
• Directions questionnaire (Form N180 or Form N181)
• Draft directions
• Precedent H ('Budget') (if multi-track)
• Disclosure report (Form N263) (if multi-track)
• Reply to defence
Timing:
• Directions questionnaire: by the date specified in it (not less than 28 days after the date it is deemed served (14 days in small-track cases) (the reply must be filed and served at the same time)
• Precedent H and draft directions: same date as directions questionnaire (if no date is specified, 7 days before the first CMC
• Disclosure report (Form N263): not less than 14 days before the CMC
DIRECTIONS AND CASE MANAGEMENT CONFERENCE
• Disclosure
• Witness statements
• Expert evidence
PRE-TRIAL CHECKLIST
NB. Fee payable - £1,090 (Multi-track) (as at September 2015)
If applying for costs file and serve Form N260 24 hours before hearing
TRIAL

PRACTICE NOTE

See also Procedural Guide (PG) A4 in *The Red Book (Family Court Practice)*.

Potential applicants

Applications under the Trusts of Land and Appointment of Trustees Act 1996 ('**TLATA 1996**') are commonly brought by cohabitants (rather than spouses or civil partners). Section 14 of TLATA 1996 allows a trustee, or anyone who has an interest in property subject to a trust of land, to apply for:

- an order declaring the nature or extent of a person's interest in the trust of land; or
- an order relating to the exercise by the trustees of any of their functions (including the power to exclude or the power of sale).

The applicant must be either:

- a trustee of land; or
- a person who has an interest in property subject to a trust of land.

Midland Bank v Pike [1988] 2 All ER 434 states that an applicant can be:

- a trustee;
- a joint legal or beneficial owner; or
- a judgment creditor holding a charging order.

Essentially a TLATA 1996 claim is brought by an applicant who cannot use the Matrimonial Causes Act 1973 ('**MCA 1973**') or the Civil Partnership Act 2004 ('**CPA 2004**'). See *Jones v Kernott* [2012] 1 FLR 45.

Applications by spouses or civil partners under TLATA 1996 are rare (and are generally discouraged – see *Miller-Smith v Miller-Smith* [2010] 1 FLR 1402) as the provisions for property adjustment under the MCA 1973 and the CPA 2004 are more suitable and the court has far wider powers under those statutes.

Also see Procedural Guide A4 (PG) in *Family Court Practice* (*the Red Book*).

Follow pre-action conduct practice direction

Claims under TLATA 1996 are governed by the Civil Procedure Rules 1998 ('**CPR 1998**'), as opposed to the Family Procedure Rules 2010 ('**FPR 2010**').

There is some debate as to whether TLATA 1996 claims should be made under Part 7 or Part 8 of the CPR 1998. The Part 8 procedure should be used when the applicant 'seeks the court's decision on a question which is unlikely to involve a substantial dispute of fact' (CPR 1998, r 8.1(2)(a)). This practice note outlines the Part 7 procedure; see the Contested applications under Trusts of Land and Appointment of Trustees Act 1996, s 14, under CPR 1998 Part 8 practice note for guidance on the procedure to be followed under Part 8 (available online at Practice Plus).

Whether a claim is made under Part 7 or Part 8 the Pre-Action Conduct Practice Direction ('**PAC PD**') will apply. The aim of the PAC PD is to encourage parties to reach settlement without the need for court proceedings. The parties are required to consider Alternative Dispute Resolution (PAC PD para 8).

The PAC PD sets out the following requirements:

Prior to issue

Before issuing proceedings the parties are expected to have exchanged sufficient information to:

(a) understand each other's position;
(b) make decisions about how to proceed;
(c) try to settle the issues without proceedings;
(d) consider a form of Alternative Dispute Resolution (ADR) to assist with settlement;
(e) support the efficient management of those proceedings; and
(f) reduce the costs of resolving the dispute (PAC PD, para 3).

Letter before claim

The claimant is required to send to the defendant a letter before claim. The letter should contain concise details of the claim including the basis on which the claim is made, a summary of the facts, what the claimant wants from the defendant, and if money, how the amount is calculated (PAC PD, para 6(a)).

Defendant's reply

The defendant should send a letter in response within a reasonable time – 14 days where the case is straight forward and no more than 3 months where the case is very complex. The response should include confirmation that the claim is accepted or, if it is not accepted, the reasons why, together with an explanation as to which facts and parts of the claim are in dispute. The letter should also detail any counterclaim if applicable (PAC PD, para 6(b)).

Claimant's response

Prior to 29 April 2015 the PAC PD stated that the claimant must provide any documents requested by the defendant within as short a period of time as is practicable (or explain in writing why the documents will not be provided) and further, if the defendant has made a counter-claim, that the claimant must provide a full response.

This provision is not included in the updated Practice Direction but it may be prudent to continue to adopt this requirement.

Issue

Documents

Claim form (Form N1)

See CPR 1998, Part 7 and PD 7A for guidance as to the content of the claim form. Rules regarding the content of a claim form are also found at CPR 1998, r 16.2 and PD 16 supplements this.

If the particulars of claim are to be served later the claim form should state that the particulars of claim are to follow (CPR 1998, r 16.2(2)).

The claim form must be verified by a statement of truth (PD 7A para 7.1).

See leaflet N1A for further guidance on completing the claim form.

Particulars of claim

Under the Part 7 procedure the particulars of claim can either be included in the claim form or filed separately later. If the particulars of claim are not included in the claim form they must be filed at court 7 days after service on the defendant (CPR 1998, r 7.4(3)) (see below at Service for further information about service of the particulars on the defendant).

CPR 1998, r 16.4 sets out the required content of particulars of claim and PD 16 supplements this. If not included in the claim form the particulars of claim must be verified by a statement of truth (PD 16, para 3.4).

When drafting the particulars of claim reference should be made to TLATA 1996, s 15 which sets out the matters to which the court will have regard when determining an application for an order under s 14.

The following points should be included in the particulars of claim:

- the background facts;
- explanation of the claimant's case with regards to:
  - whether there was an agreement between the claimant and respondent about their interests in the property;
  - any contributions made by the claimant; and
  - any detrimental reliance by the claimant.

Reference should be made to the application of the facts in the specific case to the check list in *Stack v Dowden* [2007] 1 FLR 1858 at [69]. Also see *Oxley v Hiscock* [2004] 2 FLR 669, CA; *Jones v Kernott* [2012] 1 FLR 45; *Smith v Bottomley* [2013] EWCA Civ 953; [2014] 1 FLR 626; *Thompson v Hurst* [2014] 1 FLR 238; *Southwell v Blackburn* [2014] EWCA Civ 1347 and *O'Kelly v Davies* [2014] EWCA Civ 1606.

For further guidance see the notes to TLATA 1996, s 15 *Family Court Practice (the Red Book)*. Also see *Duckworth's Matrimonial Property and Finance*, para A1[1] to para A1[68], *Emergency Remedies in the Family Courts*, para F[3.1] to para F[3.18] and the notes to precedent H1 (*Family Law Precedents Service*).

For a viewpoint on practical tips in TLATA applications see Recurring Misconceptions in TLATA Cases at http://www.familylaw.co.uk/news_and_comment/recurring-misconceptions-in-tolata-cases#.VcMxzvlVhBc.

Which court?

Either the **County Court** or the **High Court**.

- **County Court** – if issued in the County Court the claim form must be marked 'Chancery Business' (CPR 1998, PD 7A, para 2.5).
- **High Court** – should be the Chancery Division and the claim form must be marked 'Chancery Division'. However if the TLATA 1996 claim is issued together with a Sch 1 Children Act 1989 claim it may be possible to issue the claim in the Family Court. Proceedings may not be issued in the High Court if the value of the claim is £100,000 or less (CPR 1998, PD 7A, para 2.1).

Also see Procedural Guide A4 (PG) in *Family Court Practice (the Red Book)*.

Tips:

- Remember to include enough copies of the claim form (normally three – one for the claimant, one for the court and one for the defendant).
- Do not forget to check the court fee (in the High Court £480 and in the county court £280 as at September 2015) and include a cheque or postal order payable to 'HM Courts and Tribunals Service' or 'HMCTS'. The fee can also be paid in cash or by debit/credit card.
- If service is to be carried out by the claimant's solicitor remember to ask the court for 'solicitor service' at the time of filing the documents at court.

Serve

The following documents are required to be served on the defendant(s):

(1) claim form;

(2) particulars of claim (if separate to the claim form);

(3) a form for defending the claim (Form N9D);

(4) a form for admitting the claim (Form N9C); and

(5) a form for acknowledging service (Form N9).

CPR 1998, Part 6 governs the service of documents. Also see CPR 1998, PD 6A. The court will serve the documents on the defendant(s) unless 'solicitor' service is requested at the time of filing the document at court.

Timing

The claim form must be served before **12.00 midnight on the calendar day four months** after the date of issue of the claim form (CPR 1998, r 7.5). The particulars of claim can be served separately to the claim form but must be served within **14 days after service of the claim form** but no later than the latest time for serving the claim form (CPR 1998, r 7.4(1)). If the particulars of claim are served separately from the claim form they must be filed at Court within **7 days** of service on the defendant.

The claimant can apply to extend the timeframe for service of the claim form (CPR 1998, r 7.6). The defendant may also serve notice on the claimant to serve the claim form before the four month deadline has passed (CPR 1998, r 7.7).

Methods of service (CPR 1998, r 7.5)

- *Service by post or DX*
  Service must be by first class post, document exchange or other service which provides for delivery on the next business day. The step required to be taken before the deadline is 'posting, leaving with, delivering to or collection by the relevant service provider'. The defendant must be served at his usual or last known residence (CPR 1998, r 6.9) (unless the defendant has given another address to be served at (CPR 1998, r 6.8) or the claimant has been notified in writing that the defendant's solicitor is instructed to accept service on the defendant's behalf (CPR 1998, r 6.7)). If the usual or last known residence is not known the claimant must take reasonable steps to ascertain the defendant's current address (CPR 1998, r 6.9(3)). If, following reasonable steps, the defendant's current address cannot be ascertained the claimant can make an application to court to authorise service by an alternative method or at an alternative place (CPR 1998, r 6.9(5) and 6.15). See further CPR 1998, PD 6A 9.1 – 9.3.

- *Service by delivery*
  Delivering to or leaving the document at the relevant place.
- *Personal service*
  A claim form is served personally on an individual by leaving it with that individual (CPR 1998, r 6.5(3)). A claim form cannot be personally served if the claimant has been notified in writing that the defendant's solicitor is instructed to accept service on the defendant's behalf (CPR 1998, r 6.7).
- *Service by fax*
  The step required to be taken before the deadline is 'completing the transmission of the fax'. The defendant or his or her solicitor must have indicated that they are willing to accept service by fax. See further CPR 1998, PD 6A 4.1.
- *Other electronic method*
  The step required to be taken before the deadline is 'sending the e-mail or other electronic transmission'. The defendant or his or her solicitor must have indicated that they are willing to accept service by the electronic method. See further CPR 1998, PD 6A 4.1 – 4.3.

For service out of the jurisdiction see CPR 1998, Part 6, Part IV and PD 6B. An application may also be made to dispense with service in exceptional circumstances (see CPR 1998, r 6.16).

Service deemed

A claim form served within the United Kingdom is deemed to be served on the second business day after completion of the relevant step under r 7.5(1) (CPR 1998, r 6.14).

Tips:

- If instructing a process server, remember to provide them with a photograph of the defendant if possible. It is a good idea to take a copy of the documents to be served by the process server.

Defendant file acknowledgment of service

A defendant may file an acknowledgment of service if he or she is unable to file a defence within the period specified in r 15.4 (see below) or he or she wishes to dispute the court's jurisdiction (CPR 1998, r 10.1(3)).

Document

Acknowledgment of service (Form N9)

The acknowledgment of service must be signed by the defendant (or his or her legal representative) (CPR 1998, r 10.5(1)(a)). It must give an address for service (CPR 1998, r 10.5(1)(b)).

See leaflet N1C for further guidance.

Timing

- If the claim form and particulars of claim are served at the same time, the acknowledgement of service should be filed within **14 days** (CPR 1998, r 10.3(1)(b)).
- If the claim form states that the particulars of claim are to follow the acknowledgment of service does not need to be filed until **14 days** after service of the particulars of claim (CPR 1998, r 10.3(1)(a)).

Exceptions to the general 14-day rule above will occur if the claim form was served out of the jurisdiction, in which case either:

- the time period in CPR 1998, r 6.35; or
- the time period specified by the court under r 6.37(5) (when making an order giving permission to serve a claim form out of the jurisdiction)

will apply instead.

The court may also have specified a different period under r 6.12(3).

The court will notify the claimant in writing of receipt of the acknowledgment of service (CPR 1998, r 10.4).

Defendant file and serve defence

If a defendant wishes to defend all or part of a claim he or she must file a defence (CPR 1998, r 15.2).

Nb. If a defendant admits the claim they should complete Form N9C and the parties should refer to CPR 1998, Part 14.

Document

Defence (Form N9D)

Rules regarding the content of a defence are found at CPR 1998, r 16.5 and PD 16 supplements this.

The defence must be verified by a statement of truth (PD 15, para 2.1).

See leaflet N1C for further guidance.

Timing

- If no acknowledgment of service has been filed the defence should be filed within **14 days** after service of the particulars of claim (CPR 1998, r 15.4(1)(a)).
- If the defendant files an acknowledgment of service the defence should be filed **28 days** after service of the particulars of claim (CPR 1998, r 15.4(1)(b)).

An exception to the general rules above will occur if the claim form was served out of the jurisdiction, in which case see CPR 1998, r 6.35 or 6.37.

The court may also have specified a period under r 6.12(3) and so the general rules will not apply.

The parties can agree to extend the time for filing the defence by up to **28 days**, in which case the defendant should notify the court in writing (CPR 1998, r 15.5).

When a defence does not have to be filed:

The defendant will not have to file a defence before the relevant hearing if:

- the defendant is disputing the court's jurisdiction under CPR 1998, r 11 (CPR 1998, r 15.4(2)(b));

- the claimant has applied for summary judgment before the defendant has filed a defence (CPR 1998, r 15.4(2)(c) and r 24.4(2)).

Service

A copy of the defence must be served on every other party (CPR 1998, r 15.6).

Counterclaim

The defendant may make a counterclaim (see further CPR 1998, Part 20).

Default judgement

Step 1 – File a certificate of service

Before a claimant can obtain default judgment they must file a certificate of service (CPR 1998, r 6.17(2)(b)). If the defendant does not file an acknowledgment of service (and the claimant – as opposed to the court – served the claim form and particulars of claim) the claimant must file a certificate of service within **21 days** of service of the particulars of claim (CPR 1998, r 6.17(2)(a)).

Document

Certificate of service (Form N215)

Under CPR 1998, r 6.17 the certificate of service must state the category of address at which the claimant believes the claim form has been served and:

- for personal service – the date of personal service;
- for post/DX – the date of posting or leaving with, delivering to or collection by the relevant service provider;
- for delivery – the date when the document was delivered to or left at the permitted place;
- for fax – the date of completion of the transmission;
- for other electronic method – the date of sending the email or other electronic transmission; or
- for an alternative method/place – as set out by the court.

Step 2 – Apply for default judgment

'Default judgment' means judgment without trial (CPR 1998, r 12.1).

The claimant may obtain default judgment if:

- the defendant fails to file an acknowledgment of service within the period specified in r 10.3 (see above) (CPR 1998, r 10.2); and
- does not within that period file a defence in accordance with Part 15 (CPR 1998, r 15.3) or serve or file an admission in accordance with Part 14 (see above) (CPR 1998, r 10.2(2)).

See further CPR 1998, Pt 12 and PD 12.

Directions questionnaire, directions, budget, disclosure report and reply

Upon receipt of the defence the court will provisionally decide the track which appears most suitable for the claim (CPR 1998, r 26.3). It will then send to each of the parties notice of the proposed allocation which will also contain directions for filing the documents below (CPR 1998 r 26.3).

Documents

Directions questionnaire (Form N180 or Form N181)

The directions questionnaire asks the parties to set out which track the case should be allocated to.

The choices are:

- small-claims (value not more than £10,000) (CPR 1998, r 26.6(3));
- fast-track (value more than £10,000 but not more than £25,000, the trial no longer than one day and expert evidence limited to two per party (in two different expert fields)) (CPR 1998, r 26.6(4) and (5)); or
- multi-track (claims that do not fit the criteria for small claims track or fast track (CPR 1998, r 26.6(6)).

See leaflet EX305 for further details. TLATA 1996 claims are normally allocated to the multi-track. The directions questionnaire for multi-track and fast-track cases is the Form N181 (the Form N180 is for small track cases). The court will not send the parties a copy of a directions questionnaire to complete, but instead will inform them how to obtain a copy.

The directions questionnaire (for multi-track and fast-track cases) requires that the following information is provided (the directions questionnaire for small track claims requires slightly different information):

- whether a stay of one month is required to try to reach a settlement through Alternative Dispute Resolution (and if not, why not);
- details of potential witnesses;
- details of potential experts;
- whether an agreement has been reached as to the scope of disclosure (and whether a Form N263 has been filed – see below);
- a time estimate for the final hearing; and
- an estimate of costs so far, and to the trial.

Parties are required to consult one another and co-operate in completing the directions questionnaires (CPR 1998, PD 26, para 2.3)

Draft directions

The directions questionnaire asks for proposed directions to be attached to the questionnaire. The proposed directions for multi-track cases must be based on the directions at www.justice.gov.uk/courts/procedure-rules/civil (CPR 1998, r 29.1). All proposed directions for fast track cases must be based on CPR 1998, Part 28. See precedent H2 (*Family Law Precedents Service*) for examples of TLATA specific directions. If possible the parties should agree proposed directions (CPR 1998, PD 26, para 2.3). (For more information about Directions see below at Directions and Case Management Conference).

Precedent H ('Budget') (if multi-track)

All parties (except litigants in person) have to file and exchange a 'budget', in the form of Precedent H (CPR 1998, r 3.13) (if it is a multi-track case). If a party fails to file a budget despite being required to do so they will be treated as having filed a budget comprising only the applicable court fees (CPR 1998, r 3.14). Care should be taken in preparing the budget as the court will have regard to the budget when making case management decisions and will take into account the costs involved in each procedural step (CPR 1998, r 3.17). Guidance for filling in a Precedent H can be found here http://www.justice.gov.uk/courts/procedure-rules/civil/pdf/update/new-precedent-h-guidance.pdf . Bear in mind that if there are significant developments in the litigation each party should revise their budget, either upwards or downwards, if warranted (CPR 1998, PD 3E, para 7.6). Parties should submit their amended budgets to the other parties for agreement. If no agreement is reached the revised budget must be submitted to court for approval. The approved budget must be re-filed and re-served (see CPR 1998, PD 3E, paras 7.6 and 7.7 for further details).

Disclosure report (Form N263) (if multi-track)

All parties have to file and serve a disclosure report in the form of Form N263 (CPR 1998, r 31.5) (if it is a multi-track case). The parties then have to confer (not less than seven days before the first case management conference, and on any other such occasion as the court may direct) by telephone or in a meeting discuss and seek to agree a proposal in relation to disclosure that meets the overriding objective.

The parties should also consider CPR 1998, PD 31B and completing an Electronic Documents Questionnaire (Form N264).

Reply to defence

If the claimant is to file a reply to the defence, he or she should file the reply at the same time as filing his or her directions questionnaire (CPR 1998, r 15.8). The reply must be served on the other parties at the same time as it is filed. The reply must be verified by a statement of truth (CPR 1998, Part 22).

The parties may not file or serve any statement of case after a reply without the permission of the court (CPR 1998, r 15.9).

Timing

- The **directions questionnaire** must be filed and served on all other parties by the date specified by the court in the notice of the proposed allocation (not less than **28 days** after the date when it is deemed to be served on the parties, or **14 days** in small track cases) (CPR 1998, r 26.3(6)).
- The **Precedent H** must be filed and exchanged by the same date, or, if no date is specified, **seven days** before the first case management conference (CPR 1998, r 3.13).
- **Draft directions** should be attached to the directions questionnaire but in any event should be filed at least **seven days** before the case management conference (CPR 1998, r 29.4).
- The **disclosure report** (Form N263) (and Electronic Documents Questionnaire if applicable – Form N264) must be filed and served not less than **14 days** before the first case management conference (CPR 1998, r 31.5).

The parties cannot agree to vary the date for filing the directions questionnaire (CPR 1998, r 26.3(6A)).

Allocation

The court will notify the parties of which track the case is allocated to (CPR 1998, r 26.9). CPR 1998, r 26.7 and 26.8 set out the matters to which the court will have regard when making the allocation.

Directions and case management conference

The court will provide directions when providing notice of the allocation. Most TLATA 1996 claims are allocated to the multi-track. CPR 1998, Part 29 governs the procedure for multi-track cases.

There is no standard procedure for multi-track claims but commonly the court gives directions and lists a case management conference (CPR 1998, r 29.2).

Directions

When drafting directions in multi-track cases both the parties and the court should take as their starting point any relevant model directions and standard directions which can be found online at www.justice.gov.uk/courts/procedure-rules/civil and adapt them as appropriate to the circumstances of the particular case (CPR 1998, r 29.1). The directions questionnaire requires agreed directions to be attached so normally directions will be filed at the same time as the directions questionnaire. In any event the parties must endeavour to agree appropriate directions and submit agreed directions (or their respective proposals) at least **seven days** before any case management conference (CPR 1998, r 29.4) (see above at Directions Questionnaire, Budget, Disclosure Report and Reply). See precedent H2 (*Family Law Precedents Service*) for examples of TLATA specific directions.

Usually the court will give dates for:

- disclosure and inspection;
- exchange of witness statements;
- instructing an expert (preferably a single joint expert);
- asking questions of the expert;
- filing the pre-trial checklist (see below); and
- a period of time when the trial will take place.

The parties can agree informally to vary directions but they cannot agree to vary the date of the case management conference, pre-trial review or date for filing the pre-trial checklist (CPR 1998, r 29.5). See CPR 1998, PD 29, para 5.1 – 5.9 for further guidance regarding varying directions in multi-track cases.

If the parties have been able to agree directions (including a proposed trial date) and the court considers the directions suitable it will approve them without a hearing and vacate the case management conference (CPR 1998, r 29.4). See CPR 1998, PD 29, para 6.1 – 6.5 for further guidance regarding directions in multi-track cases.

- ***Disclosure***
  CPR 1998, Part 31 provides very detailed rules regarding the disclosure process. Also see CPR 1998, PDs 31A and 31B. The parties will have been required to file and serve a disclosure report, Form N263, (in multi-track cases) and are required to try to agree a proposal in relation to disclosure (see above at Directions Questionnaire, Budget, Disclosure

Report and Reply). The disclosure list should then be made on Form N265. Disclosure in TLATA 1996 claims is likely to cover documents such as:
— Land Registry documents (in particular a TR1);
— mortgage documents;
— conveyancing files;
— bank statements; and
— emails between the parties regarding the property.

- *Witness statements*
  CPR 1998, r 32.8 states that witness statements should be in the format set out in CPR 1998, PD 32 (see paras 17.1 – 25.2). A witness statement should be verified by a statement of truth (CPR 1998, Part 22).
- *Expert evidence*
  CPR 1998, Part 35 sets out the rules regarding expert evidence. Also see CPR 1998, PD 35. Where possible a Single Joint Expert should be instructed. Likely expert evidence required in TLATA 1996 claims will be evidence from a chartered surveyor/valuer as to the value of the property.

Case management conference

At the case management conference the court will review the progress made by the parties and give further directions to ensure that the case is ready for trial. As well as complying with any specific directions given by the court the following preparation for case management conferences should be undertaken:

- The parties should ensure that at least **14 days** before any case management conference a disclosure report is filed (see above) (CPR 1998, r 31.5).
- The parties should ensure that at least **seven days** before any case management conference draft directions and a budget are filed (see above) (CPR 1998, r 29.4 and r 3.13).
- The parties should make sure that the court has all the relevant documents at the hearing (i.e. witness statements, expert reports etc.) (CPR 1998, PD 29, para 5.6).
- The claimant should prepare a case summary (if it is thought useful). A case summary should set out a brief chronology and the issues of fact which are agreed or in dispute and the evidence needed to decide them. It should not be more than 500 words in length. It should be agreed with the defendant if possible (CPR 1998, PD 29, para 5.7).
- The parties should consider what orders they wish to be made and give notice to each other (it is good practice to prepare a draft order) (CPR 1998, PD 29, para 5.6).

A party's legal advisor must attend the case management conference (and if the person attending is 'inadequate' or their instructions are inadequate an order for wasted costs may be made) (CPR 1998, r 29.3(2)).

Bear in mind that if there are significant developments in the litigation each party should revise their budget, either upwards or downwards, if warranted (see CPR 1998, PD 3E, paras 7.6 and 7.7 for further details). The court may also set a time table or given further directions for future reviews of the budget (CPR 1998, PD 3E, para 7.5).

See CPR 1998, PD 29, paras 5.1 – 5.9 for further guidance regarding case management conferences in multi-track cases.

Costs management orders

The court may at any time make an order recording agreement between the parties of their budgets or where not agreed revise and approve budgets. The court will make a costs management order to control the costs that each party may recover unless it is satisfied that the litigation can be conducted justly and at proportionate cost in accordance with the overriding objective without such an order being made (CPR 1998, r 3.15). See *Seagrove v Sullivan* [2014] EWHC 4110 (Fam) where the parties legal costs far outweighed the equity in the property at the centre of the litigation.

File pre-trial checklist and pre-trial review

The court will specify the date by which the parties must file a pre-trial checklist before the trial (CPR 1998, r 29.2).

Documents

Pre-trial check list (Form N170)

The parties should discuss the content of the pre-trial check lists and try to agree them (CPR 1998, PD 29, para 8.1(5)).

Revised costs budget (Precedent H)

If no costs management order has been made each should attach to their pre-trial checklist a costs estimate in the form of Precedent H. Bear in mind that if there have been significant developments in the litigation each party should revise their budget, either upwards or downwards, if warranted (CPR 1998, PD 3E, para 7.6). Parties should submit their amended budgets to the other parties for agreement. If no agreement is reached the revised budget must be submitted to court for approval. The approved budget must be re-filed and re-served (see CPR 1998, PD 3E, paras 7.6 and 7.7 for further details). The court may also have set a time table or given further directions for reviewing the budget (CPR 1998, PD 3E, para 7.5).

Timing

The parties should complete and file the pre-trial checklist by the date directed by the court (CPR 1998, r 29.6(2)). This will be no later than 8 weeks before the trial date (CPR 1998, PD 29, para 8.1(3)).

Fees

£1,090 (multi-track) (as at September 2015).

Pre-trial review

If a pre-trial review is listed at that hearing directions will be given for final preparation for the trial and the running of the trial itself, for example:

- the trial timetable;
- the order of witnesses to be called;
- time estimates; and
- preparation of trial bundles.

Trial

Bundles

CPR 1998, PD 39A must be followed for the preparation of court bundles (CPR 1998, r 39.5). The Practice Direction sets out very precise rules regarding the preparation of bundles and should be referred to directly.

In summary:

- the paginated bundle(s) should be prepared by the claimant's legal representative (CPR 1998, r 39.5 and PD 39, para 3.4);
- PD 39A, paras 3.2 and 3.5 – 3.8 set out the content and format of the bundle(s);
- if possible the content of the bundle(s) should be agreed between the parties (PD 39A, para 3.9);
- the bundle(s) should be filed at court **not more than 7 but not less than 3 working days** before the hearing (CPR 1998, r 39.5); and
- identical copies of the bundle(s) should be provided to all parties and for use by witnesses (PD 39A, para 3.10).

Note:

FPR 2010, PD 27A must be followed for the preparation of court bundles (FPR 2010, r 27.6 and FPR 2010, PD 27A, para 2.1) if the hearing is:

- before a judge sitting in the Family Division of the High Court wherever the court may be sitting; and;
- in the Family Court.

The Practice Direction sets out very precise rules regarding the preparation of bundles and should be referred to directly.

Re W (Strict Compliance with Court Orders) [2014] EWHC 22, [2015] 1 FLR 1092, *J v J* [2014] EWHC 3654 (Fam) and also *Re L (Procedure: Bundles: Translation)* [2015] 1 FLR 1417 indicate that PD 27A (in relation to bundles in family proceedings) *must* be complied with. Practice Direction 27A does not apply to claims under TLATA 1996, however it is recommended that practitioners follow the same principle and ensure compliance with PD 39A.

Form N260

If applying for costs the applicant should file and serve a Form N260 'not less than 24 hours before the hearing' (CPR 1998, PD 44, para 9.5(4)(b)). However, have regard to any cost management orders the court may have made as only agreed or approved costs may be recovered unless there is good reason to depart from the budget (see further CPR 1998, Part 3).

Publicity

The final hearing will be in public (CPR 1998, r 39.2(1)).

An application can be made for the final hearing to be in private if:

- publicity would defeat the object of the hearing (CPR 1998, r 39.2(3)(a));
- it involves matters relating to national security (CPR 1998, r 39.2(3)(b));

- it involves confidential information (including information relating to personal financial matters) and publicity would damage that confidentiality (CPR 1998, r 39.2(3)(c));
- a private hearing is necessary to protect the interests of any child or protected party (CPR 1998, r 39.2(3)(d));
- it is a hearing of an application made without notice and it would be unjust to any respondent for there to be a public hearing (CPR 1998, r 39.2(3)(e));
- it involves uncontentious matters arising in the administration of trusts or in the administration of a deceased person's estate (CPR 1998, r 39.2(3)(f)); or
- the court considers this to be necessary, in the interests of justice (CPR 1998, r 39.2(3)(g)).

Points (c) and (d) are the most likely to apply to TLATA 1996 claims.

The court may order that the identity of any party or witness must not be disclosed if it considers non-disclosure necessary in order to protect the interests of that party or witness (CPR 1998, r 39.2(4)).

Attendance

Under CPR 1998, r 39.3 the court may proceed with a trial in the absence of a party but can strike out a party's case if they do not attend (or the whole of the proceedings if neither party attends).

Order

See precedent H3 (*Family Law Precedents Service*). A proposed draft final TLATA order in the style of the standardised family orders can be found at http://www.familylaw.co.uk/news_and_comment/a-proposed-draft-final-tolata-order#.

Cost generally (eg Part 36 offers)

As TLATA 1996 claims are governed by the CPR 1998, Part 36 will apply and therefore any offer to settle should be considered carefully with reference being made to Part 36 and the various costs consequences of accepting or rejecting the offer.

Practitioners should bear in mind the provisions of PD 36A to CPR 1998 which came into force on 6 April 2015 and which supplements PD 36 (available at http://www.justice.gov.uk/courts/procedure-rules/civil/pdf/preview/78th-pd-update.pdf).

CHILD ARRANGEMENTS (PART 1) – PRE-PROCEEDINGS TO FHDRA

FLOWCHART

Family Law

Child arrangements (Part 1) – pre-proceedings to FHDRA

PRACTICE PLUS

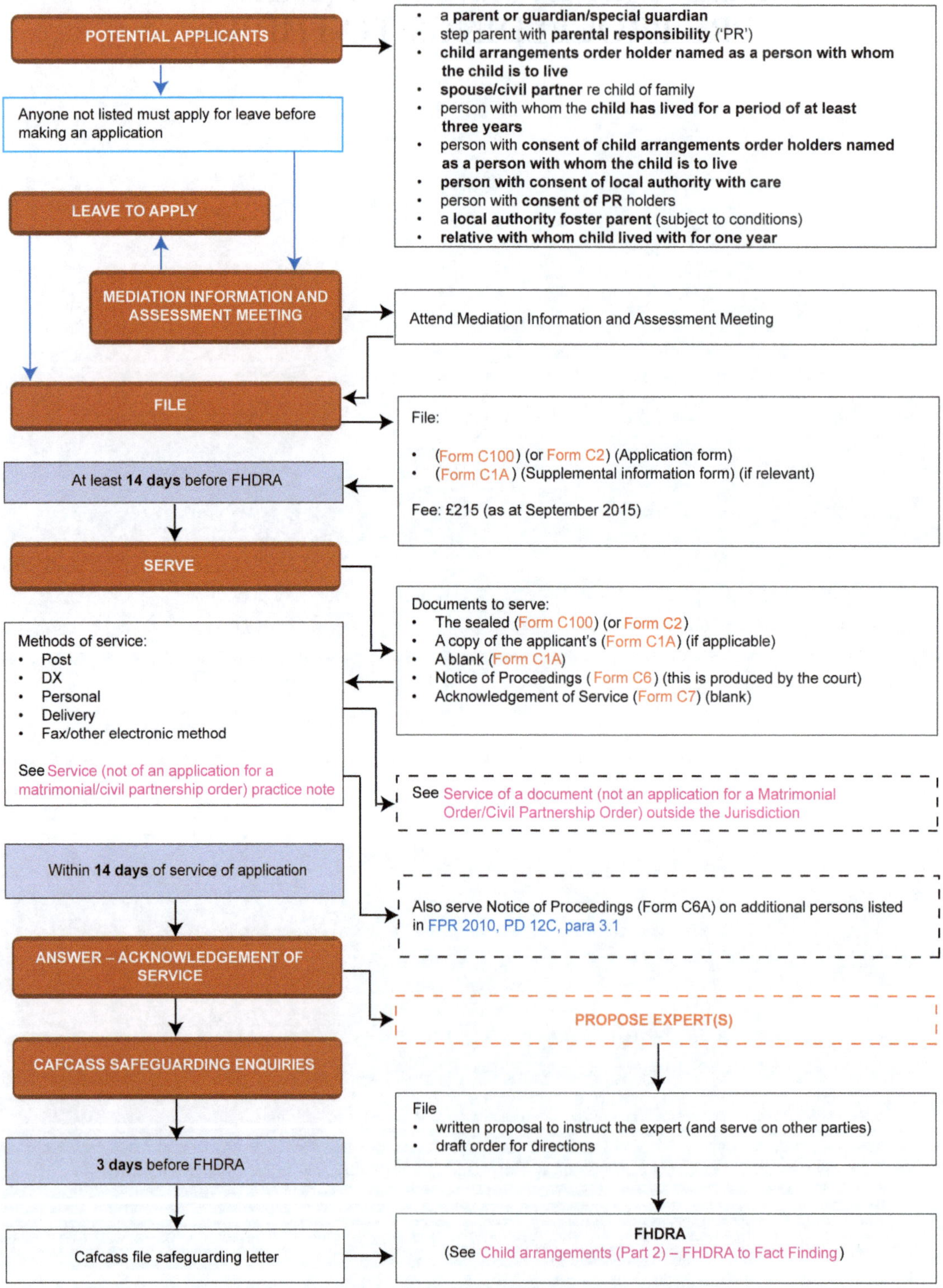

PRACTICE NOTE

See also Procedural Guide (PG) D7 in *The Red Book (Family Court Practice)*.

Potential applicants

The Children and Families Act 2014 made significant changes in readiness for the relaunched family court system implemented on 22 April 2014. With the ethos of the Family Court focussed on non-court dispute resolution and parents working together, the amendment to s 1 of the Children Act 1989 has been brought into force so there is a presumption of involvement of each parent in a child's life (unless the contrary is shown) (CFA 2014, s 11).

Section 8 orders have been amended by s 12 of the 2014 Act which replaced contact orders and residence orders with child arrangements orders which regulate with whom a child is to live, spend time or otherwise have contact, and when a child is to live, spend time or otherwise have contact with any person (CFA 2014, s 12(3)).

Possible applicants for a child arrangements order are:

- a **parent or guardian/special guardian** (CA 1989, s 10(4)(a));
- any person who by virtue of s 4A has **parental responsibility** for the child (a step-parent) (CA 1989, s 10(4)(aa));
- any **person** who is named in a child arrangements order that is in force with respect to the child as a person with whom the child is to live (CA 1989, s 10(4)(b));
- any **party to a marriage/civil partnership** (whether or not subsisting) in relation to whom the child is a child of the family (CA 1989, s 10(5)(a), (aa));
- any person with whom the **child has lived for a period of at least three years** (the three years need not be continuous but must not have begun more than five years before, or ended more than three months before, the making of the application) (CA 1989, s 10(5)(b), (10));
- in any case where a there is a child arrangements order regulating arrangements relating to with whom the child is to live or when the child is to live with any person, has the consent of each of the persons named in the order as a person with whom the child is to live (CA 1989, s 10(5)(c)(i));
- in any case where the child is in the care of a local authority, a person who has the consent of that authority (CA 1989, s 10(5)(c)(ii));
- in any other case a person who has the **consent of each of those (if any) who have parental responsibility** for the child (CA 1989, s 10(5)(c)(iii));
- any person who has parental responsibility for the child by virtue of provision made under CA 1989, s 12(2A).

Further possible applicants for a child arrangements order are:

- a **local authority foster parent** is entitled to apply for a child arrangements order where the order with respect to the child regulates arrangements relating to with whom the child is to live or when the child is to live with any person, with respect to a child if the child has lived with him for a period of at least one year immediately preceding the application (also see CA 1989, s 9) (CA 1989, s 10(5A) and 10(5C));
- **a relative** of a child is entitled to apply for a child arrangements order where the order with respect to the child regulates arrangements relating to with whom the child is to live or when the child is to live with any person, with respect to the child if the child has **lived with the relative for a period of at least one year** immediately preceding the application (CA 1989, ss 10(5B) and 10(5C)).

If a person is not included in the above list they must first apply for permission from the court to make an application (see below at 'Leave to Apply') (CA 1989, s 10(2)(b)).

The court may also make a child arrangements order even if no application has been made (CA 1989, s 10(1)(b)).

The court cannot make a child arrangements order in favour of a local authority and a local authority foster parent has to fulfil certain conditions before being able to make an application for leave to make an application for a child arrangements order (CA 1989, s 9(2), (3)).

Variation/Discharge

The procedure for applying to vary or discharge a child arrangements order is the same as the procedure for applying for an order.

In addition to those persons listed above (ie anybody who can apply for a child arrangements order can apply to vary or discharge) other potential applicants to apply to vary or discharge a child arrangements order are:

- a previous applicant (CA 1989, s 10(6)(a)); or
- a person named in the order (in the case of a child arrangements order, that person is named in provisions of the order regulating arrangements relating to with whom the child concerned is to spend time or otherwise have contact, or when the child is to spend time or otherwise have contact with any person (CA 1989, s 10(6)(b)(i) and (ii))).

For further guidance regarding the variation or discharge of child arrangements orders see *Children Law and Practice*, para B[351A], B[351B], B[351C], B[351D] and B[921]-[925] and *Children Act Private Law Proceedings: A Handbook*, Chapters 10 and 11.

Mediation Information and Assessment Meeting

Non-Court dispute resolution

The court must consider, at every stage in the proceedings, whether non-court dispute resolution is appropriate (FPR 2010, r 3.3(1)) and must consider whether a Mediation Information and Assessment Meeting (**'MIAM'**) took place (see below), whether a MIAM exemption was claimed/mediator's exemption confirmed and whether the parties attempted mediation/another form of non-court dispute resolution and the outcome (FPR 2010, r 3.3(2)).

The court can adjourn proceedings if it considers non-court dispute resolution is appropriate. See FPR 2010, r 3.1 for further details.

Mediation Information and Assessment Meeting

Before filing an application for a child arrangements order/prohibited steps/specific issue order the applicant is required to attend a MIAM (CFA 2014, s 10(1) and FPR 2010, r 3.6). Any application for private law proceedings relating to children (specified in FPR 2010, PD 3A, para 12) must be accompanied by a form containing either (a) a confirmation from an authorised family mediator that the prospective applicant has attended a MIAM; (b) a claim by the prospective applicant that one of the MIAM exemptions applies; or (c) a confirmation from an authorised family mediator that a mediator's exemption applies (Form C100 – see below).

MIAM exemptions:

Domestic violence

- there is evidence of domestic violence, as specified in PD 3A (FPR 2010, r 3.8(1)(a).

Child protection concerns

- a child would be the subject of the application; and that child or another child of the family who is living with that child is currently the subject of enquiries by a local authority under s 47, CA 1989 or the subject of a child protection plan put in place by a local authority (FPR 2010, r 3.8(1)(b)).

Urgency

- the application must be made urgently because (FPR 2010, r 3.8(1)(c)):
  - there is risk to the life, liberty or physical safety of the prospective applicant or his or her family or his or her home or any delay caused by attending a MIAM would cause a risk of harm to a child; a risk of unlawful removal of a child from the United Kingdom, or a risk of unlawful retention of a child who is currently outside England and Wales; a significant risk of a miscarriage of justice; unreasonable hardship to the prospective applicant; or irretrievable problems in dealing with the dispute (including the irretrievable loss of significant evidence); or
  - there is a significant risk that in the period necessary to schedule and attend a MIAM, proceedings relating to the dispute will be brought in another state in which a valid claim to jurisdiction may exist, such that a court in that other State would be seised of the dispute before a court in England and Wales.

Previous MIAM attendance or MIAM exemption

- in the 4 months prior to making the application, the person attended a MIAM or participated in another form of non-court dispute resolution relating to the same or substantially the same dispute or at the time of making the application, the person is participating in another form of non-court dispute resolution relating to the same or substantially the same dispute (FPR 2010, r 3.8(1)(d));
- in the 4 months prior to making the application, the person filed a relevant family application confirming that a MIAM exemption applied and that application related to the same or substantially the same dispute(FPR 2010, r 3.8(1)(e));
- the application would be made in existing proceedings which are continuing and the prospective applicant attended a MIAM before initiating those proceedings (FPR 2010, r 3.8(1)(f));
- the application would be made in existing proceedings which are continuing a MIAM exemption applied to the application for those proceedings (FPR 2010, r 3.8(1)(g)).

Other

- there is evidence that the prospective applicant is bankrupt, as specified in FPR 2010, PD 3A and the proceedings would be for a financial remedy (FPR 2010, r 3.8(1)(h));
- the prospective applicant does not have sufficient contact details for any of the prospective respondents to enable a family mediator to contact any of the prospective respondents for the purpose of scheduling the MIAM (FPR 2010, r 3.8(1)(i));
- the application would be made without notice (see further FPR 2010, PD 18A, para 5.1) (FPR 2010, r 3.8(1)(j));

- the prospective applicant is or all of the prospective respondents are subject to a disability or other inability that would prevent attendance at a MIAM unless appropriate facilities can be offered by an authorised mediator; the prospective applicant has contacted as many authorised family mediators as have an office within fifteen miles of his or home (or three of them if there are three or more), and all have stated that they are unable to provide such facilities; and the names, postal addresses and telephone numbers or e-mail addresses for such authorised family mediators, and the dates of contact, can be provided to the court if requested (FPR 2010, r 3.8(1)(k));
- the prospective applicant or all of the prospective respondents cannot attend a MIAM because he or she is, or they are, as the case may be:
  - in prison or any other institution in which he or she is or they are required to be detained;
  - subject to conditions of bail that prevent contact with the other person; or
  - subject to a licence with a prohibited contact requirement in relation to the other person (FPR 2010, r 3.8(1)(l));
- the prospective applicant or all of the prospective respondents are not habitually resident in England and Wales (FPR 2010, r 3.8(1)(m));
- a child is one of the prospective parties by virtue of FPR 2010 r 12.3(1) (FPR 2010, r 3.8(1)(n));
- the prospective applicant has contacted as many authorised family mediators as have an office within fifteen miles of his or her home (or three of them if there are three or more), and all of them have stated that they are not available to conduct a MIAM within fifteen business days of the date of contact; and the names, postal addresses and telephone numbers or e-mail addresses for such authorised family mediators, and the dates of contact, can be provided to the court if requested (FPR 2010, r 3.8(1)(o));
- there is no authorised family mediator with an office within fifteen miles of the prospective applicant's home (FPR 2010, r 3.8(1)(p)).

Mediator's exemptions

An authorised family mediator confirms in the relevant form that he or she is satisfied that:

- mediation is not suitable as a means of resolving the dispute because none of the respondents is willing to attend a MIAM (FPR 2010, r 3.8(2)(a));
- mediation is not suitable as a means of resolving the dispute because all of the respondents failed without good reason to attend a MIAM appointment (FPR 2010, r 3.8(2)(b));
- mediation is otherwise not suitable as a means of resolving the dispute (FPR 2010, r 3.8(2)(c));

Only an authorised family mediator may conduct a MIAM. FPR 2010, r 3.9(2) sets out what a mediator must do at a MIAM (for example, provide information and assess suitability, the risk of domestic violence and the risk of harm to a child).

If the party making the application uses one of the MIAM exemptions listed above the court can inquire into whether the exemption was validly claimed (FPR 2010, r 3.10(1)). If the court finds it was not validly claimed the court can adjourn proceedings and direct the parties to attend a MIAM (FPR 2010, r 3.10(2)). In deciding whether to adjourn for a MIAM the court will have regard to the factors listed at FPR 2010, r 3.10(3).

FPR 2010, PD 3A supplements FPR 2010, Part 3 and should be referred to directly. In particular it provides useful information about:

- What evidence can be used for the domestic violence MIAM exemption and the bankruptcy MIAM exemption.

- How to find an authorised family mediator.
- How to fund a MIAM (Legal Aid is available for MIAMs).

In children proceedings the Form FM1 has been incorporated into the Form C100. A mediator should complete Part 14 of the Form C100 if a MIAM has been attended or to confirm a Mediator's exemption.

Tips:

- Consider all forms of dispute resolution, for example arbitration (see ifla.org.uk) and collaborative law, as well as mediation. See also www.resolution.org.uk/alternatives_to_court.
- See the *Family Law Directory* and at www.familymediationcouncil.org.uk for help finding a local mediator.

Leave to apply

A person who wishes to apply for a child arrangements order who is not one of the people listed in CA 1989, s 10 as entitled to apply (see above) must first apply for leave from the court. The court will have regard to:

- the nature of the proposed application for the s 8 order (CA 1989, s 10(9)(a));
- the applicant's connection with the child (CA 1989, s 10(9)(b));
- any risk there might be of that proposed application disrupting the child's life to such an extent that he would be harmed by it (CA 1989, s 10(9)(c)); and
- where the child is being looked after by a local authority (CA 1989, s 10(9)(d));
  - — the authority's plans for the child's future; and
  - — the wishes and feelings of the child's parents.

For case-law relating to applications for leave prior to the Children and Families Act 2014 under (CA 1989, s 10(9) see *Re M (Care: Contact: Grandmother's Application for Leave)* [1995] 2 FLR 86, *Re G (Child Case: Parental Involvement)* [1996] 1 FLR 857, *Re J (Leave to Issue Application for Residence Order)* [2003] 1 FLR 114, *Re B (A Child)* [2012] 2 FLR 1358; *Re H (Leave to Apply for Residence Order)* [2008] EWCA Civ 503, [2008] 2 FLR 848, *Re E (Adopted Child: Contact: Leave)* [1995] 1 FLR 57, *Re S (Contact: Application by Sibling)* [1998] 2 FLR 897, *Re W (Care Proceedings: Leave to Apply)* [2005] 2 FLR 468, *Re M (Prohibited Steps Order: Application for Leave)* [1993] 1 FLR 275, *Re E (Adopted Child: Contact: Leave)* [1995] 1 FLR 57, *Re A (Section 8 Order: Grandparent Application)* [1995] 2 FLR 153, *Re W (Contact: Application by Grandparent)* [1997] 1 FLR 793, FD, *Re G (A Minor); Re Z (A Minor)* [2013] 1 FLR 1334).

If the person applying for leave is the child concerned the court may only grant leave if it is satisfied that he or she has sufficient understanding to make the proposed application for the s 8 order (CA 1989, s 10(8)).

If a special guardianship order is in force an application for a child arrangements order made by someone other than the special guardian can only be made with leave of the court (CA 1989, s 10(7A) and 7(B)).

A leave application is made using the Part 18 procedure. The documents required to be filed are set out below but see Part 18 practice note for further guidance as to the rest of the procedure.

Documents:

Application for leave (Form C100)

See precedent E2 (*Family Law Precedents Service*).

Before 22 April 2014 when applying for leave to make an application, Form C2 was required to accompany Form C100. Since 22 April 2014, Form C100 has been adapted and now covers an application for leave to start proceedings and the requirement to attend a mediation meeting is also incorporated so a separate Form FM1 is not necessary.

Statement

See precedent E5 (*Family Law Precedents Service*).

Draft application for child arrangement orders (Form C100 (as above) – and Form C1A and Form C8 if applicable)

See below at 'File'.

Draft order

See precedent E8 (*Family Law Precedents Service*).

Family mediation information and assessment form (Form FM1)

FPR 2010, PD 3A states that in private law proceedings relating to children the MIAM requirement applies. Private law proceedings relating to children are defined at FPR 2010, PD 3A, para 12 and include proceedings for 'a child arrangements order and other orders with respect to a child or children under s 8 of the Children Act 1989', which could arguably include applications for leave for a child arrangements order. However, the Form C100 has been merged with the Form FM1 and therefore, if you are attaching a completed draft Form C100, it may be unnecessary to have both the Form C100 and Form FM1 filled in.

Note that applications for leave should normally be on notice (see further *Re M (Prohibited Steps Order: Application for Leave)* [1993] 1 FLR 275; *Re F and R (Section 8 Order: Grandparent's Application)* [1995] 1 FLR 524; and *Re W (Contact Application: Procedure)* [2000] 1 FLR 263).

If granted leave the applicant can proceed with the application for a child arrangements order, subject to any directions given by the court.

Tips:

- When filing the application at court remember to include enough copies of the documents (normally four – one for the applicant, one for the court, one for the respondent and one for Cafcass).
- Do not forget to check the court fee (£215 as at September 2015) and include a cheque or postal order payable to 'HM Courts and Tribunals Service' or 'HMCTS'. The fee can also be paid in cash or by debit/credit card.

- Keep in mind that where a court has power to make a s 8 order, it may do so at any time during the course of the proceedings in question even though it is not in a position to dispose finally of those proceedings.

File

An application for a child arrangements order is classed as 'private law proceedings' (FPR 2010, r 12.2) and FPR 2010, Part 12 applies (FPR 2010, r 12.1(1)(b)). The Child Arrangements Programme, contained in FPR 2010, PD 12B, also applies. FPR 2010, PD 12B, paras 1.1 – 1.3 set out the background to and the principles underpinning the programme, which include furthering the 'overriding objective' (see FPR 2010, r 1.1).

Reference should be made to:

- **Child Arrangements Programme: Flow Chart** which accompanies the **Child Arrangements Programme** and outlines the stages of a dispute concerning arrangements for children.
- **President's Guidance on the use of Prescribed Documents (Private Law)** which supports the Child Arrangements Programme and identifies documents to be used to maintain compliance.
- **President's Guidance on Allocation and Gatekeeping for Proceedings under Part II of the Children Act 1989 (Private Law)** and the accompanying **Schedule** to ensure all private law proceedings are allocated appropriately.
- **President's Guidance on Continuity and Deployment (Private Law)** to assist with appropriate prioritisation of cases, case management and judicial continuity.

See Procedural Guide D7 (PG) (*Family Court Practice*) or precedent E2 (*Family Law Precedents Service*). Also see *Children Law and Practice*, Division B, Sections 3 and 4 and *Children Act Private Law Proceedings: A Handbook*, Chapters 10 and 11.

Guidance on making an application is set out in leaflet CB1 (also available at http://hmctsformfinder.justice.gov.uk/HMCTS/FormFinder.do).

Documents

Application form (Form C100)

In children proceedings the Form FM1 has been incorporated into the Form C100. A mediator should complete Part 14 of the Form C100 if a MIAM has been attended or to confirm a Mediator's exemption.

See precedent E2 (*Family Law Precedents Service*).

If proceedings already exist the application for a child arrangements order should be made on Form C2 (however the Form C100 may now be more appropriate even in ongoing proceedings – see precedent E7 (*Family Law Precedents Service*) and notes to precedent E2 (*Family Law Precedents Service*)).

If applying to vary or discharge a child arrangements order remember to attach a copy of the relevant order.

Allegations of harm and domestic violence (supplemental information form) (Form C1A)

This form should only be completed and filed if it is alleged that the child has suffered, or is at risk of suffering, any harm from:

- any form of domestic abuse;
- violence within the household;
- child abduction; or
- other conduct or behaviour

by any person who is or has been involved in caring for the child or lives with, or has contact with, the child.

See precedent E4 (*Family Law Precedents Service*).

Also see Notes for Guidance for Supplemental Information Form C1A (also available at http://hmctsformfinder.justice.gov.uk/HMCTS/FormFinder.do).

Confidential contact details (Form C8)

This form should only be completed if the applicant wishes to keep his or her (or the child's) address/contact details confidential (as per FPR 2010, r 29.1). If this form is filed, the parts of the Form C100 that require details of the applicant and/or child's address/contact details do not have to be completed. Care should be taken to ensure that the Form C8 is not served on the respondent in error.

See precedent E31 (*Family Law Precedents Service*).

Who is the respondent?

FPR 2010, r 12.3 sets out the respondents:

- every person whom the applicant believes to have parental responsibility for the child; and
- where the child is the subject of a care order, every person whom the applicant believes to have had parental responsibility immediately prior to the making of the care order.

If the application is to vary or discharge a child arrangements order the respondents will be (in **addition** to those set out above) the parties in the application for the order to be varied or discharged.

Which court?

The Family Court or High Court (CA 1989, s 92(7)) – although note FPR 2010, r 5.4 which says where both the Family Court and High Court have jurisdiction the proceedings must be started in the Family Court (subject to the exceptions FPR 2010, r 5.4(2)). The level of judge that the case will be allocated to is determined by The Family Court (Composition and Distribution of Business) Rules 2014 and the President's Guidance on Allocation and Gatekeeping for Proceedings under Part II of the Children Act 1989 (Private Law) (including the Schedule).

Without notice applications

Applications for child arrangements (or to vary/discharge such orders) should normally be made on notice. However, it is possible for an application to be made without notice, although short notice, or even informal notice, is preferred in most cases (see for example *Croydon LBC v A (No 3)* [1992] 2 FLR 350; *Re B (A Minor) (Residence Order: Ex Parte)* [1992] 2 FLR 1, CA).

The documents (see above) should be filed at the same time as making a without notice application (FPR 2010, r 12.16(2)).

A without notice application can be made by telephone. If so, the hard copy documents (ie. the Form C100 etc – see above) should be filed at court the next business day (FPR 2010, r 12.16(2)(a)). See FPR 2010, PD 12E (Urgent Business) for details of the procedure for out of hours applications.

An order made on a without notice application is unlikely to be a final order, it will usually be an interim order and the court has emphasised that save in exceptional circumstances, a without notice order should not be for longer than 7 days (*Re Y (A Minor) (Ex Parte Interim Orders)* [1994] Fam Law 127).

The court may require the applicant (or his or her solicitors) to give undertakings with regards to issuing the application, swearing evidence and serving the application on the respondent(s) within strict time limits (eg the next day) – see the guidelines set out in *Re S (Ex Parte Orders)* [2001] 1 FLR 308, *Re W (Ex Parte Orders)* [2000] 2 FLR 927 and *KY v DD* [2012] 2 FLR 200 and the commentary in *Family Court Practice* to FPR 2010, r 12.16.

See further *Re G* [1993] 1 FLR 910; *Re P* [1993] 1 FLR 915, *M v C (Children Orders: Reasons)* [1993] 2 FLR 584, *Re B (Minors) (Care: Procedure)* [1994] Fam Law 72, *Re J (Children: Ex Parte Orders)* [1997] 1 FLR 606.

If the application is made without notice the application form and any order made by the court must be served on the respondent(s) as soon as possible after the order is made and in any event within **48 hours** (FPR 2010, r 12.16(4)). The order must also be served on:

- any person who has actual care of the child or who had such care immediately prior to the making of the order; and
- in the case of an emergency protection order and a recovery order, the local authority in whose area the child lives or is found (FPR 2010, r 12.16(5)).

Directions

A party may want to ask for directions straight away, at the same time as filing the application (eg as to timetable for the proceedings, submission of evidence, transfer of proceedings to another court). A written request for directions must be made on Form C2 together with Form C1A if necessary. In accordance with FPR 2010, PD 12B, para 9.4 the gatekeepers are able to issue directions (see Standard Order – CAP01) in respect of a MIAM, urgent issues and/or evidence.

Withdrawal of the application

A party can seek to withdraw their application only with permission (FPR 2010, r 29.4). The application may be granted orally if the parties and the welfare officer are present. Otherwise this can be done by written request using Form C2 outlining the reasons for withdrawal and serving the same on all parties (using the Part 18 procedure – see Part 18 practice note).

Tips:

- When filing the application at court remember to include enough copies of the Form C100 and any supporting documents (eg Form C1A if applicable) (normally four – one for the applicant, one for the court, one for the respondent and one for Cafcass).
- Do not forget to check the court fee (£215 as at September 2015) and include a cheque or postal order payable to 'HM Courts and Tribunals Service' or 'HMCTS'. The fee can also be paid in cash or by debit/credit card. If a fee has already been paid when applying for leave a second fee does not need to be paid.
- If making an application without notice it is sensible to phone the court in advance to check availability of judges and to give them some prior warning.
- Consider any other orders you may wish to seek (for example a specific issue order or prohibited steps order) to save making further applications at a later date.

Serve

The court application shall be considered by a Gatekeeper within one working day of the date of receipt (FPR 2010, PD 12B, para 9.2) and directions given in prescribed Standard Order – CAP01 (Order – Directions at Gatekeeping/Allocation).

At the time of issuing the proceedings, or if not possible no later than **one working day** after issue, or in courts where applications are first considered on paper, by no later than **two working days** after issue, the court shall give notice of the FHDRA (FPR 2010, r 12.31) and shall send or hand to the applicant and send to Cafcass the following (FPR 2010, r 12.7 (1) and (2) and PD 12B, para 8.7):

- a copy of the Application (Form C100);
- the applicant's completed Supplemental Information Form C1A (if provided);
- the Notice of Hearing (Form C6);
- the Acknowledgment Form (Form C7);
- a blank Form C1A;
- information leaflets for the parties (this must include the CB7 leaflet).

It is no longer the applicant's responsibility to serve these documents. The court will serve the documents unless the applicant requests to do so or the court directs the applicant to do so (FPR 2010, r 12.8(2)).

In proceedings for an application for a child arrangements order there are two groups of people who need to be served. The first group is the respondent(s), and they need all of the documents served on them as set out below. The second group is people who only need notice of the hearing to be served on them, not all of the documents. The people who need only a notice of the hearing (the '**additional persons**') are (FPR 2010, PD 12C, para 3.1):

- a local authority providing accommodation for the child;
- persons who are caring for the child at the time when the proceedings are commenced;
- in the case of proceedings brought in respect of a child who is alleged to be staying in a refuge which is certified under CA 1989, s 51(1) or (2), the person who is providing the refuge;
- every person whom the applicant believes
  - (i) to be named in a court order with respect to the same child, which has not ceased to have effect;
  - (ii) to be party to pending proceedings in respect of the same child; or
  - (iii) to be a person with whom the child has lived for at least 3 years prior to the application,

unless, in a case to which (i) or (ii) applies, the applicant believes that the court order or pending proceedings are not relevant to the application.

There will not always be additional persons to serve in every case.

The following documents will be served on the **respondent**(s) (FPR 2010, r 12.8(a) and PD 12C, para 1.1):

(1) The Form C100 (or Form C2) (Application form).
(2) A copy of the applicant's Form C1A (if applicable) (Supplemental Information).
(3) A blank Form C1A.
(4) Notice of Proceedings (Form C6) (this is produced by the court).
(5) Acknowledgement of Service (Form C7) (blank).

In addition, if the court has provided the applicant with information leaflets, as suggested in FPR 2010, PD 12B, para 8.7, a copy of those relevant to the respondent(s) should be included with the documents served.

The following document will be served on the **additional persons** (FPR 2010, r 12.8(b) and PD 12C, para 3.1):

(1) Notice of Proceedings/Hearing/Directions Appointment to Non-Parties (Form C6A) (this is produced by the court).

Methods of service

The court will generally serve the documents although if you have requested to serve the documents instead (or have been directed to do so by the court) (FPR 2010, r 12.8(2)) see the methods below.

- *Service by Post/DX* (FPR 2010, r 6.23(b))
- *Personal service* (FPR 2010, r 6.23(a))
- *Delivery* (FPR 2010, r 6.23(c))
- *Fax or other means of electronic communication* (FPR 2010, r 6.23(d))

See Service (not of an application for a matrimonial/civil partnership order) practice note for further guidance. Also see leaflet CB3 (Serving the forms – Children Act 1989) (available at http://hmctsformfinder.justice.gov.uk/courtfinder/forms/cb3-eng.pdf).

Timing

The documents must be served on the respondent(s) **at least 14 days** before the hearing (FPR 2010, PD 12C, para 2.1) although the court can abridge this time limit if necessary (FPR 2010, PD 12B, para 14.2). The notice of proceedings to be served on the additional persons must be served at the same time (FPR 2010, PD 12C, para 1.4).

If it is an application for a child arrangements order relating to a child who is the subject of a care order the documents must be served on the respondent(s) **at least 7 days** before the hearing (FPR 2010, PD 12C, para 2.1). The notice of proceedings to be served on the additional persons must be served at the same time (FPR 2010, PD 12C, para 1.4).

Giving notice to a person with foreign parental responsibility

FPR 2010, r 12.4 provides for notice to be given to a person whom it is believed to hold parental responsibility for the child under the law of another State but who otherwise would not be required to be joined as a respondent under FPR 2010, r 12.3 (see FPR 2010, r 12.4 for further specific details).

Answer – acknowledgement of service

The respondent(s) must file and serve an answer (FPR 2010, r 12.32).

Documents:

Acknowledgement of service form (Form C7)

The respondent must give contact details for him or herself and his or her solicitor (if represented). The respondent is to indicate whether the application is defended, but does not have to set out his or her case at this point.

See precedent E30 (*Family Law Precedents Service*).

Where the prescribed forms are not applicable, the respondent's written answer should be drafted from scratch. It is suggested the format used is similar to the prescribed form and the same sort of matters covered.

Allegations of harm and domestic violence (supplemental information form) (Form C1A) (if applicable)

If the applicant has completed a Form C1A the respondent may want to comment (at Section 2 of the blank Form C1A) on the allegations made by the applicant.

Even if the applicant has not completed a Form C1A the respondent may need to complete their own Form C1A if their answer to Question 7 of the Form C7 is in the affirmative (they allege that the child has suffered, or is at risk of suffering, any harm from domestic abuse etc).

See precedent E4 (*Family Law Precedents Service*).

Also see Notes for Guidance for Supplemental Information Form C1A (available at http://hmctsformfinder.justice.gov.uk/HMCTS/FormFinder.do).

Timing

The respondent(s) must file and serve the Form C7 within **14 days** beginning on the date on which the application for a child arrangements order was served on them (FPR 2010, r 12.32). FPR 2010, PD 12B, para 14.3 states that the respondent should file a response on the Forms C7/C1A no later than 10 working days before the hearing.

If the respondent was served outside of the jurisdiction FPR 2010, r 6.42 applies and the period for filing the Form C7 will likely be longer (see further FPR 2010, PD 6B and Service (not of an application for a Matrimonial/Civil Partnership order) outside the jurisdiction practice note).

Cafcass safeguarding enquiries

Before the FHDRA Cafcass must carry out safeguarding enquiries (FPR 2010, PD 12B, para 13.1).

In order to inform the court of possible risks of harm to the child in accordance with its safeguarding framework, Cafcass:

- must carry out safeguarding enquiries, including checks of local authorities and police, and telephone risk identification interviews with the parties;
- if risks of harm are identified, may invite parties to meet separately with the Cafcass Officer before the FHDRA to clarify any safety issue;
- shall record and outline any safety issues for the court.

Cafcass will confine the enquiries to safety issues **only**, and any discussions about any other issues (for example relating to the substance of applications or replies or about issues concerning matters of welfare or the prospects of resolution) should be deferred to the FHDRA. This is so that there is equality between the parties and a full discussion can take place at the FHDRA with any safety issues which have been identified by Cafcass being taken into account.

Cafcass will not initiate contact with the child prior to the FHDRA (FPR 2010, PD 12B, para 13.6).

Safeguarding letter

Within 17 working days of receipt by Cafcass of the application, and at least 3 working days before the hearing, the Cafcass Officer shall report to the court, in a Safeguarding letter, the outcome of the risk identification work which has been undertaken (FPR 2010, PD 12B, para 13.7).

Also see *Children Act Private Law Proceedings: A Handbook*, Chapter 19.

Propose expert(s)

Permission from the court must be sought before an expert is instructed for any purpose relating to children proceedings (CFA 2014, s 13(1)). Permission from the court must also be obtained to file an expert's report (CFA 2014, s 13(5)). A child cannot be medically or psychiatrically examined, or otherwise assessed, for the purpose of preparation of expert evidence for use in the proceedings without the court's permission (CFA 2014, s 13(3)). Any evidence resulting from instructions given or an assessment made without permission is inadmissible (CFA 2014, s 13(2) and (4)). An application for permission should be made using the Part 18 procedure (see Part 18 practice note) (FPR 2010, r 25.7(1)). The latest point at which an application for permission should be made is the FHDRA (FPR 2010, r 25.6(b)).

Note that expert evidence will be restricted to that which is 'necessary' to assist the court to resolve the proceedings (CFA 2014, s 13(6)) and the court will have regard to the overriding objective (FPR 2010, r 1.1) and its case management powers under FPR 2010, Part 4 when using its discretion to direct that expert evidence is filed (see further *Re H-L (A Child)* [2013] 2 FLR 1434). When deciding whether to give permission, the court will have particular regard to the factors listed at CFA 2014, s 13(7) and the court must have regard to any failure to comply with FPR 2010, r 25.6 (when to apply for permission).

Note that expert evidence may not always be required and therefore the steps below may not need to be completed. Possible experts that may be required in child arrangements proceedings could be:

- child psychologist; and
- drugs/alcohol tester

It is important to find out early on the costs of instructing an expert and to agree with your client and the other parties how the expert is to be funded. If prior authority needs to be sought from the Legal Aid Agency it is sensible to ask the expert for a detailed costs estimate as soon as possible. See further *JG (A Child) v The Legal Services Commission* [2013] 2 FLR 1174.

The Law Society provides useful pro form templates dealing with proposing an expert at http://www.lawsociety.org.uk/advice/family-expert-templates/.

Practice Direction 25B, FPR 2010 (The Duties of an Expert, the Expert's Report and Arrangements for an Expert to Attend Court) sets out (in the annex) the standards for expert witnesses in children proceedings in the Family Court. See http://www.familylaw.co.uk/news_and_comment/fpr-practice-direction-25b-updated-october-2014.

Single joint experts

The court may direct that a single joint expert is instructed ('SJE') (FPR 2010, r 25.11).

PD 25C states that wherever possible a single joint expert should be instructed (FPR 2010, PD 25C, para 2.1).

To that end, well in advance of the FHDRA:

- a party wishing to instruct an expert should first give the other party a list of the names of one or more proposed suitable experts (FPR 2010, PD 25C, para 2.1);
- **within 5 business days** after receipt of the list of proposed experts, the other party should indicate any objection to one or more of the named experts and, if so, supply the name(s) of one or more experts whom they consider suitable (FPR 2010, PD 25C, para 2.2);
- each party should disclose whether they have already consulted any of the proposed experts about the issue(s) in question (FPR 2010, PD 25C, para 2.3); and
- if there is agreement to instruct an SJE, **before applying to the court for permission and directions for the use of an SJE** the parties should so far as appropriate:
  - — comply with the guidance in paragraphs FPR 2010, PD 25C, para 3.2 (Preliminary inquiries of the expert), para 3.10 (the application), para 3.11 (the draft order) (FPR 2010, PD 25C, para 2.6(a));
  - — have received the expert's confirmation in response to the preliminary enquiries referred FPR 2010, PD 25B, para 8.1 (FPR 2010, PD 25C, para 2.6(b) and 3.5); and
  - — have agreed in what proportion the SJE's fee is to be shared between them (at least in the first instance) and when it is to be paid (and if applicable, have obtained agreement for public funding) (FPR 2010, PD 25C, para 2.6(c) and (d))

Take care to follow the extra guidance in FPR 2010, PD 25C, paras 3.3 and 3.4, as children proceedings are confidential and therefore when making preliminary enquiries of experts you should be careful only to give sufficient information about the case to decide whether or not he or she is in a position to accept instructions.

(See further precedents J6 (preliminary enquiries) and J7 (checklist on obtaining response), precedent J8 (application to instruct expert), and precedents J1 – J4 (sample orders) (*Family Law Precedents Service*)).

If the parties cannot agree who should be the SJE the court can select the expert from a list compiled by the parties or direct that the expert be selected by another method (FPR 2010, r 25.11(2)). Commonly the court will direct that one party put forward the names of, say, three potential experts, and that the other party choose one from that list. The parties should make preliminary enquiries of each proposed expert and obtain confirmation from them in accordance with FPR 2010, PD 25C, para 3.2 and 3.5 (FPR 2010, PD 25C, para 3.6).

Separate experts

If the parties agree to instruct separate experts they should agree in advance that the reports will be disclosed (FPR 2010, PD 25C, para 2.5) and should make preliminary enquiries, obtain confirmations, and draft an application for permission attaching a draft order as set out in FPR 2010, PD 25C, paras 3.2 – 3.5, 3.10 and 3.11 (see above under Single Joint Experts).

Also see *Children Act Private Law Proceedings: A Handbook*, Chapter 18.

See the *Family Law Directory* for help in identifying an expert.

When drafting proposed directions for the First Hearing Dispute Resolution Appointment, include provision for forward-looking directions such as questions to the expert(s), a timetable for answers, discussion between the experts if applicable. This may avoid the need for a further hearing. See further FPR 2010, r 25.7 which sets out what should be included in an application for permission (nb in children proceedings the application for permission must state the questions which the expert is to be required to answer) (see further FPR 2010, PD 25C, para 3.10). Note that a draft order should be attached – see further FPR 2010, r 25.7(2)(b) and PD 25C, para 3.11.

CHILD ARRANGEMENTS (PART 2) – FHDRA TO FACT FINDING

FLOWCHART

Family Law

Child arrangements (Part 2) – FHDRA to Fact Finding

PRACTICE PLUS

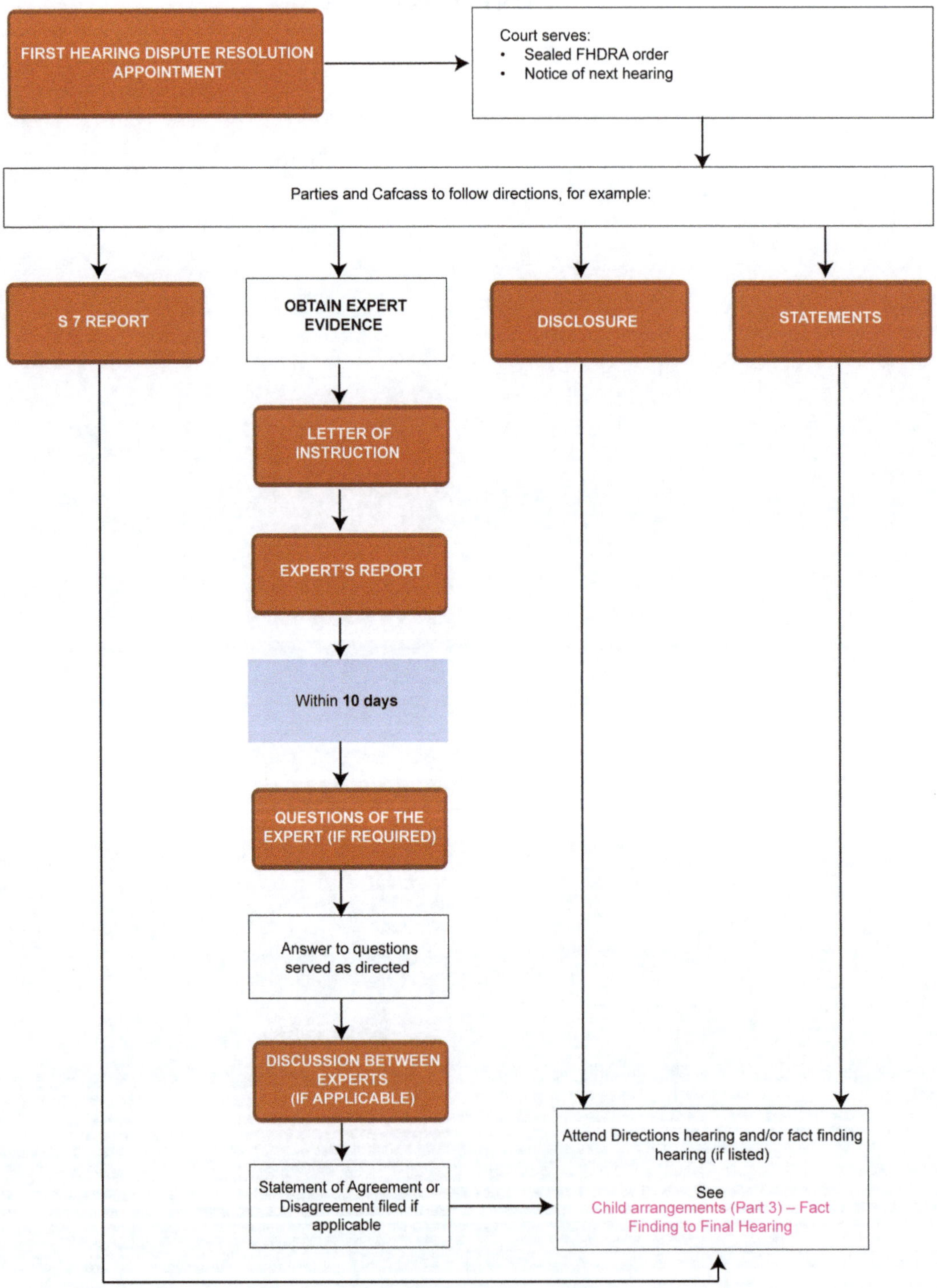

PRACTICE NOTE

See also Procedural Guide (PG) D7 in *The Red Book (Family Court Practice)*.

First hearing dispute resolution appointment

A first hearing dispute resolution appointment (FHDRA) may (where time for service on the respondent(s) has been abridged) take place within 4 weeks, but should ordinarily take place in week 5 following the issuing of the application for a child arrangements order (FPR 2010, PD 12B, para 14.1). The Child Arrangements Programme in FPR 2010, PD 12B applies to proceedings for a child arrangements order.

The court needs the following documents for the FHDRA (FPR 2010, PD 12B, para 14.10):

- Applicant's Form C100 application, and Form C1A (if any).
- Notice of Hearing.
- Respondent's Form C7 response and Form C1A (if any).
- Safeguarding letter (from Cafcass).

These documents should already be on the court file but it is sensible to bring an extra set of the documents to the FHDRA just in case. Practice Direction 27A applies when preparing a bundle – see 'Bundles' and 'Preliminary documents' sections of Child arrangements (Part 3) – Fact Finding to Final Hearing practice note.

Privilege

The hearing is not privileged (FPR 2010, PD 12B, para 14.9) and therefore what is said at the FHDRA can be referred to at later hearings.

Attendance

It is essential that both parties and their legal advisers attend (FPR 2010, r 12.14 and PD 12B, para 14.4). In some courts there are facilities to allow children to attend (normally over the age of 9) if it is considered appropriate.

Adjournment

If a party wishes to apply to adjourn the FHDRA (or any other hearing) they should make the application on Form C2 (or Form C100 in light of the adapted form since 22 April 2014), using the Part 18 procedure (see Part 18 practice note). Note that an adjournment will not be given automatically on request and there will need to be a very good reason for the application to adjourn (if, for example another form of dispute resolution is appropriate (FPR 2010, PD 12B, para 6.3)). It is sensible to apply for the adjournment as early as possible and to try to agree the adjournment with the other party, to avoid a costs order being made. If the other party agrees to the adjournment it is good practice to file with the Form C2 (or Form C100) a covering letter signed by both parties (or their solicitors) explaining the reasons for requesting an adjournment.

If the court considers that another form of dispute resolution is appropriate, it may direct that the proceedings or a particular hearing be adjourned for a specified period to enable the parties to obtain information and advice about non-court dispute resolution; and where appropriate for non-court dispute resolution to take place (FPR 2010, PD 12B, para 6.3).

What happens

The FHDRA is an opportunity for the parties to be helped to reach agreement as to, and understanding of, the issues that divide them (FPR 2010, PD 12B, para 14.8). A Cafcass officer will attend, as well as the judge (FPR 2010, PD 12B, para 14.6). A mediator may attend where available (FPR 2010, PD 12B, para 14.6). The Cafcass officer and court (and mediator if available) will attempt to assist the parties in reaching a resolution (FPR 2010, PD 12B, para 14.11) and there will be a period of time set aside specifically for the Cafcass officer to engage in discussions with the parties to facilitate conciliation (FPR 2010, PD 12B, para 14.13). The specific procedure to be followed in this regard will differ between courts and will be determined by local arrangements between Cafcass and the court (FPR 2010, PD 12B, para 14.13)).

The court's considerations

The court will consider in particular (FPR 2010, PD 12B, para 14.13):

Safeguarding

- The court shall inform the parties of the content of the safeguarding letter by Cafcass (where it has not already been sent to the parties, unless it considers that to do so would create a risk of harm to a party or the child). Further, whether, and if so how any information contained in the checks should be disclosed to the parties if Cafcass have not disclosed the letter (FPR 2010, PD 12B, para 14.13);
- Whether a fact finding hearing is needed to determine allegations which are not accepted, and whose resolution is likely to affect the decision of the court;
- Risk identification followed by active case management including risk assessment, and compliance with the PD 12J.
- If the safeguarding information is (contrary to the arrangements set out in PD 12B) not available at the FHDRA, the court should adjourn the application until the safeguarding checks are available. Interim orders (unless to protect the safety of a child) should not be made in the absence of safeguarding checks.
- Where the court so directs, a safeguarding letter ought to be attached to any referral to a supported or supervised child contact centre in the event the court directs supported or supervised contact.

Mediation Information and Assessment Meeting

The court will consider whether a MIAM exemption has been claimed and if this has been done validly, and whether the respondent has attended a MIAM. If the court finds that a MIAM exemption has not been validly claimed the court will direct the applicant (or the parties) to attend a MIAM and if necessary adjourn the proceedings to enable this to take place. At-Court Mediation assessment and other Dispute Resolution including allowing the parties the time and opportunity to engage in non-court dispute resolution will also be considered.

S 7 reports (CA 1989, s 7)

The court must consider whether it should order a report from Cafcass or the local authority to address welfare issues or other considerations. FPR 2010, PD 12B, para 14.13 makes clear that the court should consider alternative ways of working with the parties before ordering a report.

If the court considers a s 7 report necessary:

- the report should be directed specifically towards and limited to those issues in CA 1989, s 7 (FPR 2010, PD 12B, para 14.13);
- general requests should be avoided (FPR 2010, PD 12B, para 14.13);
- the court should state in the Order the specific factual and other issues that are to be addressed in a focused report (FPR 2010, PD 12B, para 14.13);
- the court should determine whether a request for a report should be directed to the relevant local authority or to Cafcass, by considering such information as Cafcass has provided about the extent and nature of the local authority's current or recent involvement with the subject of the application and the parties, and any relevant protocol between Cafcass and the Association of Directors of Children's Services (FPR 2010, PD 12B, para 14.13);
- a copy of the order requesting the report and any relevant court documents are to be sent to Cafcass or, in the case of the local authority, to the Legal Adviser to the Director of the Local Authority Children's Services and, where known, to the allocated social worker by the court forthwith (FPR 2010, PD 12B, para 14.13).

The court should also consider whether there is a need for an investigation under s 37 Children Act 1989 (see below at 'S 7 Report').

Expert(s) report(s)

The court must consider whether any expert is required (FPR 2010, PD 12B, para 14.3). See 'Propose Expert(s)' section of Child arrangements (Part 1) – pre-proceedings to FHDRA practice note. The court must give a date for the expert to provide their written report (FPR 2010, r 25.8(1)(b)) (note the need to balance the needs of the court and those of the expert – see FPR 2010, PD 25B, para 7.1). The court must also, in children proceedings, give directions approving the questions which the expert is required to answer and specifying the date by which the expert is to receive the letter of instruction (FPR 2010, r 25.8(2)). The court will need to consider carefully the future conduct of proceedings where the preparation of an expert report is necessary but where the parties are unrepresented and are unable to fund such a report (FPR 2010, PD 12B, para 14.13) (see the discussion in *Q v Q; Re B; Re C* [2015] 1 FLR 324, and similarly (albeit different facts and circumstances) in *Re D (A Child) (No 2)* [2015] EWFC 2 and *Re K and H (Children: Unrepresented Father: Cross-Examination of Child)* [2015] EWFC 1 although this has now been superseded by *Re K and H* [2015] EWCA Civ 534.

Practice Direction 25B of the FPR 2010 (The Duties of an Expert, the Expert's Report and Arrangements for an Expert to Attend Court) sets out (in the annex) the standards for expert witnesses in children proceedings in the Family Court. See http://www.familylaw.co.uk/news_and_comment/fpr-practice-direction-25b-updated-october-2014.

Wishes and feelings of the child

In line with the Family Justice Young People's Board Charter, children and young people should be at the centre of all proceedings. Each decision should be assessed on its impact on the child. The court must consider the wishes and feelings of the child, ascertainable so far as is possible in light of the child's age and understanding and circumstances. Specifically, whether the child is aware of the proceedings and whether the wishes and feelings of the child are available, and able to be ascertained. How the child is to be involved in the proceedings – whether for example they should meet the judge/lay justices, be encouraged to write to the court, or have their views reported by Cafcass or by a local authority and who will inform the child of the outcome of the case, where appropriate? (FPR 2010, PD 12B, para 14.13). Reference should also be made to the reports from the Children and Vulnerable Witnesses Working Group, September [2014] Fam Law 1325 and the final report, April [2015] Fam Law 443.

Case management and allocation

Case management and the allocation decision must be considered including the following (see FPR 2010, PD 12B, para 14.13):

- What, if any, issues are agreed and what are the key issues to be determined?
- Should the matter be listed for a fact-finding hearing?
- Are there any interim orders which can usefully be made (eg indirect, supported or supervised contact) pending Dispute Resolution Appointment or final hearing?
- What directions are required to ensure the application is ready for a Dispute Resolution Appointment or final hearing – statements, reports etc?
- Should the application be listed for a Dispute Resolution Appointment (it is envisaged that most cases will be so listed)?
- Should the application be listed straightaway for a final hearing?
- Judicial continuity should be actively considered (especially if there has been or is to be a fact finding hearing or a contested interim hearing).
- If it is necessary to transfer the case to another court within the DFJ area or another area, or re-allocate it, the court shall state the reasons for transfer/re-allocation, and shall specifically make directions for the next hearing in the court.

Consent orders

If the parties reach an agreement a consent order can be drawn up and submitted to the court. The court is not a rubber stamp and will scrutinise it before approving it. The making of a final order may be deferred if any safeguarding checks or risk assessment work remain outstanding and in such circumstances the court shall adjourn the case for no longer than **28 days** to a fixed date (FPR 2010, PD 12B, para 14.13). The parties should write to Cafcass and inform it of the work required to avoid any delays. Cafcass should carry out the work and provide written notification of it before the adjourned hearing, within the timescale specified by the court. If satisfactory information is available at the adjourned hearing the court can make the order without the parties in attendance. If Cafcass are not able to provide satisfactory information by the adjourned hearing it will be adjourned again for further consideration with an opportunity for the parties to make further representations (FPR 2010, PD 12B, para 14.13).

Order

If no agreement is reached in conciliation/discussions with Cafcass/the court, the court will proceed to consider the issues between the parties and then make an order containing case management directions for the future resolution of the case (see Standard Order – CAP02 or Standard Order – CAP02 Lite).

The order must set out:

- the issues about which the parties are agreed;

- the issues that remain to be resolved;
- the steps that are planned to resolve the issues;
- any interim arrangements pending such resolution, including arrangements for the involvement of children;
- the timetable for such steps and, where this involves further hearings, the date of such hearings;
- a statement as to any facts relating to risk or safety; in so far as they are resolved the result will be stated and, in so far as not resolved, the steps to be taken to resolve them will be stated;
- whether the parties are to be assisted by participation in mediation, Separated Parents Information Programme, WT4C, or other types of parenting intervention, and to detail any activity directions or conditions; imposed by the court;
- the date, time and venue of the next hearing;
- whether the author of any section 7 report is required to attend the hearing, in order to give oral evidence. A direction for the Cafcass officer or WFPO to attend court will not be made without first considering the reason why attendance is necessary, and upon what issues the Cafcass officer or WFPO will be providing evidence;
- where both parties are Litigants in Person, the court may direct HMCTS to produce a Litigant in Person bundle; and
- the judge will, as far as possible, provide a copy of the order to both parties before they leave the courtroom, and will, if necessary, go through and explain the contents of the order to ensure they are clearly understood by both parties. The parties should know the date, time and venue of any further hearing before they leave the court (FPR 2010, PD 12B, para 14.13).

FPR 2010, r 12.12 also gives guidance as to the directions the court may give and should be referred to directly.

The parties can agree proposals for the management of the proceedings and if the court considers that the proposals are suitable it may approve them without a hearing and give directions in the terms proposed (FPR 2010, r 12.15). Bear in mind *Re W (Strict Compliance with Court Orders)* [2015] 1 FLR 1092 in which the President emphasised that the parties are not permitted to amend a timetable fixed by the court without the prior approval of the court. There is an obligation on every party, spelt out in the standard form of case management order, to inform the Court immediately in the event of any non-compliance. Failure to do so may result in sanctions – see for example *HU v SU* [2015] EWFC 18, where a wasted costs order was made against solicitors for failure to comply with the court timetable. See also *Re L (Procedure: Bundles: Translation)* [2015] 1 FLR 1417 for further guidance, particularly on the court's stance on adherence to PD 27A.

Note that the court has the power to make an order of its own initiative, even if an application has not been made for that particular order (FPR 2010, r 4.3). The emphasis is on robust case management. See further *Re TG (A Child)* [2013] 1 FLR 1250 and *Re C (Children)* [2013] 1 FLR 1089.

If an interim child arrangements order is made the court can make an activity direction. An activity direction is a direction requiring an individual who is a party to the proceedings concerned to take part in an activity that would, in the court's opinion, help to establish, maintain or improve the involvement in the life of the child concerned of that individual, or another individual who is a party to the proceedings, for example programmes, classes and counselling or guidance sessions (see further CA 1989, s 11A and 11B).

Publicity

The proceedings will be held in private (FPR 2010, r 27.10). This means that members of the public are not allowed access to the court room. Accredited members of the press are **not** allowed access to the court room where the judge is playing an active part in the conciliation process (FPR 2010, PD 27B, para 2.1). However accredited members of the press are entitled to be in court in the parts where the judge plays no part in the conciliation or where the conciliation part is complete and the judge is adjudicating upon the issues between the parties (FPR 2010, r 27.11(2)(f)) unless the court directs that they shall not be allowed access (FPR 2010, r 27.11(3)). Accredited members of the press are not entitled to attend conciliation meetings or negotiations between the Cafcass officer and the parties. See *Family Court Practice* notes to FPR 2010, r 27.11 and FPR 2010, PD 27B (particularly para 2.1) for further information. See also *City and County of Swansea v XZ and others* [2014] 2 FLR 1091 for a further case involving reporting restrictions.

Transparency in the Family Court continues to be an area of development. Following the Practice Guidance in February [2014] Fam Law 222 and various views (see *12th View from the President's Chambers: The process of reform: next steps* in July [2014] Fam Law 978) the President released Transparency – The Next Steps: A Consultation Paper, September [2014] Fam Law 1331. Also see *Re J (A Child)* [2014] 1 FLR 523 and *Re P (Enforced Caesarean: Reporting Restrictions)* [2014] 2 FLR 410.

Costs

The court may at any time make such order as to costs as it thinks just (FPR 2010, r 28.1). Costs are governed by CPR 1998, Parts 43, 44 (except rr 44.3(2) and (3), 44.9 to 44.12C, 44.13(1A) and (1B), and 44.18 to 44.20), 47 and 48 and r 45.6. See *Costs in Private Law Children Proceedings: What now?* Family Law Journal, September [2014] Fam Law 1305 and further *H v W* [2013] 1 FLR 420 about costs at FHDRAs.

Tips:

- If a CA 1989, s 7 report is anticipated it is sensible for Cafcass to be contacted to find out how long it will take for a report to be prepared and to fix the court timetable for the filing of the report, as well as the filing of evidence/disclosure and any further hearings, to fit with this timescale (see further *B v B (Minors) (Interviews and Listing Arrangements)* [1994] 2 FLR 489, CA; *Re A and B (Minors) (No 2)* [1995] 1 FLR 351).
- It is sensible to prepare and take along to the FHDRA a draft order containing the directions you require if an agreement is not reached. If possible speak to the listing office to ascertain likely dates for any future hearings and work backwards from those dates in calculating a timetable for directions.
- If the facilities exist, it may be sensible to phone ahead and book a consultation room at court, particularly if you anticipate there being negotiations.
- Prepare the client to expect delays and explain that shuttle negotiations may mean that they find themselves on their own for periods, but that this is normal.
- If a single joint expert is being instructed try to agree at court: the questions to be asked, who will be responsible for drafting the letter of instruction and what documents should be enclosed with the letter. If possible it is helpful to bring to the hearing a draft letter of instruction and the parties can amend and agree this whilst outside court (see Letter of Instruction below).
- If medical records are required bring appropriate consent letters for to the client to sign at court so that these can be sent off as soon as possible (see precedent C14 (*Family Law Precedents Service*), which gives an outline of the type of letter of authority but which will need to be amended appropriately). Also make enquiries of the GP/hospital/other record

keeper to ascertain whether there will be any charge for obtaining copies of the records and ensure it is made clear (preferably in the court's order) whose responsibility it is for paying any charges.

- In the rising number of situations where practitioners may find themselves dealing with Litigants in Person, the Bar Council, Chartered Institute of Legal Executives (CILEx) and The Law Society have produced guidelines to assist http://www.familylaw.co.uk/news_and_comment/surge-in-diy-justice-sparks-guidelines-for-lawyers#.VXVey89VhBc.

S 7 Report

The court will, as soon as practicable after the issue of proceedings:

- consider whether to ask an officer of the service or a Welsh family proceedings officer for advice relating to the welfare of the child (ie a Cafcass officer) (FPR 2010, r 12.6(c));
- consider whether a report relating to the welfare of the child is required, and if so, request such a report in accordance with CA 1989, s 7 (FPR 2010, r 12.6(d)).

The court can direct that a welfare report be prepared when it is considering 'any question with respect to a child under the CA 1989' which includes the question of whether a child arrangements order should be granted (CA 1989, s 7(1)). A welfare report can be prepared by a Cafcass officer (an 'officer of the Service or a Welsh family proceedings officer' CA 1989, s 7(1)(a)) and/or an officer of the local authority (normally a social worker) (CA 1989, s 7(1)(b)). As to the differences between their roles see *Re W (Welfare Reports)* [1995] 2 FLR 142.

If a Cafcass officer has been involved in conciliation with the parties before a s 7 report is ordered a different Cafcass officer should prepare the report (see also *Re H (Conciliation: Welfare Reports)* [1986] 1 FLR 476).

In order to prepare a s 7 report the Cafcass officer will investigate the situation, which will involve interviewing the parties and child and any other people considered appropriate (for example, step parents, teachers etc). See further *Re R (A Minor) (Court Welfare Report)* [1993] Fam Law 722 – duty to see all relevant parties and, whenever possible, the child with each of the protagonists. The Cafcass officer's role in preparing a s 7 report is not to facilitate conciliation although he or she may encourage the parties to settle if the issue comes up during his or her investigations.

See further FPR 2010, r 16.33 and PD 16A, paras 9.1-9.4.

In cases where allegations of domestic violence have been made the court should have regard to PD 12J – Child Arrangements & Contact Order: Domestic Violence and Harm.

The court may also order a CA 1989, s 37 report if it appears that a care or supervision order may be made for the child (see the commentary to CA 1989, s 37 in *Family Court Practice* for further information).

Timescales

Obtaining a welfare report can take several weeks/months and there are often delays due to the practicalities of scheduling interviews etc. Before ordering the report the court will have had to balance the harm of not obtaining the report against the harm caused by the inevitable delay in obtaining the report (bearing in mind the welfare principle and the no delay principle in CA 1989, s 1(1) and (2)) (see *Re H (Minors) (Welfare Reports)* [1990] 2 FLR 172, CA).

For further commentary in relation to s 7 reports see the notes to CA 1989, s 7 in *Family Court Practice.*

Risk assessment

In addition to the court directing that a s 7 report be produced, a Cafcass officer is required to produce a risk assessment if he or she has cause to suspect that a child is at risk of harm (CA 1989, s 16A). The Practice Direction FPR 2010, PD 12L *Risk Assessments under Section 16A* applies if a risk assessment under s 16A is made.

The Cafcass officer must file the risk assessment with the court and the court will serve it on the parties in accordance with FPR 2010, r 12.34.

Letter of instruction

If a court directs that an expert should be instructed, the letter of instruction should be prepared, filed and served by the date given by the court pursuant to FPR 2010, r 25.8(2)(b). See *Re H-L (Expert Evidence: Test for Permission)* [2013] 2 FLR 1434.

The Law Society provides useful pro-forma templates dealing with proposing an expert at http://www.lawsociety.org.uk/advice/family-expert-templates/.

To an expert (not an SJE)

The letter of instruction should comply with paras 4.1 and 6.1 of PD 25C (FPR 2010, PD 25C, para 2.5(b)). Note the enclosures, including a copy of the guidance in PDs 25B, 25C, 25E and, where appropriate, 15B.

The instructions to the expert are **not** privileged against disclosure (FPR 2010, r 25.14(3)).

To a single joint expert ('SJE')

The instructions to a SJE should be in an agreed joint letter (FPR 2010, r 25.12(1)). If the letter cannot be agreed the letter of instruction can be determined by the court (FPR 2010, r 25.12(2)). If the court directs that the instructions to the expert can be in separate letters the parties must send a copy of the letter to each other when sending the letter to the expert (FPR 2010, r 25.12(3)).

The letter of instruction should comply with paras 4.1 and 6.1 of PD 25C (FPR 2010, PD 25C, para 2.7). Note the enclosures, including a copy of the guidance in PDs 25B, 25C, 25E and, where appropriate, 15B. Family Procedure Rules PD 25B (The Duties of an Expert, the Expert's Report and Arrangements for an Expert to Attend Court) sets out (in the annex) the standards for expert witnesses in children proceedings in the Family Court. See http://www.familylaw.co.uk/news_and_comment/fpr-practice-direction-25b-updated-october-2014.

For example letters of instruction see precedents J9, J9A and J9B (*Family Law Precedents Service*). Also see Annex A to FPR 2010, PD 25C.

Unless the court directs otherwise, the relevant parties are jointly and severally liable for the payment of the expert's fees and expenses (FPR 2010, r 25.12(6)).

The instructions to the expert are **not** privileged against disclosure (FPR 2010, r 25.14(3)).

Tips:

- If medical records or other similar records are required remember to prepare appropriate consent letters for your client so that these can be sent off as soon as possible, if you haven't done so already (see precedent C14 (*Family Law Precedents Service*), which gives an outline of the type of letter of authority but which will need to be amended appropriately). Also make enquiries of the GP/hospital/other record keeper to ascertain whether there will be any charge for obtaining copies of the records and ensure it is made clear (preferably in the court's order – see First Hearing Dispute Resolution Appointment above) whose responsibility it is for paying any charges.

Expert's report

FPR 2010, r 25.14 states that an expert's report must comply with the requirements set out in PD 25B. Paragraph 9.1 of the Practice Direction sets out the requirements and should be consulted directly.

At the end of an expert's report there must be a statement that the expert understands and has complied with their duty to the court (FPR 2010, r 25.14(2)). It is the expert's overriding duty to help the court on matters within their expertise (FPR 2010, r 25.3 and PD 25B, para 3.1). The duties of the expert are listed at FPR 2010, PD 25B, para 4.1.

Any party can use a disclosed expert's report as evidence at any hearing where an issue to which the report relates is being considered (FPR 2010, r 25.15).

Questions of the expert

Within **10 days** beginning on the date on which the expert's report was served a party may put written questions to the expert (FPR 2010, r 25.10(2)(c)). The questions must also be served on the other party at the same time (FPR 2010, r 25.10(2)(e)). The questions must be proportionate and for the purpose only of clarification of the report (FPR 2010, r 25.10(2)(a) and (d)). The questions can only be put once (FPR 2010, r 25.10(2)(b)).

These requirements apply unless the court directs otherwise or a practice direction provides otherwise (FPR 2010, r 25.10(2)).

The court will set out a timetable for answering the questions (FPR 2010, r 25.10(3)(a)).

The expert's answers are treated as part of the expert's report (FPR 2010, r 25.10(3)(b)).

If the expert does not answer a question the court can order that the party may not rely on the evidence of that expert and/or that the party may not recover the fees and expenses of that expert from any other party (FPR 2010, r 25.10(4)).

If a party is dissatisfied with a SJE's report, even after receiving answers to questions put, the party can put forward a '*Daniels v Walker (Practice Note)* [2000] 1 WLR 1382' argument to apply for the court to order that another expert report be filed. As a last resort both experts will be cross examined.

Discussions between experts

The court can direct that there be a discussion between experts for the purpose of identifying and discussing the expert issues in the proceedings; and where possible, reaching an agreed opinion on those issues (FPR 2010, r 25.16(1)).

The court may specify which issues the experts should discuss and may direct that the experts prepare a joint statement summarising which issues they agree and which they do not (a 'Statement of Agreement and Disagreement') (FPR 2010, r 25.16(2) and (3)).

See FPR 2010, PD 25E for the specific requirements of setting up a discussion between experts. In summary:

- within **15 business days** after the experts' reports have been filed and copied to the parties the 'nominated professional' (see FPR 2010, PD 25E, para 3.1) should make arrangements for the experts to meet/communicate;
- **5 business days** before the discussion/meeting the nominated professional should formulate an agenda for the meeting (normally a list of questions);
- the agenda should be sent to the experts no later than **2 business days** before the discussion/meeting;
- if a Statement of Agreement and Disagreement is required by the court it should be served and filed not later **than 5 business days** after the discussion/meeting.

Disclosure

The court may direct that the parties file disclosure, for example:

- hospital/GP records;
- school reports;
- police reports; or
- copies of letters/cards.

In private law proceedings (which includes an application for a child arrangements order), strictly speaking a court order for disclosure against a third party cannot be made (for example, the police cannot be ordered to disclose records and in fact may not be permitted to disclose evidence obtained for other purposes – see *X, Commissioner of Police for the Metropolis, the Secretary of State v Z, a Local Authority* [2015] 1 FLR 1100). However, in the case of *Re A and B (Minors) (No 2)* [1995] 1 FLR 351 the court said that it could order such third party disclosure so long as undertakings were provided to protect the confidentiality and the use of any material disclosed.

For an explanation of the issues surrounding a request for disclosure from a Multi-Agency Risk Assessment Conference see the notes to FPR 2010, r 12.12 in *Family Court Practice*.

Statements

The court will sometimes direct that the parties produce and serve statements outlining their case in further detail.

FPR 2010, PD 22A sets out the requirements as to the format and contents of a witness statement and should be referred to directly.

When drafting the statement practitioners should have regard to the requirements of CA 1989:

- CA 1989, s 1(1) sets out the welfare principle. This states that in making an order the child's welfare must be the court's paramount consideration.
- CA 1989, s 1(2) sets out the no-delay principle. This reminds the court that any delay in determining a question relating to a child's upbringing is likely to prejudice the welfare of the child.
- CA 1989, s 1(3) sets out the welfare checklist:
  - the ascertainable wishes and feelings of the child concerned (considered in the light of his or her age and understanding);
  - his or her physical, emotional and educational needs;
  - the likely effect on him or her of any change in his or her circumstances;
  - his or her age, sex, background and any characteristics of his or hers which the court considers relevant;
  - any harm which he or she has suffered or is at risk of suffering;
  - how capable each of his or her parents, and any other person in relation to whom the court considers the question to be relevant, is of meeting his or her needs;
  - the range of powers available to the court under the CA 1989 in the proceedings in question.
- CA 1989, s 1(5) sets out the no-order principle which provides that where a court is considering whether or not to make an order, it shall not make the order unless it considers that doing so would be better for the child than making no order at all.
- CA 1989, s 1(2A) and (2B) set out a presumption that, unless the contrary is shown, the involvement of each parent in the life of the child concerned will further the child's welfare. 'Involvement' means involvement of some kind, either direct or indirect, but not any particular division of the child's time. CA 1989, s 1(6) restricts a 'parent' in subsection (2A) to a parent can be involved in the child's life in a way that does not put the child at risk of suffering harm.

Regard should also be had to the case-law and to the types of order that can be made (see 'Orders' section of Child arrangements (Part 3) – Fact Finding to Final Hearing practice note). For case-law see further:

Contact

- Grandparents: *Re A (Section 8 Order: Grandparent Application)* [1995] 2 FLR 153; *Re W (Contact: Application by Grandparent)* [1997] 1 FLR 793.
- Step-parents: *Re H (A Minor) (Contact)* [1994] 2 FLR 776.
- Importance of biological parentage: *Re H (A Child)* [2012] 2 FLR 627; *A v B and C (Lesbian Co-parents: Role of Father)* [2012] 2 FLR 607; *Re SAB* [2014] 2 FLR 1197.
- Intractable contact cases: *Re J (A Minor) (Contact)* [1994] 1 FLR 729; *Re D (Contact: Reasons for Refusal)* [1997] 2 FLR 48 (meaning of 'implacably hostile); *Re W (A Minor) (Contact)* [1994] 2 FLR 441; *Re F (Contact: Restraint Order)* [1995] 1 FLR 956; *Re M (Intractable Contact Dispute: Interim Care Order)* [2003] 2 FLR 636; *Re E* [2011] EWHC 2521 (Fam); *Re S (Contact: Intractable Dispute)* [2010] 2 FLR 1517; *Re M (Contact)* [2013] 1 FLR 1403; *Re Y (Private Law: Fact Finding)* [2014] EWHC 486 (Fam); *Re A and B (Children)* [2013] EWHC 4150 (Fam); *Re G (Intractable Contact Dispute)* [2014] Fam Law 23; *Re H-B (Contact)* [2015] EWCA Civ 389 and *K v D (Parental Conflict)* [2015] EWFC 49.
- Duty on parents to work together to put aside differences: *Re W (Direct Contact)* [2013] 1 FLR 494; *Re W (Contact: Permission to Appeal)* [2013] 1 FLR 609. Also *Re J and K* [2015] 1 FLR 86 where the parents were seemingly able to resolve their differences.
- Determining with whom a child lives: *Re H (Contact: Adverse Finding of Fact)* [2011] 2 FLR 1201.

- Domestic violence: *Re L (Contact: Domestic Violence); Re V (Contact: Domestic Violence); Re M (Contact: Domestic Violence); Re H (Contact: Domestic Violence)* [2000] 2 FLR 334, and see FPR PD 12J *Child Arrangements & Contact Order: Domestic Violence and Harm; Re Z (Unsupervised Contact: Allegations of Domestic Violence)* [2009] 2 FLR 877; *Re W (Children: Domestic Violence)* [2014] 1 FLR 260; *Re H A Child* [2014] 1 FLR 41; *AB v BB and C, D, E and F (By their Children's Guardian)* [2014] 1 FLR 178; *Re A (A Child) (Supervised Contact Order: Assessment of Impact of Domestic Violence)* [2015] EWCA Civ 486.
- Human rights: (ECHR 1950 and HRA 1998) particularly with regard to unmarried fathers *Elsholz v Germany* [2000] 2 FLR 486; *Ciliz v The Netherlands* [2000] 2 FLR 469; *Elsholz v Italy* [2000] Fam Law 680; *Glaser v UK (Case No 32346/96)* [2001] 1 FLR 153; *S and G v Italy* [2000] 2 FLR 771; *Sahin v Germany; Sommerfeld v Germany; Hoffmann v Germany* [2002] 1 FLR 119; *Hoppe v Germany* [2003] 1 FLR 384; *Sylvester v Austria* [2003] 2 FLR 210; *Hansen v Turkey (Application No 36141/97)* [2004] 1 FLR 142; *Kosmopoulou v Greece* [2004] 1 FLR 800; *Bove v Italy* [2005] Fam Law 752; *Zawadka v Poland* [2005] 2 FLR 897; *Gluhakovic v Croatia* [2011] 2 FLR 294; *Re C (Direct Contact: Suspension)* [2011] 2 FLR 912 at [47].

Living Arrangements (formerly Residence)

- Importance of biological parentage: *Re G (Children)* [2006] 2 FLR 629, HL; *Re B (A Child)* [2010] 1 FLR 551, but also see *Re E-R (A Child)* [2015] EWCA Civ 405.
- Shared living arrangements: *Re F (Shared Residence Order)* [2003] 2 FLR 397; *Re P (Shared Residence Order)* [2006] 2 FLR 347; *Re M (Residence Order)* [2008] 1 FLR 1087; *Re K (Shared Residence Order)* [2008] 2 FLR 380; *A v A (Shared Residence)* [2004] 1 FLR 1195; *Re W (Shared Residence Order)* [2009] 2 FLR 436; *Re R (Residence: Shared Care: Children's Views)* [2006] 1 FLR 491; *Re W (Shared Residence Order)* [2009] 2 FLR 436; *Re G (Residence: Same-Sex Partner)* [2005] 2 FLR 957; *Re A (Joint Residence/Parental Responsibility)* [2008] 2 FLR 1593; *D v D (Shared Residence Order)* [2001] 1 FLR 495.
- Transferring living arrangements (in light of repeated breaches of child arrangements orders): *Re A (Residence Order)* [2010] 1 FLR 1083, CA; *Re C (Residence Order)* [2008] 1 FLR 211; *Re S (Transfer of Residence)* [2011] 1 FLR 1789; *Re D (Children)* [2009] EWCA Civ 1467; *Re M (Contact)* [2012] EWHC 1948; *Re Y (Private Law: Interim Change of Residence)* [2014] EWHC 1068 (Fam).

Relocation

If a child arrangements order regulating living arrangements for a child is in force, written consent from everyone with parental responsibility is required to remove the child from the UK (s 13, CA 1989). If no child arrangements order regulating living arrangements is in force, a prohibited steps order may be used to prevent a parent removing a child from the jurisdiction. A specific issue order should be used if no child arrangements order regulating living arrangements is in force and the applicant wishes to relocate the child outside the jurisdiction, without the consent of all parental responsibility holders. External relocation cases are also known as Leave to Remove cases. See further – *Payne v Payne* [2001] 1 FLR 1052; *K v K (Relocation: Shared Care Arrangement)* [2012] 2 FLR 880 and *Re F (Relocation)* [2013] 1 FLR 645.

The law relating to child arrangements is large and complex and has been subject to a wealth of reform. This practice note sets out only a very brief summary and is by no means exhaustive. Reference should be made to further detailed commentary which can be found in:

- *Family Court Practice* (in particular see commentary to CA 1989, s 8); and
- *Children Law and Practice*, Division B, Section 3
- *Children Act Private Law Proceedings: A Handbook*, Chapters 10 and 11

The Children and Families Act 2014 reiterated the ethos that it is in a child's welfare interests to have both parents involved in their lives, unless the contrary is shown. The presumption wording in the Act is careful not to express this in terms of a presumption of equal division of time, but the developing case law should be noted with interest in terms of how child arrangements orders take shape.

CHILD ARRANGEMENTS (PART 3) – FACT FINDING TO FINAL HEARING

FLOWCHART

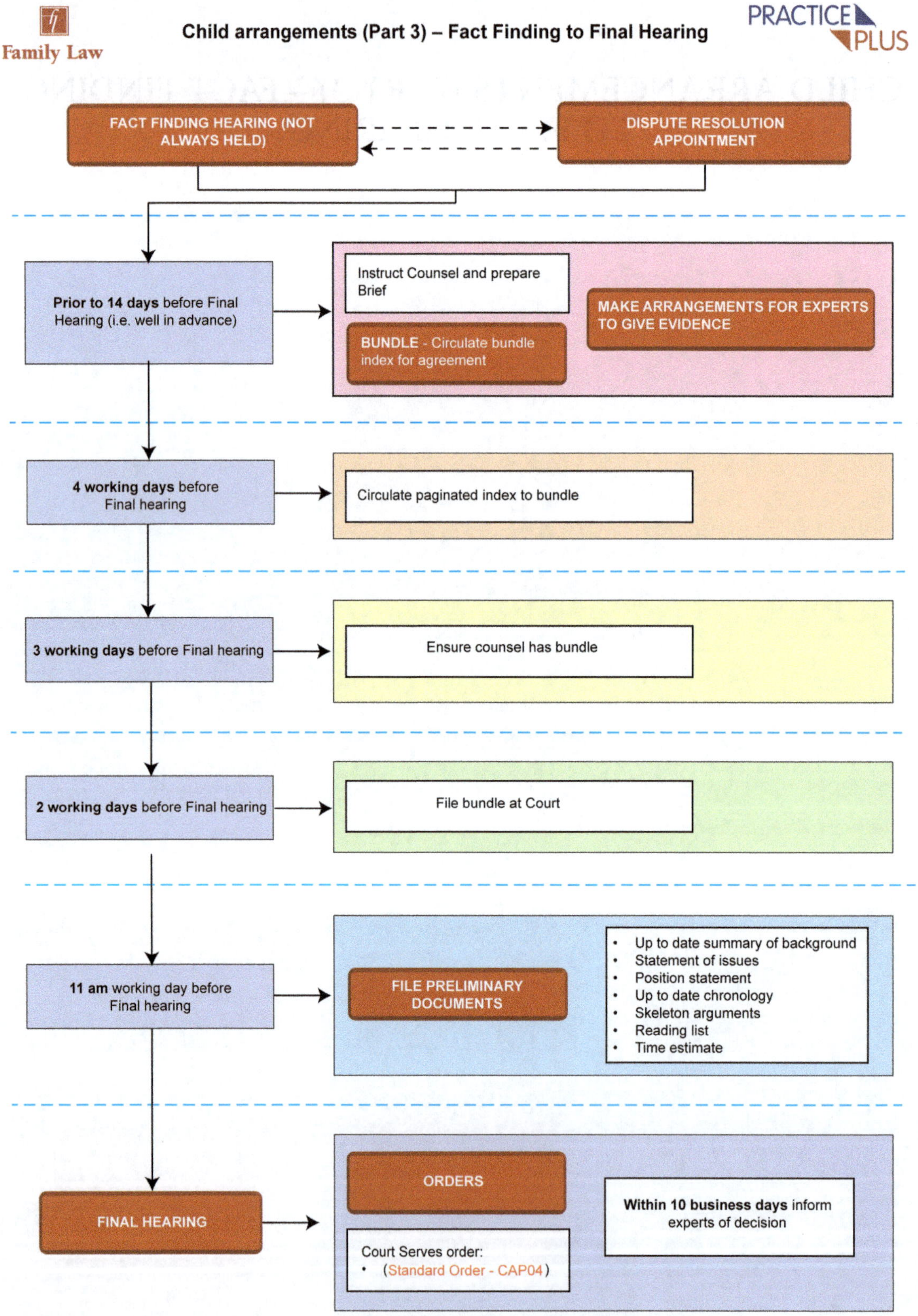
Family Law
Child arrangements (Part 3) – Fact Finding to Final Hearing
PRACTICE PLUS
FACT FINDING HEARING (NOT ALWAYS HELD)
DISPUTE RESOLUTION APPOINTMENT
Prior to 14 days before Final Hearing (i.e. well in advance)
Instruct Counsel and prepare Brief
BUNDLE - Circulate bundle index for agreement
MAKE ARRANGEMENTS FOR EXPERTS TO GIVE EVIDENCE
4 working days before Final hearing
Circulate paginated index to bundle
3 working days before Final hearing
Ensure counsel has bundle
2 working days before Final hearing
File bundle at Court
11 am working day before Final hearing
FILE PRELIMINARY DOCUMENTS
Up to date summary of background
Statement of issues
Position statement
Up to date chronology
Skeleton arguments
Reading list
Time estimate
FINAL HEARING
ORDERS
Court Serves order:
(Standard Order - CAP04)
Within 10 business days inform experts of decision

PRACTICE NOTE

See also Procedural Guide (PG) D7 in *The Red Book (Family Court Practice)*.

Dispute Resolution Appointment

The court shall list a Dispute Resolution Appointment ('DRA') to follow the preparation of section 7 or other expert report, or Separated Parenting Information Programme (SPIP), if this is considered likely to be helpful in the interests of the child (FPR 2010, PD 12B, para 19.1).

The author of the section 7 report will only attend this hearing if directed to do so by the Court (FPR 2010, PD 12B, para 19.2).

At the DRA the court will:

- Identify the key issue(s) (if any) to be determined and the extent to which those issues can be resolved or narrowed at the DRA (FPR 2010, PD 12B, para 19.3(1));
- Consider whether the DRA can be used as a final hearing (FPR 2010, PD 12B, para 19.3(2));
- Resolve or narrow the issues by hearing evidence (FPR 2010, PD 12B, para 19.3(3));
- Identify the evidence to be heard on the issues which remain to be resolved at the final hearing (FPR 2010, PD 12B, para 19.3(4));
- Give final case management directions including filing of further evidence/a statement of facts/issues remaining to be determined (FPR 2010, PD 12B, para 19.3(5)(a)(b));
- Filing of a witness template and / or skeleton arguments (FPR 2010, PD 12B, para 19.3(5)(c));
- Ensuring Compliance with FPR 2010, PD 27A (FPR 2010, PD 12B, para 19.3(5)(d));
- Listing the Final Hearing (FPR 2010, PD 12B, para 19.3(5)(e)).

If a party considers a case to be drifting, or if they would like the court to make a specific direction, they can make an application for directions using the Part 18 procedure (using Form C2 (or Form C100 in light of the amendments made to the form following 22 April 2014), see further Part 18 practice note).

Note that for any hearings before a judge sitting in the Family Division of the High Court wherever the court may be sitting, and all hearings in the Family Court (save for hearings of any urgent application if and to the extent it would be impossible to comply with the Practice Direction (PD 27A, paras 2.1 and 2.4)) FPR 2010, PD 27A will apply and a bundle will need to be prepared and lodged and preliminary documents filed – see 'Bundles' and 'Preliminary documents' below.

The court will make an order in prescribed Standard Order – CAP03 (Order – Dispute Resolution Appointment).

Adjournment

If a party wishes to apply to adjourn the directions hearing (or any other hearing) they should make the application on Form C2 (or Form C100), using the Part 18 procedure (see Part 18 practice note). Note that an adjournment will not be given automatically on request and there will need to be a very good reason for the application to adjourn. It is sensible to apply for the adjournment as early as possible and to try to agree the adjournment with the other party, to avoid a costs order being made. If the other party agrees to the adjournment it is good practice to file with the Form C2 (or Form C100) a covering letter signed by both parties (or their solicitors) explaining the reasons for requesting an adjournment.

Fact finding hearing (not always held)

The court may direct that a fact-finding hearing should be held. The purpose of a fact-finding hearing is for the court to make findings of fact on issues identified by the parties or the court. A fact finding hearing will not always be required – see the President's *Guidance in Relation to Split Hearings* (May 2010) which warns that split hearings (where the first limb of the hearing is a fact finding hearing) had been taking place when they should not be. See also *Re S (Split Hearing)* [2014] 1 FLR 1421.

In the context of applications for child arrangements orders a fact-finding hearing may be listed in order for the court to make findings of fact in relation to allegations of domestic violence or abuse (which may be one of the reasons put forward by the respondent against the making of a child arrangements order). See further *Re H (A Child)* [2014] 1 FLR 41.

In accordance with FPR 2010, PD 12B, para 20.1 if the court considers that a fact-finding hearing is necessary it shall conduct that hearing in accordance with FPR 2010, PD 12J.

Preparation for a fact finding hearing

A bundle will need to be prepared and lodged and preliminary documents filed in accordance with FPR 2010, PD 27A in all hearings PD 27A must be followed (see for example *Re W (Strict Compliance with Court Orders)* [2015] 1 FLR 1092, *J v J* [2014] EWHC 3654 (Fam), *Re L (Procedure: Bundles: Translation)* [2015] 1 FLR 1417) before a judge sitting in the Family Division of the High Court wherever the court may be sitting, and all hearings in the Family Court save for hearings of any urgent application if and to the extent it would be impossible to comply with the Practice Direction (PD 27A, paras 2.1 and 2.4) – see 'Bundles' and 'Preliminary documents' below.

The court may have given directions for the following documents to be filed by a particular date ahead of a fact finding hearing:

- a concise schedule of the allegations the applicant/respondent relies on for the purpose of the fact finding hearing;
- a concise schedule of the answer to the allegations the applicant/respondent relies on for the purpose of the fact finding hearing.

If experts are to give evidence preparation for them to do so must be made in advance – see 'Make Arrangements for Experts to Give Evidence' below.

Order of evidence

FPR 2010, r 12.21 states that, subject to any directions given by the court, evidence should be heard in the following order:

- the applicant;
- any party with parental responsibility for the child (the respondent(s));
- other respondents (if applicable);
- the children's guardian (if applicable); and
- the child, if the child is a party to the proceedings and there is no children's guardian.

Evidence can be given by video link or by other means (FPR 2010, r 22.3). See further FPR 2010, PD 22A, para 17.1 and Annex 3. See also *Re R (Children)* [2015] EWCA Civ 167 where the child was permitted to give evidence against the wishes of other parties.

In cases where allegations of domestic violence have been made the court should have regard to PD 12J – Child Arrangements & Contact Order: Domestic Violence and Harm. *Re M (Children)* [2013] EWCA Civ 388 gives guidance on the status of an allegation which is found not to be proved. Where a party is unrepresented and would need to cross-examine a witness who has made allegations against him or her, perhaps of domestic violence, consideration will need to be given as to how this is best achieved – see *Re K and H (Children: Unrepresented Father: Cross-Examination of Child)* [2015] EWFC 1, although this has now been superseded by *Re K and H* [2015] EWCA Civ 543.

Adjournment

If a party wishes to apply to adjourn the fact finding hearing (or any other hearing) they should make the application on Form C2 (or Form C100), using the Part 18 procedure (see Part 18 practice note). Note that an adjournment will not be given automatically on request and there will need to be a very good reason for the application to adjourn. It is sensible to apply for the adjournment as early as possible and to try to agree the adjournment with the other party, to avoid a costs order being made. If the other party agrees to the adjournment it is good practice to file with the Form C2 (or Form C100) a covering letter signed by both parties (or their solicitors) explaining the reasons for requesting an adjournment. Remember to inform any experts or other witnesses.

Make arrangements for experts to give evidence

The court can direct that an expert should give evidence at the final hearing. The court will only direct that an expert should attend court if it is necessary to do so in the interests of justice (FPR 2010, r 25.9(2)) – often only the expert's written report will be required and their attendance at court will not be necessary. FPR 2010, PD 25B (The Duties of an Expert, the Expert's Report and Arrangements for an Expert to Attend Court) sets out (in the annex) the standards for expert witnesses in children proceedings in the Family Court. See http://www.familylaw.co.uk/news_and_comment/fpr-practice-direction-25b-updated-october-2014. Where the court has directed that the expert should attend court the party who is responsible for the instruction of the expert must, by a date specified by the court prior to the hearing at which the expert is to give oral evidence, ensure that:

- a date and time (if possible, convenient to the expert) are fixed for the court to hear the expert's evidence, substantially in advance of the hearing at which the expert is to give oral evidence and no later than a specified date prior to that hearing (FPR 2010, PD 25B, para 10.1(a));
- if the expert's oral evidence is not required, the expert is notified as soon as possible (FPR 2010, PD 25B, para 10.1(b));
- the witness template accurately indicates how long the expert is likely to be giving evidence, in order to avoid the inconvenience of the expert being delayed at court (FPR 2010, PD 25B, para 10.1(c));
- consideration is given in each case to whether some or all of the experts participate by telephone conference or video link, or submit their evidence in writing, to ensure that minimum disruption is caused to professional schedules and that costs are minimised (FPR 2010, PD 25B, para 10.1(d)).

All parties shall ensure that:

- the parties' advocates have identified (whether at an advocates' meeting or by other means) the issues which the experts are to address (FPR 2010, PD 25B, para 10.2(a));
- wherever possible, a logical sequence to the evidence is arranged, with experts of the same discipline giving evidence on the same day (FPR 2010, PD 25B, para 10.2(b));

- the court is informed of any circumstance where all experts agree but a party nevertheless does not accept the agreed opinion, so that directions can be given for the proper consideration of the experts' evidence and opinion and of the party's reasons for not accepting the agreed opinion (FPR 2010, PD 25B, para 10.2(c));
- in the exceptional case the court is informed of the need for a witness summons (FPR 2010, PD 25B, para 10.2(d) see Form FP25).

See *Re H-L (Expert Evidence: Test for Permission)* [2013] 2 FLR 1434.

Bundles

Bundles

Practice Direction 27A must be followed (see for example *Re W (Strict Compliance with Court Orders)* [2015] 1 FLR 1092, *J v J* [2014] EWHC 3654 (Fam), *Re L (Procedure: Bundles: Translation)* [2015] 1 FLR 1417) for the preparation of court bundles (FPR 2010, r 27.6). The Practice Direction sets out very precise rules regarding the preparation of the bundle and should be referred to directly. It applies to all hearings before a judge sitting in the Family Division of the High Court wherever the court may be sitting, and all hearings in the Family Court save for hearings of any urgent application if and to the extent it would be impossible to comply with the Practice Direction (PD 27A, paras 2.1 and 2.4).

In summary:

- A bundle must be provided by the party in the position of applicant (or, if there are cross-applications, by the party whose application was first in time) or, if that person is a litigant in person, by the first listed respondent who is not a litigant in person. (PD 27A, para 3.1);
- PD 27A, para 4.1 sets out the content of the bundle and paras 5.1 – 5.3 set out the format of the bundle;
- if possible the content of the bundle should be agreed between the parties (PD 27A, para 3.2);
- a paginated index to the bundle should be circulated to all parties 4 working days before the hearing (FPR 2010, PD 27A, para 6.1);
- the paginated bundle should be sent to counsel by the person instructing them **3 working days** before the hearing (PD 27A, para 6.2); and
- the bundle should be lodged at court not less than 2 working days before the hearing (FPR 2010, PD 27A, para 6.3). It is advisable to obtain a receipt if possible or to seek confirmation from the court that the bundle has arrived if sent by post/DX (if the case is to be heard in the RCJ a receipt or proof of postage must be obtained and brought to the hearing – PD 27A, para 7.6).

Re L (Procedure: Bundles: Translation) [2015] 1 FLR 1417 provides further guidance, particularly on the court's stance on adherence to PD 27A.

Number of sets of bundles:

- Applicant
- Counsel
- Court
- Witness (if relevant. And note, the witness bundle should not be sent to the court beforehand as per PD 27A)

- Respondent – The applicant should request an undertaking that the respondent will pay for reasonable copying charges before producing the respondent's bundle. The applicant should also enquire whether the respondent's counsel will need a copy and, if so, whether the respondent would like it delivered straight to chambers. The respondent should meet the copying charges for his or her counsel's bundle.

Tips:

- The bundle should be contained in one A4 size ring binder or lever arch file and limited to no more than 350 pages of single-sided text (FPR 2010, PD 27A). Follow the Practice Guidance carefully to ensure only the necessary documents are contained and no space is wasted.
- Try to avoid duplication – for example if medical records are attached to a witness statement and to an expert's report, only put them in the bundle once and put a note in to guide the user to their location (eg a page marked 'Medical records can be found at page 166').

File preliminary documents

Preliminary documents

PD 27A, para 4.3 sets out the preliminary documents that should be prepared and lodged by **11 am the day before the hearing** (PD 27A, para 6.4):

- an up to date summary of the background to the hearing confined to those matters which are relevant to the hearing and the management of the case and limited, if practicable, to four A4 pages (PD 27A, para 4.3(a));
- a statement of the issue or issues to be determined at that hearing and at the final hearing (PD 27A, para 4.3(b));
- a position statement by each party including a summary of the order or directions sought by that party at that hearing and at the final hearing (PD 27A, para 4.3(c));
- an up to date chronology (PD 27A, para 4.3(d));
- skeleton arguments, if appropriate, with copies of all authorities relied on (PD 27A, para 4.3(e));
- a list of essential reading for the hearing (PD 27A, para 4.3(f)); and
- the time estimate (PD 27A, para 4.3(g)).

If possible there should only be one set of preliminary documents, agreed between the parties (PD 27A, para 4.6). If agreement is not possible the fact of the parties' disagreement and their differing contentions should be set out at the appropriate places in the document. The preliminary documents should be as short and succinct as possible and should state on the front page immediately below the heading the date when it was prepared and the date of the hearing for which it was prepared (FPR 2010, PD 27A, para 4.4). The preliminary documents should be cross referenced to the relevant pages of the bundle (FPR 2010, PD 27A, para 4.5).

Copies of all authorities relied on must be contained in a separate composite bundle agreed between the advocates and must be lodged in hard copy (FPR 2010, PD 27A, para 6.4).

Tip:

- Take extra copies of the preliminary documents to court on the day of the final hearing, in case they have not made their way onto the court file.
- When lodging preliminary documents at the court, request a receipt to retain on file as confirmation they have been submitted.

Final hearing

Attendance

All parties must personally attend unless the court directs otherwise (FPR 2010, r 27.3 and r 12.14(2)).

If the respondent does not attend the court can proceed in his or her absence if he or she received reasonable notice of the date of the hearing or the court is satisfied that the circumstances of the case justify proceeding in his or her absence (FPR 2010, r 27.4(2) and (3) and r 12.14(5) and (6)). If an order is made in the respondent's absence the court may provide that the respondent can apply to set it aside or vary it within a certain number of days of the order being served on him or her.

If the applicant does not attend, the court may refuse the application or, if sufficient evidence has previously been received, proceed without him or her (FPR 2010, r 27.4(4) and r 12.14(7)).

If neither party appears, the court may refuse the application (FPR 2010, r 27.4(5) and r 12.14(8)).

Evidence

FPR 2010, r 12.21 states that, subject to any directions given by the court, evidence should be heard in the following order:

- the applicant;
- any party with parental responsibility for the child (the respondent(s));
- other respondents (if applicable);
- the children's guardian (if applicable); and
- the child, if the child is a party to the proceedings and there is no children's guardian.

Evidence can be given by video link or by other means (FPR 2010, r 22.3). See further FPR 2010, PD 22A, para 17.1 and Annex 3.

Publicity

The proceedings will be held in private (FPR 2010, r 27.10). This means that members of the public are not allowed access to the court room. However accredited members of the press are entitled to be in court (FPR 2010, r 27.11(2)(f)) unless the court directs that they shall not be allowed access (FPR 2010, r 27.11(3)). See notes to FPR 2010, r 27.11 and FPR 2010, PD 27B for further information. See also *City and County of Swansea v XZ* [2014] 2 FLR 1091.

Transparency in the Family Court continues to be high on the agenda. Following the Practice Guidance in February [2014] Fam Law 222 and various views (see *12th View from the President's Chambers: The process of reform: next steps* in July [2014] Fam Law 978 the President released a consultation paper Transparency – The Next Steps: A Consultation Paper, September [2014] Fam Law 1331 and also see *Re J (A Child)* [2014] 1 FLR 523 and *Re P (Enforced Caesarean: Reporting Restrictions)* [2014] 2 FLR 410.

The law

The court will have regard to the requirements of CA 1989:

- CA 1989, s 1(1) sets out the welfare principle. This states that in making an order the child's welfare must be the court's paramount consideration.
- CA 1989, s 1(2) sets out the no-delay principle. This reminds the court that any delay in determining a question relating to a child's upbringing is likely to prejudice the welfare of the child.
- CA 1989, s 1(3) sets out the welfare checklist:
  - the ascertainable wishes and feelings of the child concerned (considered in the light of his or her age and understanding) (see *Re SK (Permission to Appeal Residence and Contact Orders)* [2013] EWCA Civ 1247 for an example of the wishes and feelings of older children being overridden);
  - his or her physical, emotional and educational needs;
  - the likely effect on him or her of any change in his or her circumstances;
  - his or her age, sex, background and any characteristics of his or hers which the court considers relevant;
  - any harm which he or she has suffered or is at risk of suffering;
  - how capable each of his or her parents, and any other person in relation to whom the court considers the question to be relevant, is of meeting his or her needs;
  - the range of powers available to the court under the CA 1989 in the proceedings in question.
- CA 1989, s 1(5) sets out the no-order principle which provides that where a court is considering whether or not to make an order, it shall not make the order unless it considers that doing so would be better for the child than making no order at all.
- CA 1989, s 1(2A) and (2B) set out a presumption that, unless the contrary is shown, the involvement of each parent in the life of the child concerned will further the child's welfare. 'Involvement' means involvement of some kind, either direct or indirect, but not any particular division of the child's time. CA 1989, s 1(6) restricts a 'parent' in subsection (2A) to a parent can be involved in the child's life in a way that does not put the child at risk of suffering harm.

Regard should also be had to the case law and to the types of order that can be made (see 'Orders' below and 'Statements' section of Child arrangements (Part 2) – FHDRA to Fact Finding practice note).

The Court must give reasons if it decides not to follow the recommendations of the Cafcass officer (see further the notes to CA 1989, s 7 in *Family Court Practice* and *Re P (Custody of Children: Split Custody Order)* [1991] 1 FLR 337; *Re J (Children) (Residence: Expert Evidence)* [2001] 2 FCR 44; *Re R (Residence Order)* [2010] 1 FLR 509; *Re V (Residence: Review)* [1995] 2 FLR 1010, CA; *Re CB (Access: Attendance of Court Welfare Officer)* [1995] 1 FLR 622; *Re C (Section 8 Order: Court Welfare Officer)* [1995] 1 FLR 617); and *Re S (A Child): Child Arrangements Order: Effect of Long-Term Supervised Contact on* Welfare [2015] EWCA Civ 689.

Form of order

The order should be in Standard Order – CAP04.

See precedents below for child arrangements:

- Precedent E6 (*Family Law Precedents Service*) – Temporary child arrangements order incorporating a prohibited steps order

- Precedent E7 (*Family Law Precedents Service*) – Application for a child arrangements order in existing proceedings (Form C100 or Form C2)
- Precedent E8 (*Family Law Precedents Service*) – Defined child arrangements order (contact/spending time)
- Precedent E9 (*Family Law Precedents Service*) – Child arrangements order: example of order for the use of a contact centre
- Precedent E10 (*Family Law Precedents Service*) – Child arrangements: example of order for indirect contact

Also see 'Orders' section below.

Costs

The court may at any time make such order as to costs as it thinks just (FPR 2010, r 28.1). Costs are governed by CPR 1998, Parts 43, 44 (except rr 44.3(2) and (3), 44.9 to 44.12C, 44.13(1A) and (1B), and 44.18 to 44.20), 47 and 48 and r 45.6. See further *HH v BLW (Appeal: Cost: Proportionality)* [2013] 1 FLR 420 and *Re G (Contact Proceedings: Cost)* [2014] 1 FLR 517.

Inform experts

If an expert has been instructed, **within 10 business days after the Final Hearing,** the solicitor instructing the expert shall inform the expert in writing of the outcome of the case, and of the use made by the court of the expert's opinion (FPR 2010, r 25.19(1)). Unless the court directs otherwise the final order and transcript must be sent to the expert (within 10 days of the order and transcript being received) (FPR 2010, r 25.19(2)).

Adjournment

If a party wishes to apply to adjourn the final hearing (or any other hearing) they should make the application on Form C2 (or Form C100), using the Part 18 procedure (see Part 18 practice note). Note that an adjournment will not be given automatically on request and there will need to be a very good reason for the application to adjourn (for example if another form of dispute resolution is appropriate, to enable the parties to obtain information and advice about non-court dispute resolution; and where the parties agree, to enable non-court dispute resolution to take place FPR 2010, PD 12B, para 6.3). It is sensible to apply for the adjournment as early as possible and to try to agree the adjournment with the other party, to avoid a costs order being made. If the other party agrees to the adjournment it is good practice to file with the Form C2 (or Form C100) a covering letter signed by both parties (or their solicitors) explaining the reasons for requesting an adjournment. Remember to inform any experts or other witnesses.

Orders

Child arrangements orders

Child arrangements orders (save for those which apply to regulate a child's living arrangements (CA 1989, s 9(6B)):

- cannot have effect for a period that will end after the child has reached the age of 16, unless the circumstances of the case are exceptional (CA 1989, s 9(6));
- cannot be made after a child has reached the age of 16 (other than to vary or discharge an existing order) unless the circumstances of the case are exceptional (CA 1989, s 9(7));

- will cease to have effect if the parents with parental responsibility live together for a continuous period of more than six months (CA 1989, s 11(6));
- must have a warning notice attached if made or varied after 8 December 2008 setting out the consequences of not complying with the order (ie an enforcement order (for unpaid work) (ss 11J–N), an order for financial compensation (ss 11O, 11P), and sanctions for contempt of court. The warning notice must also make clear the person to whom it is addressed, and the exact provisions of the order to which it relates (CA 1989, s 11I). For further information regarding enforcement see Enforcement Orders and Financial Compensation Orders (Child Arrangements Orders) practice note.

Directions and conditions

The court has the option to make directions or impose conditions when making a child arrangements order (CA 1989, s 11(7)). It also has the following options:

- Activity directions – the court can make a direction requiring an individual who is a party to the proceedings concerned to take part in an activity that would, in the court's opinion, help to establish, maintain or improve the involvement in the life of the child concerned, for example programmes, classes and counselling or guidance sessions (see further CA 1989, s 11A and 11B). An activity direction should only be made when the court gives an interim order in child arrangements proceedings and cannot be made with a final order (CA 1989, s 11A(7));
- Activity conditions – the court can impose a condition requiring an individual (falling within s 11C(3)) to take part in an activity that would, in the court's opinion, help to establish, maintain or improve the involvement in the life of the child concerned, as above (programmes, classes etc) (see further CA 1989, s 11C and 11D).

CA 1989, s 11E sets out the matters the court must satisfy itself of before making an activity direction or condition. They are:

- that the activity proposed is appropriate in the circumstances of the case (CA 1989, s 11E(2));
- that the person proposed to be specified as the provider of the activity is suitable to provide the activity (CA 1989, s 11E(3));
- that the activity proposed is provided in a place to which the individual who would be subject to the direction (or the condition) can reasonably be expected to travel (CA 1989, s 11E(4)).

In addition, before making an activity direction or condition, the court must obtain and consider information about the individual who would be subject to it and the likely effect of the direction or the condition on him or her, including any conflict with the individual's religious beliefs or working hours (CA 1989, s 11E(5) and (6)).

CA 1989, s 11E(7) allows the court to ask a Cafcass officer to provide it with information with regard to these matters (subsections (2) to (5)) (also see FPR 2010, r 16.38 and r 12.12(3) and (4)).

Financial assistance may be available to assist an individual required by an activity condition or direction to take part in an activity (see further CA 1989, s 11F).

Monitoring

Cafcass may be required to monitor compliance with a child arrangements order, activity direction or condition (see further CA 1989, s 11G and 11H).

Child arrangement orders – living arrangements

Child arrangements orders which apply to a child's living arrangements:

- can have effect for a period after the child has reached the age of 16, but not after the age of 18 years (these orders are the exception – all other s 8 orders cannot take effect after age 16) (CA 1989, s 9(6));
- cannot be made after a child has reached the age of 16 (other than to vary or discharge an existing order) unless the circumstances of the case are exceptional (CA 1989, s 9(7));
- will cease to have effect if the parents with parental responsibility live together for a continuous period of more than six months (CA 1989, s 11(5));
- can be suspended (see the pre-child arrangements case *Re A (Suspended Residence Order)* [2010] 1 FLR 1679, *Re D (Children)* [2010] EWCA Civ 496).

Note that the court has the option to make directions or impose conditions when making a child arrangements order which applies to regulate a child's living arrangements (CA 1989, s 11(7)).

Parental responsibility and child arrangements orders

- If the court makes a child arrangements order naming the father as a person with whom the child is to live, the court shall, if the father would not otherwise have it, make a parental responsibility order under s 4 giving him that responsibility. The same applies to a woman who is a parent of the child by virtue of s 43 of the Human Fertilisation and Embryology Act 2008 and she will gain parental responsibility under s 4ZA (CA 1989, s 12(1)).
- If the court makes a child arrangements order naming the father as a person with whom the child is to spend time or otherwise have contact (but not a person with whom the child is to live) the court shall decide whether it would be appropriate for him to have parental responsibility and, if so must also make an order under section 4 giving him that responsibility (CA 1989, s 12(1A)). The same applies to a woman who is a parent of the child by virtue of section 43 of the Human Fertilisation and Embryology Act 2008 and if considered appropriate, she will gain parental responsibility under section 4ZA.
- If the court makes a child arrangements order naming a person (other than the parent or guardian of the child) as a person with whom the child is to live, that person shall have parental responsibility for the child while the order for living arrangements remains in force (CA 1989, s 12(2)).
- If a child arrangements order is in force with respect to the living arrangements of that child, no person may cause the child to be known by a new surname or remove him or her from the UK for a month or more without either the written consent of every person who has parental responsibility for the child or the leave of the court (CA 1989, s 13).

Finances and child arrangements orders

- The court can, on making, varying or discharging provision in a child arrangements order with respect to the living arrangements of a child, exercise any of its powers under Sch 1, CA 1989 even if no application has been made for such an order (Children Act 1989, Sch 1, para 1(6)). Note however that there is no principle of 'sharing' or of compensation for the other parent in Sch 1 claims – see *Re A (A Child)* [2014] EWCA Civ 1577.

Family assistance orders

The court can make a Family Assistance Order ('FAO') when making a child arrangements order (CA 1989, s 16). A FAO requires a Cafcass officer or local authority officer to be made available to advise, assist and (where appropriate) befriend any person named in the order. A FAO can only last for a maximum of 12 months (CA 1989, s 16(5)). The court must have the consent of everyone named in the order (except the child) before it can make a FAO (CA 1989, s 16(3)).

If the court makes a FAO together with a child arrangements order it can direct that the officer concerned reports to the court on matters relating to the child arrangements order as the court may require (including the question whether the order ought to be varied or discharged) (CA 1989, s 16(6)) (also see FPR 2010, r 16.38 and r 12.12(3) and (4)).

Also see FPR 2010, PD 12M Family Assistance Orders: Consultation.

S 91(14) orders

When dealing with an application for a child arrangements order the court can decide to make a s 91(14) order. Such an order prevents the person named in it from making any further applications under CA 1989 unless they have leave of the court. S 91(14) orders should be used sparingly. See *Re P (Section 91(14) Guidelines) (Residence and Religious Heritage)* [1999] 2 FLR 573; *Re M (Parental Responsibility Order)* [2014] 1 FLR 339; *Re K (Contact Order: Posed Risk By Father)* [2014] 2 FLR 1140; *Re G (Intractable Contact)* [2013] EWHC B16 (Fam); and *Re T (A Child) (Suspension of Contact) (Section 91(14) CA 1989)* [2015] EWCA Civ 719.

For further guidance in this regard see the notes to s 91(14) in *Family Court Practice* and *Children Law and Practice*, B[910]-[911].

Adjournment

If a party wishes to apply to adjourn the final hearing (or any other hearing) they should make the application on Form C2 (or Form C100), using the Part 18 procedure (see Part 18 practice note). Note that an adjournment will not be given automatically on request and there will need to be a very good reason for the application to adjourn. It is sensible to apply for the adjournment as early as possible and to try to agree the adjournment with the other party, to avoid a costs order being made. If the other party agrees to the adjournment it is good practice to file with the Form C2 (or Form C100) a covering letter signed by both parties (or their solicitors) explaining the reasons for requesting an adjournment. Remember to inform any experts or other witnesses.

Variation/discharge of a child arrangements order

A child arrangements order may be varied or discharged by the court either in any family proceedings in which a question arises with respect to the welfare of the child, or on a free-standing application for its variation or discharge. The principles governing variation or discharge as of right, and leave to do so, are common to all s 8 orders. On a variation or discharge application the court has the full range of orders available to it, including the power to give directions or impose condition (CA 1989, s 11(7)). The child's welfare will be the paramount consideration (CA 1989, s 1(1)).

Termination of a child arrangements order

A child arrangements order may come to an end in one of three ways:

- it will cease to have effect because of the passage of time (see above under Child Arrangements Orders).
- it will be discharge by order of the court (CA 1989, s 8(2)).

- it will be discharged automatically on the making of a care order with respect to the child (CA 1989, s 91(2)).

PART 18

FLOWCHART

Family Law

Part 18

PRACTICE PLUS

When to use Part 18

When to use the Part 18 procedure:

Unless any other rule in any other Part of the FPR 2010 sets out the procedure or a practice direction provides that the Part 18 procedure may not be used, use the Part 18 procedure:

- in the course of existing proceedings
- to start proceedings
- in connection with proceedings which have been concluded
- for pre-action applications
- for applications for permission

FILE

File:

- Application notice (Form C2, Form C100, Form D11 or Form FP2)
- Statement in support (if separate from application notice)
- Draft order

Fee: £50 without notice or by consent
£155 on notice (as at September 2015)

At least **7 (or 14)** days before the hearing

SERVE

Documents to serve:

- Application notice
- Notice of Proceedings
- Copy statement in support
- Copy draft order

See Service practice note

Follow any directions given by the court (eg. filing further evidence)

HEARING

If hearing without notice, applicant must serve on respondent(s):

- Copy of the order
- Copy of the application notice
- Copy of any evidence in support

If hearing without notice respondent can apply to set aside/vary, **within 7 days** of being served with the order

PRACTICE NOTE

See also Procedural Guides (PG) A3, A9, B5, B6, B7, C1(4), C2, D22, E6(2), F2 and F4(2) in *The Red Book (Family Court Practice).*

When to use Part 18

When to use the Part 18 procedure:

- in the course of existing proceedings (FPR 2010, r 18.1(2)(a));
- to start proceedings except where some other part of the FPR 2010 prescribes the procedure to start proceedings (FPR 2010, r 18.1(2)(b));
- in connection with proceedings which have been concluded (FPR 2010, r 18.1(2)(c));
- for pre-action applications (FPR 2010, PD 18A, para 7.1); or
- for all applications for permission except where specific provision is made in another part of the FPR 2010 (FPR 2010, PD 18A, para 1.1).

Unless:

- any other rule in any other Part of the FPR 2010 sets out the procedure for that type of application (FPR 2010, r 18.1(3)(a)); or
- a Practice Direction provides that the Part 18 procedure may not be used in relation to the type of application in question (FPR 2010, r 18.1(3)(b)).

Examples:

- Application for permission to amend an application for matrimonial/civil partnership order under FPR 2010, r 7.13 (see Amending an application for divorce/dissolution (formerly a petition) practice note).
- Application for permission to file answer out of time (see Defended divorce/civil partnership dissolution practice note).
- Application for a consent order for an application/cross application for a matrimonial/civil partnership order to be stayed and for a divorce case to proceed undefended (see Defended divorce/civil partnership dissolution practice note).
- Application to stay grant of decree absolute under Matrimonial Causes Act 1973, s 10A (see Staying Grant of Decree Absolute under Matrimonial Causes Act 1973, s 10A practice note).
- Application for deemed service of an application for matrimonial/civil partnership order (see Undefended divorce/civil partnership dissolution practice note).
- Application for alternative method/place of service of an application for matrimonial/civil partnership order (see Undefended divorce/civil partnership dissolution practice note).
- Expedited application to apply for decree absolute/final order (see Undefended divorce/civil partnership dissolution practice note).
- Application on notice by respondent to apply for decree absolute/final order (see Undefended divorce/civil partnership dissolution practice note).
- Withdrawal of an application for a matrimonial/civil partnership order.
- Application for maintenance pending suit/maintenance pending outcome of proceedings/ interim periodical payment/interim variation order/any other form of interim order (see Interim financial orders practice note).
- Application for an injunction (see Application for an injunction practice note).

- Application for permission to rely on evidence at a hearing under the Part 19 procedure that has not been served in accordance with FPR 2010, r 19.13 (see Declaration of Marital/Civil Partnership Status practice note).
- Application by a child for leave to terminate a parental responsibility agreement (see Parental Responsibility Order (Part 3) – Fact Finding to Final Hearing practice note).

File

An application notice must be filed (FPR 2010, r 18.4(1)) (unless a rule or Practice Direction permits an application to be made without filing an application notice or the court dispenses with the requirement to file an application notice (FPR 2010, r 18.4(2)).

Documents

Application notice

Either:

- Form C2 (or Form C100, considering the changes post-April 2014).
  Form C2 (or Form C100) is the application for permission to start proceedings, for an order or directions in existing proceedings and to be joined as, or cease to be, a party in existing family proceedings under Children Act 1989. FPR 2010, PD 5A, para 2.2(i) states that the form should be used where the application is made in the course of or in connection with proceedings under Part 12 (proceedings relating to children except parental order proceedings and proceedings for applications in adoption, placement and related proceedings). See precedent E7 (*Family Law Precedents Service*).
- Form D11
  Form D11 is an application notice (see specific precedent Form D11s in *Family Law Precedents Service* for particular applications). FPR 2010, PD 5A, para 2.2(ii) states that the form should be used where the application is made in the course of or in connection with proceedings under Parts 7, 8 or 9 (procedure for applications in matrimonial and civil partnership proceedings, miscellaneous applications and financial remedy applications).
- Form FP2
  Form FP2 is described as 'an application notice under Part 18, FPR 2010'. See for example precedent K2 (*Family Law Precedents Service*). FPR 2010, PD 5A, para 2.2(iii) states that the form should be used 'in any other case' (where a Form C2 or Form D11 is not the correct form).

An application notice must be signed (FPR 2010, PD 18A, para 3.2). Paragraphs 3.2 – 3.7 of PD 18A set out further guidance as to the content of the application notice.

Statement

The statement does not have to be separate and can be included in box 6 of Form C2, box 10 of Form D11 or Part C of Form FP2. It must explain what order the applicant is seeking and why (FPR 2010, r 18.7(1)). It must be verified by a statement of truth (FPR 2010, r 17.3). Any written evidence in support must be filed at the same time as filing the application notice (FPR 2010, r 18.8(2)) but written evidence that has already been filed at court does not need to be filed again (FPR 2010, r 18.8(5)(a)).

Draft order

FPR 2010, r 18.7(2) requires that a draft order is attached to the application.

If the application is for a consent order the parties should ensure that they provide the court with any material it needs to be satisfied that it is appropriate to make the order (normally a letter) (FPR 2010, PD 18A, para 12.1).

Who is the respondent?

If there are existing proceedings or proceedings that have concluded:

- the parties to those proceedings (FPR 2010, r 18.3(a)(i)); and
- if the proceedings are proceedings under Part 11 (forced marriage protection), the person who is the subject of those proceedings (FPR 2010, r 18.3(a)(ii)).

If there are no existing proceedings:

- if notice has been given under s 44 of the 2002 Act (notice of intention to adopt or apply for an order under s 84 of that Act), the local authority to whom notice has been given (FPR 2010, r 18.3(b)(i)); and
- if an application is made for permission to apply for an order in proceedings, any person who will be a party to the proceedings brought if permission is granted (FPR 2010, r 18.3(b)(ii));

And any other person as the court may direct (FPR 2010, r 18.3(c)).

Timing

Every application should be made as soon as it becomes apparent that it is necessary or desirable to make it (FPR 2010, PD 18A, para 4.6). When an application must be made within a specified time, the court must receive the application notice within that time (FPR 2010, r 18.6).

Listing the hearing

Applications should, wherever possible, be made so that they are considered at any directions hearing or other hearing for which a date has been fixed or for which a date is about to be fixed (FPR 2010, PD 18A, para 4.7). Where a date for a hearing has been fixed, a party who wishes to make an application at that hearing but does not have sufficient time to file an application notice should as soon as possible inform the court (if possible in writing) and, if possible, the other parties of the nature of the application and the reason for it. That party should then make the application orally at the hearing (FPR 2010, PD 18A, para 4.9).

Which court?

An application for permission to start proceedings must be made to the court where the proceedings will be started if permission is granted (FPR 2010, r 18.2).

Tips:

- When filing the application at court remember to include enough copies of the application form and supporting documents (normally three – one for the applicant, one for the court and one for the respondent).

- Do not forget to check the court fee (£50 for applications without notice or £155 for applications on notice as at September 2015) and include a cheque or postal order payable to 'HM Courts and Tribunals Service' or 'HMCTS'. The fee can also be paid in cash or by debit/credit card.

Serve

Service

Normal service rules apply (see Service (not of an application for a matrimonial/civil partnership order) practice note).

Documents to serve:

(1) application notice;

(2) notice of proceedings (FPR 2010, r 18.8(3)(a));

(3) a copy of any witness statement in support (FPR 2010, r 18.8(3)(b)); and

(4) a copy of the draft order which the applicant has attached to the application (FPR 2010, r 18.8(3)(c)).

If written evidence has already been served on a party it does not need to be served again (FPR 2010, r 18.8(5)(b)).

Who to serve

- each respondent (FPR 2010, r 18.5(1)(a));
- in relation to proceedings under Part 11 (forced marriage protection), the person who is, or, in the case of an application to start proceedings, it is intended will be, the subject of the proceedings (FPR 2010, r 18.5(1)(b)); and
- in relation to proceedings under Parts 12 (proceedings relating to children) and 14 (adoption and related matters), the children's guardian (if any) (FPR 2010, r 18.5(1)(c)).

No service

An application may be made without serving a copy of the application notice if this is permitted by a rule, a Practice Direction or the court (FPR 2010, r 18.5(2)).

An application may be made without service of an application notice only:

- where there is exceptional urgency (FPR 2010, PD 18A, para 5.1(a));
- where the overriding objective is best furthered by doing so (FPR 2010, PD 18A, para 5.1(b));
- by consent of all parties (FPR 2010, PD 18A, para 5.1(c));
- with the permission of the court (FPR 2010, PD 18A, para 5.1(d)); or
- where para 4.9 applies (application to be made orally at a hearing) (FPR 2010, PD 18A, para 5.1(e)).

Timing

The application notice must be served as soon as possible after it is filed (FPR 2010, r 18.8(1)(a)) and in any event **at least 7 days** before the court is to deal with the application (FPR 2010, r 18.8(1)(b)(ii) and FPR 2010, PD 18A, para 6.1).

If the application is for an interim order under FPR 2010, r 9.7 the application must be served **at least 14 days** before the court is to deal with the application (FPR 2010, r 18.8(1)(b)(i)).

Where an application notice should be served but there is not sufficient time to do so, informal notification of the application should be given (unless the circumstances of the application require no notice of the application to be given) (FPR 2010, PD 18A, para 6.2). If the documents are served, but the period of notice is shorter than the period required by the FPR 2010 the court may direct that, in the circumstances of the case, sufficient notice has been given and hear the application (FPR 2010, r 18.8(4)).

Without notice applications

If the court has disposed of an application which it permitted to be made without service, where the court makes an order, whether granting or dismissing the application, the applicant must serve:

- a copy of the order;
- a copy of the application notice; and
- a copy of any evidence in support

on all the parties in the proceedings (and in relation to proceedings under Part 11 (forced marriage protection), the person who is, or, in the case of an application to start proceedings, it is intended will be, the subject of the proceedings) (FPR 2010, r 18.10).

The order must contain a statement of the right to make an application to set aside or vary the order under r 18.11 (FPR 2010, r 18.10(3)). A person who was not served with a copy of the application notice before an order was made under r 18.10 may apply to have the order set aside or varied (FPR 2010, r 18.11(1)). They must make the application within **7 days beginning** with the date on which the order was served on them (FPR 2010, r 18.11(2)).

Hearing

Without a hearing

Some applications may be dealt with without a hearing (FPR 2010, PD 18A, para 4.2).

The court may deal with an application without a hearing if:

- the court does not consider that a hearing would be appropriate (FPR 2010, r 18.9(1)(a)); or
- the parties agree a consent order or the parties agree that the court should dispose of the application without a hearing **and** the court does not consider that a hearing would be appropriate (FPR 2010, r 18.9(1)(b)).

Where the court considers that the application is suitable for consideration without a hearing but is not satisfied that it has sufficient material to decide the application immediately, it may give directions for the filing of evidence and will inform the applicant and the respondent(s) of its decision (FPR 2010, PD 18A, para 4.3).

The court will have regard to the overriding objective (FPR 2010, r 1.1) and will use its case management powers under FPR 2010, Part 4 (for example it may direct that a telephone hearing should take place – see below).

If the court refuses an application for permission to make an application in proceedings under the Children Act 1989 without a hearing the court must, at the request of the applicant, re-list the application and fix a date for a hearing (FPR 2010, r 18.9(2)).

Prior to the hearing:

Evidence

The court may give directions as to the filing of evidence prior to the hearing (FPR 2010, PD 18A, para 4.4). FPR 2010, PD 18A, paras 11.1 – 11.7 set out specific provisions about evidence (also see Part 22, FPR 2010).

Agreement

If a hearing is fixed and the parties agree a judgment or order beforehand they must inform the court immediately (normally by letter) (FPR 2010, PD 18A, para 12.2). If a hearing is fixed and the parties agree that the court should dispose of the application without a hearing they should so inform the court in writing and each should confirm that all evidence and other material on which he or she relies has been disclosed to the other parties to the application (FPR 2010, PD 18A, para 13.2).

Bundles and preliminary documents

Practice Direction 27A requires a bundle to be filed in all hearings before a judge sitting in the Family Division of the High Court wherever the court may be sitting and all hearings in the Family Court (FPR 2010, PD 27A, para 2.1). The Practice Direction sets out very precise rules regarding the preparation of bundles and should be referred to directly. *Re W (Strict Compliance with Court Orders)* [2015] 1 FLR 1092 confirms the importance of strict adherence to the Practice Direction. The bundle should be lodged not less than **2 working days** before the hearing. FPR 2010, PD 27A also sets out requirements for filing preliminary documents at **11 am the day before** the hearing. For further details see the Preliminary Documents box of the Applications for a financial order (not an interim order) under MCA 1973 or CPA 2004 FDR to Final Hearing practice note. See also *Re L (Procedure: Bundles: Translation)* [2015] 1 FLR 1417 for further guidance, particularly on the court's stance on adherence to PD 27A.

At the hearing

The parties must anticipate that at any hearing (including any directions hearing) the court may wish to review the conduct of the case as a whole and give any necessary directions. They should be ready to assist the court in doing so and to answer questions the court may ask for this purpose (FPR 2010, PD 18A, para 4.8).

FPR 2010, PD 18A, paras 8.1 – 8.5 set out specific provisions about telephone hearings. Paragraph 9.1 deals with video conference hearings (also see FPR 2010, PD 22A, Annex 3).

Attendance

If a party fails to attend the court can proceed with the hearing in their absence (FPR 2010, r 18.12(1)).

The court may, on application or of its own initiative, re-list the application if it makes an order at a hearing at which one of the parties failed to attend (FPR 2010, r 18.12(2)).

Totally without merit applications

If the Family Court dismisses an application (including an application for permission to appeal) and it considers that the application is totally without merit the court's order must record that fact and the court must at the same time consider whether it is appropriate to make a civil restraint order (FPR 2010, r 18.13).

COMMITTAL AND ARREST FOR DISOBEDIENCE OF AN INJUNCTIVE ORDER OR BREACH OF AN UNDERTAKING IN THE HIGH COURT, FAMILY COURT OR COUNTY COURT

FLOWCHART

Family Law

PRACTICE PLUS

COMMITTAL AND ARREST FOR DISOBEDIENCE OF AN INJUNCTIVE ORDER OR BREACH OF AN UNDERTAKING IN THE HIGH COURT, FAMILY COURT OR COUNTY COURT

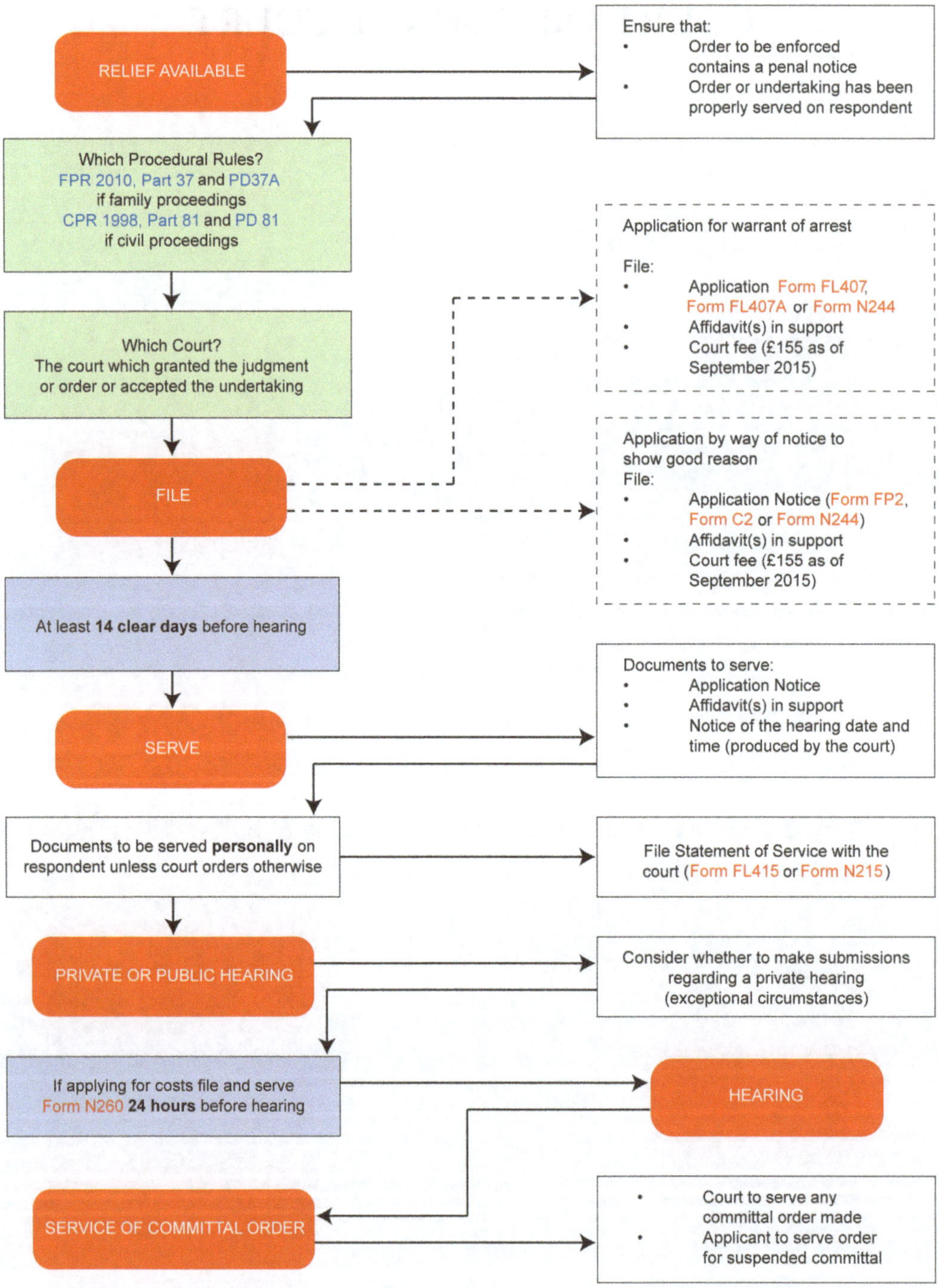

PRACTICE NOTE

See also Procedural Guide (PG) C14 in *The Red Book (Family Court Practice)*.

Relief available

An injunctive order directing a person to do an act, or to abstain from doing an act, or an undertaking with the same effect which contains a penal warning notice can be enforced by committal proceedings. This includes, but is not limited to, the following types of proceedings:

- A non-molestation order, occupation order or forced marriage protection order under the Family Law Act 1996. An undertaking given to a court under FLA 1996 is enforceable as if the court had made an order in terms corresponding to those of the undertaking (FLA 1996, s 46(4) and s 63E(4)).
- An order (or undertaking) under the Protection from Harassment Act 1997.
- An order under the Children Act 1989, s 8 to which a penal notice has been attached. A warning notice will automatically be attached to a child arrangements order, or an order varying a child arrangements order, warning of the consequences of failing to comply with the order (CA 1989, s 11I, as amended by CFA 2014).
- An order under the Family Law Act 1986 to disclose the whereabouts of a child to which a penal notice has been attached.

The person in whose favour the injunction was made, or the undertaking was given, may apply for committal (FPR 2010, r 37.3 and CPR 1998, r 81.3).

See Procedural Guide C14 (PG) (*Family Court Practice*) and *Emergency Remedies in the Family Courts*, para E[5.1]-[6.3]. Also see *Children Law and Practice*, paras B[1493]-[1515].

See Committal for breach of an order or undertaking in the Family Court and High Court – Matrimonial and Civil Partnership Financial Proceedings practice note for enforcement by committal proceedings in finance cases.

Service of original order or undertaking

An order may not be enforced by way of an application for committal unless it has been served on the respondent, or service has been dispensed with (FPR 2010, r 37.5 and CPR 1998, r 81.5). The order must have been served before the end of the time fixed for doing the act. The order should have been served personally, subject to any order dispensing with personal service (FPR 2010, r 37.6 and r 37.8 and CPR 1998, r 81.6 and 81.8). The order must contain a penal notice, a warning that disobedience of the order would be contempt of court punishable by imprisonment, a fine or sequestration of assets (FPR 2010, r 37.9(1) and CPR 1998, r 81.9(1) and FPR 2010, PD 37A, para 1.1; CPR 1998, PD 81, para 1). An undertaking contained in an order may be enforced by committal even if the order itself does not contain the penal notice (FPR 2010, r 37.9(2) and CPR 1998, r 81.9(2)).

FPR 2010, r 37.7 and CPR 1998, r 81.7 provide for the method of service of undertakings which still require service on the respondent, albeit not necessarily personal service.

However, if the respondent breaches an order pending service then the court can impose a penalty and dispense with personal service if satisfied that the respondent knew of the terms of the order (FPR 2010, r 37.8; CPR 1998, r 81.8).

Which Procedure Rules?

If the injunctive order or undertaking was made in family proceedings, for example under FLA 1996 or CA 1989, the order for committal is made in family proceedings and is governed by FPR 2010, Part 37 and PD 37A.

If the injunctive order or undertaking was made in civil proceedings, such as under PHA 1997, then committal proceedings are governed by CPR 1998, Part 81 and PD 81.

Commencing proceedings

There are three main ways in which proceedings for committal can be commenced:

- committal proceedings begun by way of notice to show good reason why an order for committal should not be made;
- committal proceedings begun by an arrest under a power of arrest attached to an occupation order, or a forced marriage protection order made before 16 June 2014; and
- committal proceedings begun by an arrest under a warrant of arrest.

Breach of a non-molestation order is a criminal offence (FLA 1996, s 42A). Breach of a forced marriage protection order made on or after 16 June 2014 is also a criminal offence (FLA 1996, s 63CA). If the respondent breaches one of these orders the police can be contacted and they will arrest the respondent who will be dealt with in criminal proceedings. Under FLA 1996, s 42A(5)(a) and s 63CA(5)(a) the maximum imprisonment is for a term not exceeding five years, or a fine, or both. If the CPS decide not to proceed, the applicant can consider bringing the matter to the Family Court for committal proceedings. However, the same conduct cannot be punished twice and must either be punished under criminal proceedings or civil committal proceedings (FLA 1996, s 42A(3) and 42A(4), s 63CA(3) and s 63CA(4)). The UK saw its first prosecution under the Forced Marriage laws, whereby a man was sentenced to 4 years' imprisonment for forcing a woman to marry him by threatening to murder her father.

Which court?

Proceedings should be issued in the court which granted the judgment or order or accepted the undertaking (CPR 1998, PD 81, para 10.1 – 10.4 and FPR 2010, r 37.10).

Potential penalties

The powers of the County Court to deal with breach of injunctive orders are the same as those of the High Court (County Courts Act 1984, s 38).

The court can:-

- commit the respondent to prison;
- make a suspended order of committal;
- impose a fine;
- make a hospital or guardianship order in relation to a person suffering from a mental illness or severe mental impairment;
- make no order, or make only an order as to costs;
- grant an order extending the injunction; or
- adjourn consideration of the penalty for a fixed period.

Lay justices' powers are more limited than those of a District Judge in the Family Court (Family Court (Contempt of Court) (Powers) Regulations 2014). The maximum committal period which can be imposed by lay justices is two months where any individual disobeys a judgment or an order of, or an undertaking given to, the Family Court. The potential fine is up to level 5 on the standard scale of fines. The guideline case on sentencing is *Hale v Tanner* [2000] 2 FLR 879 as supplemented by *Lomas v Parle* [2004] 1 FLR 812 and *Murray v Robinson* [2006] 1 FLR 365.

A District Judge or Circuit Judge may impose a maximum committal period of up to two years or a fine of up to level 5 and see Contempt of Court Act 1981, s 14(1).

A High Court Judge may impose a maximum committal period of up to two years or a fine without upper limit (Contempt of Court Act 1981, s 14(1)).

Under CCA 1981, s 14(1), the sentence for contempt imposed on any one occasion cannot exceed two years, whether or not it relates to more than one application, even if it had been dealt with on different occasions the sentences imposed for different contempts could exceed that amount in aggregate (*Villiers v Villiers* [1994] 1 FLR 647).

As at September 2015 level 5 on the standard scale is £5000.

Tips:

- Although an undertaking is enforceable on being given to and accepted by the court, a copy of it will be delivered to the respondent in accordance with FPR 2010, r 37.7 and CPR 1998, r 81.7. The court may require the respondent to have signed a statement confirming he or she understands the terms of the undertaking and the consequences of failure to comply with it and, in the Family Court, the undertaking must be endorsed with a notice setting out the consequences of disobedience (FPR 2010, PD 37A, paras 2.1 – 2.3; CPR 1998, PD 81, paras 2.1 – 2.4). See also *Hussain v Hussain* [1986] 2 FLR 271.
- If a person breaches a child arrangements order under CA 1989, s 8, in addition to the court's powers to treat the breach as contempt of court, the court can make enforcement orders and financial compensation orders. See Enforcement Orders and Financial Compensation Orders (Child Arrangements Orders) practice note.
- If the CA 1989, s 8 order which requires enforcement does not contain a penal notice, the person seeking enforcement can request that the court issues a further copy of the order endorsed with a penal notice for service on the respondent (FPR 2010, r 37.9(3)). The procedure is under FPR 2010, r 12.33. See Apply to attach a warning notice (if necessary) section of the Enforcement Orders and Financial Compensation Orders (Child Arrangements Orders) practice note.
- A person arrested under a power of arrest must be brought before the court within **24 hours** of his or her arrest (not including Sundays, Christmas Day or Good Friday) (FLA 1996, s 47(7)), and may be remanded in custody if the matter is not disposed of immediately.
- Note the case of *Re an Application by Gloucestershire County Council for the Committal to prison of Matthew John Newman (No 1)* [2015] 1 FLR 1359, which emphasises the need for committal applications to comply with FPR 2010, r 37 and PD 37 in family proceedings and confirms that injunctions cannot be enforced by committal unless they are in terms which are clear, precise and unambiguous.

File

The procedure will vary depending on how the committal proceedings are commenced. Most applications are likely to be brought under the notice to show good reason procedure.

Committal proceedings begun by way of notice to show good reason why an order for committal should not be made

The application is usually made **on notice** to the respondent (FPR 2010, r 37.10(4) and CPR 1998, r 81.10(4)).

See *Emergency Remedies in the Family Courts*, para E[10.11]-[10.12].

Documents:

Application Notice – Family Proceedings

The committal application is made by an application notice using the Part 18 procedure (FPR 2010, r 37.10(1)). See Part 18 practice note. See precedent K18 (*Family Law Precedents Service*).

The application notice must set out in full the grounds on which the committal application is made and must identify, separately and numerically, each alleged act of contempt including, if known, the date of each of the alleged acts (FPR 2010, r 37.10(3)(a)).

The application notice must contain a prominent notice stating the possible consequences of the court making a committal order and of the respondent not attending the hearing (FPR 2010, PD 37A, para 10.2(4)). An appropriate form of penal notice is attached to FPR 2010, PD 37A.

Form FP2

Form FP2 is the application notice to be used 'in any other case' (where a Form C2 or Form D11 is not the correct form) (FPR 2010, PD 5A, para 2.2(iii)). It should be used for applications to commit for breaches of injunctions and undertakings under FLA 1996.

Form C2

Form C2 is the application for permission to start proceedings, for an order or directions in existing proceedings and to be joined as, or cease to be, a party in existing family proceedings under Children Act 1989. FPR 2010, PD 5A, para 2.2(i) states that the form should be used where the application is made in the course of or in connection with proceedings under Part 12 (proceedings relating to children except parental order proceedings and proceedings for applications in adoption, placement and related proceedings).

Application Notice – Civil Proceedings

The committal application is made by an application notice using the Part 23 procedure (CPR 1998, r 81.10(1). Form N244 should be used (CPR 1998, PD 23A, para 2.1).

The application notice must set out in full the grounds on which the committal application is made and must identify, separately and numerically, each alleged act of contempt including, if known, the date of each of the alleged acts (CPR 2010, r 81.10(3)(a)).

The application notice must contain a prominent notice stating the possible consequences of the court making a committal order and of the respondent not attending the hearing (CPR 1998, PD 81, para 13.2(4)). An appropriate form of penal notice is at CPR 1998, PD 81, Annex 3.

Affidavit in support

The application notice must be supported by one or more affidavits containing all the evidence relied upon (FPR 2010, r 37.10(3)(b) and CPR 1998, r 81.10(3)(b)).

See precedent K19 (*Family Law Precedents Service*) Affidavit in support of application to commit and *Emergency Remedies in the Family Courts*, para E[6.3] statement in support for content (but note that the evidence must be given on oath).

Application for warrant of arrest under FLA 1996, s 47(8) or 63J, or PHA 1997, s 3(3)

The application can be made **without notice** to the respondent. As an alternative to applying for an order for committal, the applicant can apply to the court for a warrant for arrest. The police will then arrest the respondent and bring him or her before the court.

See *Children Law and Practice*, para G[246]-[247] and see *Emergency Remedies in the Family Courts*, para E[10.13] and E[10.15].

Documents:

Application Form FL407 (Part IV FLA 1996) or Form FL407A (Part 4A FLA 1996)

FPR 2010, PD 5A provides for the application for a warrant of arrest to be made in Form FL407 for proceedings under FLA 1996, Part IV, and Form FL407A for proceedings under FLA 1996, Part 4A.

However, practitioners will note that HMCTS forms finder does not have the Form FL407 available as of October 2014, although Form FL407A continues to be available.

The application should set out the precise parts of the order or undertaking relevant to the application and list the ways in which it is alleged that the respondent has disobeyed the order or broken the undertaking. It should also confirm whether, to the claimant's knowledge, criminal proceedings are being pursued as the respondent cannot be punished both for a criminal offence and a contempt of court for the same breach.

Application – PHA 1997

An application for a warrant of arrest under PHA 1997, s 3(3) should be made in accordance with CPR 1998, Part 23 (CPR 1998, r 65.29(1). Form N244 should be used (CPR 1998, PD 23A, para 2.1).

Affidavit

The application must be substantiated on oath (FLA 1996, s 47(9) and s 63J, PHA 1997, s 3(5)(a)) and therefore practitioners should file one or more affidavits containing all the evidence relied upon in support of the application.

Under PHA 1997, s 3(3), the affidavit in support must set out the grounds for the application, state whether the claimant has informed the police of the conduct of the defendant as described in the affidavit and state whether, to the claimant's knowledge, criminal proceedings are being pursued (CPR 1998, r 65.29(2)).

Tips:

- Do not forget to check the court fee (£155 in the Family Court as at September 2015 (FPFO 2008, as amended by the Family Proceedings Fees (Amendment) Order 2014 and Civil Proceedings Fees (Amendment) Order 2014) and include a cheque or postal order payable to 'HM Courts and Tribunals Service' or 'HMCTS'. The fee can also be paid in cash or by debit/credit card.
- See *Emergency Remedies in the Family Courts*, para E[10.28] for a checklist on preparing an application for committal for disobedience of an injunctive order or undertaking.

Serve

Committal proceedings begun by way of notice to show good reason why an order for committal should not be made

In exceptional circumstances the court may deal with an application for committal begun by way of notice to show good reason **without notice** to the respondent by dispensing with service of the summons or notice (FPR 2010, r 37.10(5)(a) and CPR 1998, r 81.10(5)(a)). See *Emergency Remedies in the Family Courts*, para E[10.12].

On notice

Where the application has been made **on notice** the following must be served on the respondent (FPR 2010, r 37.10(4) and CPR 1998, r 81.10(4)):

- Application Notice;
- Evidence in support;
- Notice of the hearing date and time.

Timing

The documents must be served not less than **14 clear days** before the date of the hearing, unless the court has abridged time for service before the application is served (FPR 2010, PD 37A, para 12.2 and CPR 1998, PD 81, para 15.2).

Method of service

The documents must be served personally on the respondent unless the court makes an order dispensing with service or ordering that it should take place by an alternative method or at an alternative place (FPR 1998, r 37.10(5) and CPR 1988, r 81.10(5)).

Certificate of service

Once service has been effected the applicant should file a certificate of service stating the time and date of personal service, containing details of how the respondent was identified as the person to be served, a description of the respondent and a detailed description of service on them. The certificate of service can be in Form FL415 in family proceedings and Form N215 in civil proceedings.

Application for warrant of arrest under FLA 1996, s 47(8) or 63J, or PHA 1997, s 3(3)

The court will only grant the warrant if they have reasonable grounds for believing that the respondent has failed to comply with the order (FLA 1996, s 47(9)(b) and s 63J(3)(b), PHA 1997, s 3(5)(b)).

The warrant of arrest will be executed in the High Court by the tipstaff, and in the Family Court and the County Court by the bailiffs. In each case the enforcement agents can call on the police to assist them with the arrest. The respondent will then be brought before the court.

A person arrested under a warrant of arrest will be brought before the court as soon as practicable.

Tips:

- If a process server is used to serve the papers, if possible provide them with a recent clear photograph of the respondent to assist with identification.
- As part of the family law reforms, draft standard orders were released by the President. These include a warrant for arrest. All the draft orders can be found at http://www.jordanpublishing.co.uk/l/family-orders and, whilst they await implementation, it is prudent to become familiar with them.

Private or public hearing

On 26 March 2015, the Lord Chief Justice issued a Practice Direction on committal for contempt of court (see http://www.familylaw.co.uk/news_and_comment/practice-direction-committal-for-contempt-of-court-open-court). It applies to all proceedings in all courts in England and Wales for committal for contempt of court, including contempt in the face of the court, whether arising under any statutory or inherent jurisdiction. The Practice Direction supersedes the Practice Guidance of 3 May 2013: *Committal for Contempt of Court*, the Practice Guidance of 4 June 2013: *Committal for Contempt of Court* and the President's Circular of 2 August 2013: *Committals*.

The Practice Direction provides that, apart from in exceptional cases, committal applications should be heard in public.

Practice Guidance has also been issued by Lord Thomas, the Lord Chief Justice, to answer various questions which have arisen on the application and interpretation of the Practice Direction which will be reviewed in October 2015 http://www.familylaw.co.uk/news_and_comment/practice-guidance-committal-for-contempt-of-court-open-court#.VZVOpflVhBc.

Summary

The Practice Guidance provides in summary as follows:

- It is a fundamental principle of the administration of justice in England and Wales that applications for committal for contempt should be heard and decided in public.
- This principle applies to committal applications in the Court of Protection and in the Family Division as well as to committal applications in any other Division of the High Court.
- The court has discretion to hear the application in private only in exceptional circumstances. The fact that the hearing is in the Court of Protection or in proceedings involving a child does not in itself justify a derogation from the general principle that the hearing will take place in public. Neither can it be justified to hold the hearing in private to constrain the release of certain material if such disclosure could be controlled with an appropriate order.

- If the court is considering hearing the application in private it must notify the media and hear submissions from the parties and/or the media.
- If, in an exceptional case, a committal application is heard in private and the court finds that a person has committed a contempt of court it must state in public (rule 188(3) of the Court of Protection Rules 2007; Order 52 rule 6(2) of the Rules of the Supreme Court 1965):
  (1) the name of that person;
  (2) in general terms the nature of the contempt of court in respect of which the committal order, including a suspended committal order, is being made; and
  (3) the punishment being imposed.
- Committal applications in the Court of Protection or the Family Division should at the outset be listed and heard in public. Whenever the court decides to exercise its discretion to sit in private the judge should, before continuing the hearing in private, give a judgment in public setting out the reasons for doing so. At the conclusion of any hearing in private the judge should sit in public to comply with the requirements set out above.
- In every case in which a committal order or a suspended committal order is made the judge should take appropriate steps to ensure that any judgment or statement complies with the above and that as soon as reasonably practicable a transcript is prepared at public expense of the judgment.
- Every judgment as referred to above is published on the BAILII website; and upon payment of any appropriate charge that may be required a copy of any such judgment is made available to any person who requests a copy.

When can a hearing be heard in private?

FPR 2010, r 37.27(5) provides that a committal application may be heard in private if one of the following apply:

(1) publicity would defeat the object of the hearing;

(2) it involves matters relating to national security;

(3) it involves confidential information (including information relating to personal financial matters) and publication would damage that confidentiality (but not if the confidentiality can be preserved by an appropriate order);

(4) a private hearing is necessary to protect the interests of any child or protected party;

(5) it is a hearing of an application made without notice and it would be unjust to any respondent for there to be a public hearing; or

(f) the court considers this to be necessary, in the interests of justice.

If the court makes a committal order against the respondent when hearing the application in private, FPR 2010, r 37.27(6) and CPR 1998, r 81.28(5) provide that the court will state in public the name of the respondent, the nature of the contempt of court in respect of which the committal order is being made in general terms and the length of the period of the committal order, as required by the Practice Direction.

Hearing

See *Emergency Remedies in the Family Courts*, para E[10.20] and see *Children Law and Practice*, para B[1520]-[1524].

Powers of court where respondent arrested under warrant or power of arrest

The court may hear the facts upon which the arrest was based, and then decide on the penalty or adjourn the case, in which case the respondent must be given no less than **2 days'** notice of the adjourned hearing. (FPR 2010, r 10.11; CPR 1998, r 65.30) Under FLA 1996, the matter must be dealt with within **14 days** beginning with the date of the arrest unless the court directs otherwise (FPR 2010, r 10.11(3)(a)) and under PHA 1997, the matter must be dealt with within **28 days** of the date the arrested person appears in court (CPR 1998, r 65.30(2)(a)).

Under FLA 1996, Sch 5 the respondent can also be remanded in custody for no more than **8 clear days.**

In proceedings under FLA 1996, where the court has reason to suspect that the respondent suffers from mental impairment or severe mental impairment the court may remand the respondent for medical examination and report for no more than **3 weeks** if on remand or **4 weeks** if on bail (FLA 1996, s 48 and s 63L).

Without notice

In exceptional circumstances the court may deal with an application begun by a notice to show cause without notice have been given to the respondent (FPR 2010, r 37.10(5)(a) and CPR 1998, r 81.10(5)(a)). The court may also dispense with service of the application summons or notice or make an order for service by an alternative method.

If the court makes a committal order without notice, the court will then fix a date and time for the respondent to be brought before the court (FPR 2010, r 37.27(7); CPR 1998, r 81.28(6)).

Levels of judiciary

In the County Court, District Judges do not have the power to hear committal proceedings (eg under PHA 1997) (CPR 1998, PD 81, para 10.2(2)).

In the Family Court, District Judges may hear committal proceedings as well as Circuit Judges (Family Court (Contempt of Court) (Powers) Regulations 2014). See Potential penalties in File section above for details of the limitations on the penalties to be imposed by the different levels of judiciary.

Attendance at court

If the respondent fails to attend court, provided he or she has been properly served, the court may proceed in his or her absence (FPR 2010, r 18.12(1), CPR 1998, r 39.3 and see *Begum v Anam* [2004] EWCA 578). The decision to proceed should be taken in the context of the case as a whole *(Re P (Committal for Breach of Contact Order: Reasons)* [2007] 1 FLR 1820).

What the court can do

The court may make directions at any time as to the service of evidence, the conduct of proceedings or to strike out an inappropriate application (FPR 2010, PD 37A, para 12.3 and para 13; CPR 1998, PD 81, para 15.1 – 15.6 and 16.1 – 16.3). This can include adjourning the application to a future date (FPR 2010, PD 37A, para 12.3(1) and CPR 1998, PD 81, para 15.4(1)). Where the court adjourns the hearing, personal service of the notice of the adjourned hearing will be required unless the respondent was present in court and told the date of the adjourned hearing.

Evidence

Unless the court otherwise permits, the applicant may not rely on any grounds other than those set out in the claim form or application notice or any evidence unless it has been served in accordance with the relevant Procedural Rules (FPR 2010, r 37.27(1) and CPR 1998, r 81.28(1)).

At the hearing the respondent is entitled to give oral evidence, whether or not he or she has filed or served written evidence, and, if doing so, may be cross-examined and, with the permission of the court, may call a witness to give oral evidence whether or not the witness has made an affidavit or witness statement (FPR 2010, r 37.27(2) and CPR 1998, r 81.28(2)).

The court may require or permit any party or other person (other than the respondent) to give oral evidence at the hearing (FPR 2010, r 37.27(3) and CPR 1998, r 81.28(3)) and may give directions requiring the attendance for cross-examination of a witness who has given written evidence (FPR 2010, r 37.27(4) and CPR 1998, r 81.28(4)).

The respondent <u>cannot</u> be compelled to give evidence (FPR 2010, r 37.27(3); CPR 1998, r 81.28(3)).

Procedural safeguards

Committal orders should only be made in exceptional circumstances and full effect must be given to ECHR, Art 6. The standard of proof is the criminal one, having regard to the possibility of imprisonment, the allegations must be proved beyond reasonable doubt (FPR 2010, PD 37A, para 8 and CPR 1998, PD 81, para 9).

Care must be taken if seeking to rely on findings made in earlier proceedings to the civil standard of proof for example as to the respondent's means. See *Prest v Prest* [2015] EWCA Civ 674 where the court of appeal confirmed the following:

- the fact that the respondent has or has had, since the date of the order or judgment, the means to pay the sum due must be proved to the criminal standard of proof;
- the fact that the respondent has refused or neglected, or refuses or neglects, to pay the sum due must also be proved to the criminal standard;
- the burden of proof is at all times on the applicant; and
- the respondent cannot be compelled to give evidence

A deliberate act (or failure to act) together with knowledge of the terms of the order must be proved.

In particular, the court will have regard to the need for the respondent:

- to have details of the alleged acts of contempt and the opportunity to respond to the committal application (FPR 2010, PD 37A, para 12.4 and CPR 1998, PD 81, para 15.5);
- to be allowed a reasonable time for responding to the committal application including, if necessary, preparing a defence (FPR 2010, PD 37A, para 12.5(1) and CPR 1998, PD 81, para 15.6(1));
- to be made aware of the possible availability of criminal legal aid and how to contact the Legal Aid Agency (FPR 2010, PD 37A, para 12.5(2) and CPR 1998, PD 81, para 15.6(2));

- to be given the opportunity, if unrepresented, to obtain legal advice (FPR 2010, PD 37A, para 12.5(3) and CPR 1998, PD 81, para 15.6(3); and
- if unable to understand English, to be allowed to make arrangements, seeking the assistance of the court if necessary, for an interpreter to attend the hearing (FPR 2010, PD 37A, para 12.5(4) and CPR 1998, PD 81, para 15.6(4)).

Procedural errors may result in the application or any subsequent committal being invalid (see *Hammerton v Harmmerton* [2007] 2 FLR 1133 and *Emergency Remedies in the Family Courts*, para E[10.5]), and practitioners should therefore take care to ensure that the application notice and supporting statement are carefully drafted with all allegations against the respondent that the applicant wishes to rely on detailed. See *Re K (Return Order: Failure to Comply: Committal: Appeal)* [2015] 1 FLR 927 where a committal order was set aside due to procedural irregularities and the court emphasised that *Hammerton v Hammerton* must be complied with. The respondent must be warned that he or she is not obliged to give evidence and must be given the opportunity to secure representation and to attempt mitigation.

A procedural defect may be waived if the court is satisfied that no injustice has been done to the respondent (FPR 2010, PD 37A, para 13.2 and CPR 1998, PD 81, para 16.2).

Potential penalty

See Potential penalties in relief available section above for details of the penalties which can be imposed and see *Children Law and Practice*, para B[1491]. The sanction is designed to reflect the seriousness of the contempt and to secure compliance with the terms of the order in the future.

The court will consider whether any sentence should be suspended (FPR 2010, r 37.28(1) and CPR 1998, r 81.29(1) and see *Slade v Slade* [2010] 1 FLR 160), however an immediate sentence is likely to be appropriate where there has been no indication of co-operation by the respondent (*London Borough of Ealing v Connors* [2014] 2 FLR 328; *Sanchez v Oboz* [2015] EWHC 235 (Fam); and *Sanchez v Oboz (No 2) (Sentencing for Contempt of Court)* [2015] EWHC 611 (Fam)).

Hale v Tanner [2000] 2 FLR 879 contains a review of the proper approach to committal proceedings and sentencing. Whilst the court could not give guidance on appropriate sentences, the following general considerations should be applied:

(1) imprisonment was not to be regarded as an automatic response to the breach of an order, although there was no principle that imprisonment was not to be imposed on the first occasion;
(2) although alternatives to imprisonment were limited, there were a number of things the court should consider, in particular where no violence was involved;
(3) if imprisonment was appropriate the length of the committal should be decided without reference to whether or not it was to be suspended;
(4) the seriousness of the contempt had to be judged not only for its intrinsic gravity but also in the light of the court's objectives both to mark its disapproval of the disobedience to the order and to secure compliance in the future;
(5) the length of the committal should relate to the maximum available, ie 2 years;
(6) suspension was possible in a wider range of circumstances than in criminal cases, and was usually the first way of attempting to secure compliance with the order;
(7) The court had to consider whether the context was mitigating or aggravating, in particular where there was a breach of an intimate relationship and/or children were involved;
(8) the court should consider any concurrent proceedings in another court, and should explain to the contemnor the nature of the order and the consequence of breach.

Any time spent on remand must be taken into account in the sentence (*Kerai v Patel* [2008] 2 FLR 2137).

The order will specify the exact details of the contempt found proved and specify the penalty imposed. Where the sentence is suspended, the order must specify the period of suspension and the exact terms and conditions of suspension (FPR 2010, r 37.28; CPR 1998, r 81.29).

Costs

The *President's Direction (Committal applications and proceedings in which a committal order may be made)* [2001] 1 FLR 949 specifies that, as with all family committal applications, CPR 1998 costs provisions apply. See CPR 1998, Part 44. If intending to seek a costs order, file and serve a Form N260 costs schedule **24 hours** before the hearing if possible.

Concurrent criminal proceedings

The following principles should be applied in cases where there are concurrent civil and criminal proceedings (*Slade v Slade* [2010] 1 FLR 160):

(a) the court is not sentencing for the criminal equivalent of what the contemnor has done;

(b) the court should have as much information as possible about the parties and any concurrent criminal proceedings relating to the same or similar facts; and

(c) the sentence for contempt of court should not be 'manifestly discrepant' with sentences passed in criminal proceedings for comparable offences.

It is not open to the judge to use the civil proceedings to impose a tougher sentence where the offence has already been punished in criminal proceedings.

The court must ensure that the respondent is not punished in criminal and civil proceedings for the same breach (FLA 1996, s 42A(3) and 42A(4), s 63CA(3) and s 63CA(4); *H v O (Contempt of Court Sentencing)* [2005] 2 FLR 329, *Slade v Slade* [2010] 1 FLR 160 and *Chelmsford County Court v Ramet* [2014] 2 FLR 1081). The judge can only pass sentence for the conduct which was not the subject of the criminal proceedings.

Tips:

- See *Emergency Remedies in the Family Courts*, para E[10.28] for a checklist on the conduct of a hearing of a notice to show good reason or following arrest under a power or warrant of arrest.
- There is no power to commit a person under 18 to prison for contempt. See *Re B (A Child: Evidence: Passport Order)* [2015] 1 FLR 871 which is also a reminder that the court cannot act outside its powers. The age of the respondent should be kept in mind. See *Emergency Remedies in the Family Courts*, para E[10.3].
- The Practice Direction of 26 March 2015 'Practice Direction: Committal for Contempt – Open Court' (available at http://www.familylaw.co.uk/news_and_comment/practice-direction-committal-for-contempt-of-court-open-court) states that whenever a committal application is being heard in public the judge and the advocates should be robed.
- If the respondent still fails to comply following the making of a committal order they can be brought back to court again at the end of the sentence and the court may impose a further sentence up to a maximum of two years. There can be successive terms of imprisonment imposed for further and repeated breaches of repeated orders. The question of whether it is justified in a particular case will turn on the facts (*London Borough of Ealing v Connors* [2014] 2 FLR 328, *Re W (Abduction: Committal)* [2012] 2 FLR 133; and *Button v Salama*

(No 3) [2014] 2 FLR 488). Practitioners should therefore consider requesting that the court makes a further mandatory injunction requiring positive action, such as the disclosure of information as to the whereabouts of a child, notwithstanding a past failure to comply with an identical request. Any failure to comply with any fresh order would expose the respondent to fresh contempt proceedings and the possibility of a further term of imprisonment.

- Public funding for respondents in contempt cases is available under the criminal scheme which covers all contempt proceedings whether arising in the context of criminal, civil or family proceedings (reg 9(v) of the Criminal Legal Aid (General) Regulations 2013). Criminal public funding can be ordered by the court.
- A committal application may not be discontinued without the permission of the court (FPR 2010, PD 37A, para 13.3 and *Re an Application by Gloucestershire County Council for the Committal to Prison of Matthew John Newman (No 2)* [2015] 1 FLR 1377) also illustrates the potential for the court to defer the sentencing aspect where the primary objective in the case, outweighing the need for an immediate custodial sentence, is to ensure that there is no repetition of the misbehaviour. Here the sentence was deferred for one year on the basis that if no further breaches occurred, the respondent would not be subject to any further order.
- Within the draft standard orders released by the President there is an order for committal and for suspended committal. All the draft orders can be found at http://www.jordanpublishing.co.uk/l/family-orders and, whilst they await implementation, it is prudent to become familiar with them.

Service of committal order

Where immediate imprisonment is ordered

Where a committal order is made, the order will be for the issue of a warrant of committal (FPR 2010, r 37.29(1); CPR 1998, r 81.30(1)). The committal order will be served by the court.

Unless the court orders otherwise, a copy of the committal order must be served on the respondent either before or at the time of the execution of the warrant of committal or, where the warrant of committal has been signed by the judge, the committal order may be served on the respondent at any time within **36 hours** after the execution of the warrant (FPR 2010, r 37.29(2); CPR 1998, r 81.30(2)).

The warrant of committal must not be enforced more than **2 years** after the date on which the warrant is issued without further order of the court (FPR 2010, r 37.29(3); CPR 1998, r 81.30(3)).

Where a suspended sentence is ordered

Where the court makes an order for suspended committal, the applicant must serve the suspended order on the respondent (FPR 2010, r 37.28(2); CPR 1998, r 81.29(2)).

Official Solicitor

The court sends a copy of every committal order and relevant details to the Official Solicitor, who reviews the case and may apply or appeal of his own motion or at the contemnor's request.

Discharge of order

See *Emergency Remedies in the Family Courts*, para E[10.23] and *Children Law and Practice*, para B[1525]-[1530].

A person committed to prison for contempt of court may apply to the court for the order to be discharged (FPR 2010, r 37.30 and CPR 1998, r 81.31).

The application must be in writing and attested by the governor of the prison (or any other officer of the prison not below the rank of principal officer) showing that the person committed to prison for contempt has purged, or wishes to purge, the contempt; and be served on the person (if any) at whose instance the warrant of committal was issued at least **1 day** before the application is made.

Under CPR 1998, r 23.7, in civil proceedings the application notice must be served as soon as practicable once it has been filed and at least **3 days** before the hearing. Under FPR 2010, r 18.8, in family proceedings application notice must be served as soon as practicable once it has been filed and at least **7 days** before the hearing.

Tips:

- An application for discharge should usually be made in accordance with FPR 2010, Part 18 or CPR 1998, Part 23 but in practice a letter from the respondent will usually suffice (*CJ v Flintshire Borough Council* [2010] 2 FLR 1224).

PART II

KEY LEGISLATION

MATRIMONIAL CAUSES ACT 1973

SECTIONS 21A–25D

21A Pension sharing orders

(1) For the purposes of this Act, a pension sharing order is an order which –

(a) provides that one party's –

(i) shareable rights under a specified pension arrangement, or
(ii) shareable state scheme rights,

be subject to pension sharing for the benefit of the other party, and

(b) specifies the percentage value to be transferred.

(1A) Where section 25E(7) applies, the reference in subsection (1) –

(a) to shareable rights under a specified pension arrangement shall include a reference to entitlement to PPF compensation (as defined in section 25E(9)); and
(b) to pension sharing shall include a reference to sharing of that compensation.

(2) In subsection (1) above –

(a) the reference to shareable rights under a pension arrangement is to rights in relation to which pension sharing is available under Chapter I of Part IV of the Welfare Reform and Pensions Act 1999, or under corresponding Northern Ireland legislation,
(b) the reference to shareable state scheme rights is to rights in relation to which pension sharing is available under Chapter II of Part IV of the Welfare Reform and Pensions Act 1999, or under corresponding Northern Ireland legislation, and
(c) "party" means a party to a marriage.

21B Pension compensation sharing orders

(1) For the purposes of this Act, a pension compensation sharing order is an order which –

(a) provides that one party's shareable rights to PPF compensation that derive from rights under a specified pension scheme are to be subject to pension compensation sharing for the benefit of the other party, and
(b) specifies the percentage value to be transferred.

(2) In subsection (1) –

(a) the reference to shareable rights to PPF compensation is to rights in relation to which pension compensation sharing is available under Chapter 1 of Part 3 of the Pensions Act 2008 or under corresponding Northern Ireland legislation;
(b) "party" means a party to a marriage;
(c) "specified" means specified in the order.

21C Pension compensation: interpretation

In this Part –

"PPF compensation" means compensation payable under the pension compensation provisions;
"the pension compensation provisions" means –

(a) Chapter 3 of Part 2 of the Pensions Act 2004 (pension protection) and any regulations or order made under it,
(b) Chapter 1 of Part 3 of the Pensions Act 2008 (pension compensation on divorce etc) and any regulations or order made under it, and
(c) any provision corresponding to the provisions mentioned in paragraph (a) or (b) in force in Northern Ireland.

Ancillary relief in connection with divorce proceedings etc

22 Maintenance pending suit

(1) On a petition for divorce, nullity of marriage or judicial separation, the court may make an order for maintenance pending suit, that is to say, an order requiring either party to the marriage to make to the other such periodical payments for his or her maintenance and for such term, being a term beginning not earlier than the date of the presentation of the petition and ending with the date of the determination of the suit, as the court thinks reasonable.

(2) An order under this section may not require a party to a marriage to pay to the other party any amount in respect of legal services for the purposes of the proceedings.

(3) In subsection (2) "legal services" has the same meaning as in section 22ZA.

22ZA Orders for payment in respect of legal services

(1) In proceedings for divorce, nullity of marriage or judicial separation, the court may make an order or orders requiring one party to the marriage to pay to the other ("the applicant") an amount for the purpose of enabling the applicant to obtain legal services for the purposes of the proceedings.

(2) The court may also make such an order or orders in proceedings under this Part for financial relief in connection with proceedings for divorce, nullity of marriage or judicial separation.

(3) The court must not make an order under this section unless it is satisfied that, without the amount, the applicant would not reasonably be able to obtain appropriate legal services for the purposes of the proceedings or any part of the proceedings.

(4) For the purposes of subsection (3), the court must be satisfied, in particular, that –

(a) the applicant is not reasonably able to secure a loan to pay for the services, and
(b) the applicant is unlikely to be able to obtain the services by granting a charge over any assets recovered in the proceedings.

(5) An order under this section may be made for the purpose of enabling the applicant to obtain legal services of a specified description, including legal services provided in a specified period or for the purposes of a specified part of the proceedings.

(6) An order under this section may –

(a) provide for the payment of all or part of the amount by instalments of specified amounts, and
(b) require the instalments to be secured to the satisfaction of the court.

(7) An order under this section may direct that payment of all or part of the amount is to be deferred.

(8) The court may at any time in the proceedings vary an order made under this section if it considers that there has been a material change of circumstances since the order was made.

(9) For the purposes of the assessment of costs in the proceedings, the applicant's costs are to be treated as reduced by any amount paid to the applicant pursuant to an order under this section for the purposes of those proceedings.

(10) In this section "legal services", in relation to proceedings, means the following types of services –

(a) providing advice as to how the law applies in the particular circumstances,
(b) providing advice and assistance in relation to the proceedings,
(c) providing other advice and assistance in relation to the settlement or other resolution of the dispute that is the subject of the proceedings, and
(d) providing advice and assistance in relation to the enforcement of decisions in the proceedings or as part of the settlement or resolution of the dispute,

and they include, in particular, advice and assistance in the form of representation and any form of dispute resolution, including mediation.

(11) In subsections (5) and (6) "specified" means specified in the order concerned.

22ZB Matters to which court is to have regard in deciding how to exercise power under section 22ZA

(1) When considering whether to make or vary an order under section 22ZA, the court must have regard to –

(a) the income, earning capacity, property and other financial resources which each of the applicant and the paying party has or is likely to have in the foreseeable future,
(b) the financial needs, obligations and responsibilities which each of the applicant and the paying party has or is likely to have in the foreseeable future,
(c) the subject matter of the proceedings, including the matters in issue in them,
(d) whether the paying party is legally represented in the proceedings,
(e) any steps taken by the applicant to avoid all or part of the proceedings, whether by proposing or considering mediation or otherwise,
(f) the applicant's conduct in relation to the proceedings,
(g) any amount owed by the applicant to the paying party in respect of costs in the proceedings or other proceedings to which both the applicant and the paying party are or were party, and
(h) the effect of the order or variation on the paying party.

(2) In subsection (1)(a) "earning capacity", in relation to the applicant or the paying party, includes any increase in earning capacity which, in the opinion of the court, it would be reasonable to expect the applicant or the paying party to take steps to acquire.

(3) For the purposes of subsection (1)(h), the court must have regard, in particular, to whether the making or variation of the order is likely to –

(a) cause undue hardship to the paying party, or
(b) prevent the paying party from obtaining legal services for the purposes of the proceedings.

(4) The Lord Chancellor may by order amend this section by adding to, omitting or varying the matters mentioned in subsections (1) to (3).

(5) An order under subsection (4) must be made by statutory instrument.

(6) A statutory instrument containing an order under subsection (4) may not be made unless a draft of the instrument has been laid before, and approved by a resolution of, each House of Parliament.

(7) In this section "legal services" has the same meaning as in section 22ZA.

23 Financial provision orders in connection with divorce proceedings etc

(1) On granting a decree of divorce, a decree of nullity of marriage or a decree of judicial separation or at any time thereafter (whether, in the case of a decree of divorce or of nullity of marriage, before or after the decree is made absolute), the court may make any one or more of the following orders, that is to say –

(a) an order that either party to the marriage shall make to the other such periodical payments, for such term, as may be specified in the order;
(b) an order that either party to the marriage shall secure to the other to the satisfaction of the court such periodical payments, for such term, as may be so specified;
(c) an order that either party to the marriage shall pay to the other such lump sum or sums as may be so specified;
(d) an order that a party to the marriage shall make to such person as may be specified in the order for the benefit of a child of the family, or to such a child, such periodical payments, for such term, as may be so specified;
(e) an order that a party to the marriage shall secure to such person as may be so specified for the benefit of such a child, or to such a child, to the satisfaction of the court, such periodical payments, for such term, as may be so specified;
(f) an order that a party to the marriage shall pay to such person as may be so specified for the benefit of such a child, or to such a child, such lump sum as may be so specified;

subject, however, in the case of an order under paragraph (d), (e) or (f) above, to the restrictions imposed by section 29(1) and (3) below on the making of financial provision orders in favour of children who have attained the age of 18.

(2) The court may also, subject to those restrictions, make any one or more of the orders mentioned in subsection (1)(d), (e) and (f) above –

(a) in any proceedings for divorce, nullity of marriage or judicial separation, before granting a decree; and
(b) where any such proceedings are dismissed after the beginning of the trial, either forthwith or within a reasonable period after the dismissal.

(3) Without prejudice to the generality of subsection (1)(c) or (f) above –

(a) an order under this section that a party to a marriage shall pay a lump sum to the other party may be made for the purpose of enabling that other party to meet any liabilities or expenses reasonably incurred by him or her in maintaining himself or herself or any child of the family before making an application for an order under this section in his or her favour;

(b) an order under this section for the payment of a lump sum to or for the benefit of a child of the family may be made for the purpose of enabling any liabilities or expenses reasonably incurred by or for the benefit of that child before the making of an application for an order under this section in his favour to be met; and
(c) an order under this section for the payment of a lump sum may provide for the payment of that sum by instalments of such amount as may be specified in the order and may require the payment of the instalments to be secured to the satisfaction of the court.

(4) The power of the court under subsection (1) or (2)(a) above to make an order in favour of a child of the family shall be exercisable from time to time; and where the court makes an order in favour of a child under subsection (2)(b) above, it may from time to time, subject to the restrictions mentioned in subsection (1) above, make a further order in his favour of any of the kinds mentioned in subsection (1)(d), (e) or (f) above.

(5) Without prejudice to the power to give a direction under section 30 below for the settlement of an instrument by conveyancing counsel, where an order is made under subsection (1)(a), (b) or (c) above on or after granting a decree of divorce or nullity of marriage, neither the order nor any settlement made in pursuance of the order shall take effect unless the decree has been made absolute.

(6) Where the court –

(a) makes an order under this section for the payment of a lump sum; and
(b) directs –

    (i) that payment of that sum or any part of it shall be deferred; or
    (ii) that the sum or any part of it shall be paid by instalments,

the court may order that the amount deferred or the instalments shall carry interest at such rate as may be specified by the order from such date, not earlier than the date of the order, as may be so specified, until the date when payment of it is due.

24 Property adjustment orders in connection with divorce proceedings etc

(1) On granting a decree of divorce, a decree of nullity of marriage or a decree of judicial separation or at any time thereafter (whether, in the case of a decree of divorce or of nullity of marriage, before or after the decree is made absolute), the court may make any one or more of the following orders, that is to say –

(a) an order that a party to the marriage shall transfer to the other party, to any child of the family or to such person as may be specified in the order for the benefit of such a child such property as may be so specified, being property to which the first-mentioned party is entitled, either in possession or reversion;
(b) an order that a settlement of such property as may be so specified, being property to which a party to the marriage is so entitled, be made to the satisfaction of the court for the benefit of the other party to the marriage and of the children of the family or either or any of them;
(c) an order varying for the benefit of the parties to the marriage and of the children of the family or either or any of them any ante-nuptial or post-nuptial settlement (including such a settlement made by will or codicil) made on the parties to the marriage, other than one in the form of a pension arrangement (within the meaning of section 25D below);
(d) an order extinguishing or reducing the interest of either of the parties to the marriage under any such settlement, other than one in the form of a pension arrangement (within the meaning of section 25D below);

subject, however, in the case of an order under paragraph (a) above, to the restrictions imposed by section 29(1) and (3) below on the making of orders for a transfer of property in favour of children who have attained the age of 18.

(2) The court may make an order under subsection (1)(c) above notwithstanding that there are no children of the family.

(3) Without prejudice to the power to give a direction under section 30 below for the settlement of an instrument by conveyancing counsel, where an order is made under this section on or after granting a decree of divorce or nullity of marriage, neither the order nor any settlement made in pursuance of the order shall take effect unless the decree has been made absolute.

24A Orders for sale of property

(1) Where the court makes an order under section 22ZA or makes under section 23 or 24 of this Act a secured periodical payments order, an order for the payment of a lump sum or a property adjustment order, then, on making that order or at any time thereafter, the court may make a further order for the sale of such property as may be specified in the order, being property in which or in the proceeds of sale of which either or both of the parties to the marriage has or have a beneficial interest, either in possession or reversion.

(2) Any order made under subsection (1) above may contain such consequential or supplementary provisions as the court thinks fit and, without prejudice to the generality of the foregoing provision, may include –

- (a) provision requiring the making of a payment out of the proceeds of sale of the property to which the order relates, and
- (b) provision requiring any such property to be offered for sale to a person, or class of persons, specified in the order.

(3) Where an order is made under subsection (1) above on or after the grant of a decree of divorce or nullity of marriage, the order shall not take effect unless the decree has been made absolute.

(4) Where an order is made under subsection (1) above, the court may direct that the order, or such provision thereof as the court may specify, shall not take effect until the occurrence of an event specified by the court or the expiration of a period so specified.

(5) Where an order under subsection (1) above contains a provision requiring the proceeds of sale of the property to which the order relates to be used to secure periodical payments to a party to the marriage, the order shall cease to have effect on the death or re-marriage of, or formation of a civil partnership by, that person.

(6) Where a party to a marriage has a beneficial interest in any property, or in the proceeds of sale thereof, and some other person who is not a party to the marriage also has a beneficial interest in that property or in the proceeds of sale thereof, then, before deciding whether to make an order under this section in relation to that property, it shall be the duty of the court to give that other person an opportunity to make representations with respect to the order; and any representations made by that other person shall be included among the circumstances to which the court is required to have regard under section 25(1) below.

24B Pension sharing orders in connection with divorce proceedings etc

(1) On granting a decree of divorce or a decree of nullity of marriage or at any time thereafter (whether before or after the decree is made absolute), the court may, on an application made under this section, make one or more pension sharing orders in relation to the marriage.

(2) A pension sharing order under this section is not to take effect unless the decree on or after which it is made has been made absolute.

(3) A pension sharing order under this section may not be made in relation to a pension arrangement which –

(a) is the subject of a pension sharing order in relation to the marriage, or
(b) has been the subject of pension sharing between the parties to the marriage.

(4) A pension sharing order under this section may not be made in relation to shareable state scheme rights if –

(a) such rights are the subject of a pension sharing order in relation to the marriage, or
(b) such rights have been the subject of pension sharing between the parties to the marriage.

(5) A pension sharing order under this section may not be made in relation to the rights of a person under a pension arrangement if there is in force a requirement imposed by virtue of section 25B or 25C below which relates to benefits or future benefits to which he is entitled under the pension arrangement.

24C Pension sharing orders: duty to stay

(1) No pension sharing order may be made so as to take effect before the end of such period after the making of the order as may be prescribed by regulations made by the Lord Chancellor.

(2) The power to make regulations under this section shall be exercisable by statutory instrument which shall be subject to annulment in pursuance of a resolution of either House of Parliament.

24D Pension sharing orders: apportionment of charges

If a pension sharing order relates to rights under a pension arrangement, the court may include in the order provision about the apportionment between the parties of any charge under section 41 of the Welfare Reform and Pensions Act 1999 (charges in respect of pension sharing costs), or under corresponding Northern Ireland legislation.

24E Pension compensation sharing orders in connection with divorce proceedings

(1) On granting a decree of divorce or a decree of nullity of marriage or at any time thereafter (whether before or after the decree is made absolute), the court may, on an application made under this section, make a pension compensation sharing order in relation to the marriage.

(2) A pension compensation sharing order under this section is not to take effect unless the decree on or after which it is made has been made absolute.

(3) A pension compensation sharing order under this section may not be made in relation to rights to PPF compensation that –

(a) are the subject of pension attachment,

(b) derive from rights under a pension scheme that were the subject of pension sharing between the parties to the marriage,
(c) are the subject of pension compensation attachment, or
(d) are or have been the subject of pension compensation sharing between the parties to the marriage.

(4) For the purposes of subsection (3)(a), rights to PPF compensation "are the subject of pension attachment" if any of the following three conditions is met.

(5) The first condition is that –

(a) the rights derive from rights under a pension scheme in relation to which an order was made under section 23 imposing a requirement by virtue of section 25B(4), and
(b) that order, as modified under section 25E(3), remains in force.

(6) The second condition is that –

(a) the rights derive from rights under a pension scheme in relation to which an order was made under section 23 imposing a requirement by virtue of section 25B(7), and
(b) that order –

(i) has been complied with, or
(ii) has not been complied with and, as modified under section 25E(5), remains in force.

(7) The third condition is that –

(a) the rights derive from rights under a pension scheme in relation to which an order was made under section 23 imposing a requirement by virtue of section 25C, and
(b) that order remains in force.

(8) For the purposes of subsection (3)(b), rights under a pension scheme "were the subject of pension sharing between the parties to the marriage" if the rights were at any time the subject of a pension sharing order in relation to the marriage or a previous marriage between the same parties.

(9) For the purposes of subsection (3)(c), rights to PPF compensation "are the subject of pension compensation attachment" if there is in force a requirement imposed by virtue of section 25F relating to them.

(10) For the purposes of subsection (3)(d), rights to PPF compensation "are or have been the subject of pension compensation sharing between the parties to the marriage" if they are or have ever been the subject of a pension compensation sharing order in relation to the marriage or a previous marriage between the same parties.

24F Pension compensation sharing orders: duty to stay

(1) No pension compensation sharing order may be made so as to take effect before the end of such period after the making of the order as may be prescribed by regulations made by the Lord Chancellor.

(2) The power to make regulations under this section shall be exercisable by statutory instrument which shall be subject to annulment in pursuance of a resolution of either House of Parliament.

24G Pension compensation sharing orders: apportionment of charges

The court may include in a pension compensation sharing order provision about the apportionment between the parties of any charge under section 117 of the Pensions Act 2008 (charges in respect of pension compensation sharing costs), or under corresponding Northern Ireland legislation.

25 Matters to which court is to have regard in deciding how to exercise its powers under ss 23, 24, 24A, 24B and 24E

(1) It shall be the duty of the court in deciding whether to exercise its powers under section 23, 24, 24A, 24B and 24E above and, if so, in what manner, to have regard to all the circumstances of the case, first consideration being given to the welfare while a minor of any child of the family who has not attained the age of 18.

(2) As regards the exercise of the powers of the court under section 23(1)(a), (b) or (c), 24, 24A, 24B and 24E above in relation to a party to the marriage, the court shall in particular have regard to the following matters –

- (a) the income, earning capacity, property and other financial resources which each of the parties to the marriage has or is likely to have in the foreseeable future, including in the case of earning capacity any increase in that capacity which it would in the opinion of the court be reasonable to expect a party to the marriage to take steps to acquire;
- (b) the financial needs, obligations and responsibilities which each of the parties to the marriage has or is likely to have in the foreseeable future;
- (c) the standard of living enjoyed by the family before the breakdown of the marriage;
- (d) the age of each party to the marriage and the duration of the marriage;
- (e) any physical or mental disability of either of the parties to the marriage;
- (f) the contributions which each of the parties has made or is likely in the foreseeable future to make to the welfare of the family, including any contribution by looking after the home or caring for the family;
- (g) the conduct of each of the parties, if that conduct is such that it would in the opinion of the court be inequitable to disregard it;
- (h) in the case of proceedings for divorce or nullity of marriage, the value to each of the parties to the marriage of any benefit which, by reason of the dissolution or annulment of the marriage, that party will lose the chance of acquiring.

(3) As regards the exercise of the powers of the court under section 23(1)(d), (e) or (f), (2) or (4), 24 or 24A above in relation to a child of the family, the court shall in particular have regard to the following matters –

- (a) the financial needs of the child;
- (b) the income, earning capacity (if any), property and other financial resources of the child;
- (c) any physical or mental disability of the child;
- (d) the manner in which he was being and in which the parties to the marriage expected him to be educated or trained;
- (e) the considerations mentioned in relation to the parties to the marriage in paragraphs (a), (b), (c) and (e) of subsection (2) above.

(4) As regards the exercise of the powers of the court under section 23(1)(d), (e) or (f), (2) or (4), 24 or 24A above against a party to a marriage in favour of a child of the family who is not the child of that party, the court shall also have regard –

- (a) to whether that party assumed any responsibility for the child's maintenance, and, if so, to the extent to which, and the basis upon which, that party assumed such responsibility and to the length of time for which that party discharged such responsibility;

(b) to whether in assuming and discharging such responsibility that party did so knowing that the child was not his or her own;
(c) to the liability of any other person to maintain the child.

25A Exercise of court's powers in favour of party to marriage on decree of divorce or nullity of marriage

(1) Where on or after the grant of a decree of divorce or nullity of marriage the court decides to exercise its powers under section 23(1)(a), (b) or (c), 24, 24A, 24B or 24E above in favour of a party to the marriage, it shall be the duty of the court to consider whether it would be appropriate so to exercise those powers that the financial obligations of each party towards the other will be terminated as soon after the grant of the decree as the court considers just and reasonable.

(2) Where the court decides in such a case to make a periodical payments or secured periodical payments order in favour of a party to the marriage, the court shall in particular consider whether it would be appropriate to require those payments to be made or secured only for such term as would in the opinion of the court be sufficient to enable the party in whose favour the order is made to adjust without undue hardship to the termination of his or her financial dependence on the other party.

(3) Where on or after the grant of a decree of divorce or nullity of marriage an application is made by a party to the marriage for a periodical payments or secured periodical payments order in his or her favour, then, if the court considers that no continuing obligation should be imposed on either party to make or secure periodical payments in favour of the other, the court may dismiss the application with a direction that the applicant shall not be entitled to make any future application in relation to that marriage for an order under section 23(1)(a) or (b) above.

25B Pensions

(1) The matters to which the court is to have regard under section 25(2) above include –

(a) in the case of paragraph (a), any benefits under a pension arrangement which a party to the marriage has or is likely to have, and
(b) in the case of paragraph (h), any benefits under a pension arrangement which, by reason of the dissolution or annulment of the marriage, a party to the marriage will lose the chance of acquiring,

and, accordingly, in relation to benefits under a pension arrangement, section 25(2)(a) above shall have effect as if "in the foreseeable future" were omitted.

(2) (*repealed*)

(3) The following provisions apply where, having regard to any benefits under a pension arrangement, the court determines to make an order under section 23 above.

(4) To the extent to which the order is made having regard to any benefits under a pension arrangement, the order may require the person responsible for the pension arrangement in question, if at any time any payment in respect of any benefits under the arrangement becomes due to the party with pension rights, to make a payment for the benefit of the other party.

(5) The order must express the amount of any payment required to be made by virtue of subsection (4) above as a percentage of the payment which becomes due to the party with pension rights.

(6) Any such payment by the person responsible for the arrangement –

(a) shall discharge so much of his liability to the party with pension rights as corresponds to the amount of the payment, and
(b) shall be treated for all purposes as a payment made by the party with pension rights in or towards the discharge of his liability under the order.

(7) Where the party with pension rights has a right of commutation under the arrangement, the order may require him to exercise it to any extent; and this section applies to any payment due in consequence of commutation in pursuance of the order as it applies to other payments in respect of benefits under the arrangement.

(7A) The power conferred by subsection (7) above may not be exercised for the purpose of commuting a benefit payable to the party with pension rights to a benefit payable to the other party.

(7B) The power conferred by subsection (4) or (7) above may not be exercised in relation to a pension arrangement which –

(a) is the subject of a pension sharing order in relation to the marriage, or
(b) has been the subject of pension sharing between the parties to the marriage.

(7C) In subsection (1) above, references to benefits under a pension arrangement include any benefits by way of pension, whether under a pension arrangement or not.

25C Pensions: lump sums

(1) The power of the court under section 23 above to order a party to a marriage to pay a lump sum to the other party includes, where the benefits which the party with pension rights has or is likely to have under a pension arrangement include any lump sum payable in respect of his death, power to make any of the following provision by the order.

(2) The court may –

(a) if the person responsible for the pension arrangement in question has power to determine the person to whom the sum, or any part of it, is to be paid, require him to pay the whole or part of that sum, when it becomes due, to the other party,
(b) if the party with pension rights has power to nominate the person to whom the sum, or any part of it, is to be paid, require the party with pension rights to nominate the other party in respect of the whole or part of that sum,
(c) in any other case, require the person responsible for the pension arrangement in question to pay the whole or part of that sum, when it becomes due, for the benefit of the other party instead of to the person to whom, apart from the order, it would be paid.

(3) Any payment by the person responsible for the pension arrangement under an order made under section 23 above by virtue of this section shall discharge so much of his liability in respect of the party with pension rights as corresponds to the amount of the payment.

(4) The powers conferred by this section may not be exercised in relation to a pension arrangement which –

(a) is the subject of a pension sharing order in relation to the marriage, or
(b) has been the subject of pension sharing between the parties to the marriage.

25D Pensions: supplementary

(1) Where –

(a) an order made under section 23 above by virtue of section 25B or 25C above imposes any requirement on the person responsible for a pension arrangement ("the first arrangement") and the party with pension rights acquires rights under another pension arrangement ("the new arrangement") which are derived (directly or indirectly) from the whole of his rights under the first arrangement, and
(b) the person responsible for the new arrangement has been given notice in accordance with regulations made by the Lord Chancellor,

the order shall have effect as if it had been made instead in respect of the person responsible for the new arrangement.

(2) The Lord Chancellor may by regulations –

(a) in relation to any provision of sections 25B or 25C above which authorises the court making an order under section 23 above to require the person responsible for a pension arrangement to make a payment for the benefit of the other party, make provision as to the person to whom, and the terms on which, the payment is to be made,
(ab) make, in relation to payment under a mistaken belief as to the continuation in force of a provision included by virtue of section 25B or 25C above in an order under section 23 above, provision about the rights or liabilities of the payer, the payee or the person to whom the payment was due,
(b) require notices to be given in respect of changes of circumstances relevant to such orders which include provision made by virtue of sections 25B and 25C above,
(ba) make provision for the person responsible for a pension arrangement to be discharged in prescribed circumstances from a requirement imposed by virtue of section 25B or 25C above,
(c), (d) (*repealed*)
(e) make provision about calculation and verification in relation to the valuation of –

(i) benefits under a pension arrangement, or
(ii) shareable state scheme rights,

for the purposes of the court's functions in connection with the exercise of any of its powers under this Part of this Act.

(2A) Regulations under subsection (2)(e) above may include –

(a) provision for calculation or verification in accordance with guidance from time to time prepared by a prescribed person, and
(b) provision by reference to regulations under section 30 or 49(4) of the Welfare Reform and Pensions Act 1999.

(2B) Regulations under subsection (2) above may make different provision for different cases.

(2C) Power to make regulations under this section shall be exercisable by statutory instrument which shall be subject to annulment in pursuance of a resolution of either House of Parliament.

(3) In this section and sections 25B and 25C above –

"occupational pension scheme" has the same meaning as in the Pension Schemes Act 1993;
"the party with pension rights" means the party to the marriage who has or is likely to have benefits under a pension arrangement and "the other party" means the other party to the marriage;
"pension arrangement" means –

(a) an occupational pension scheme,
(b) a personal pension scheme,
(c) a retirement annuity contract,
(d) an annuity or insurance policy purchased, or transferred, for the purpose of giving effect to rights under an occupational pension scheme or a personal pension scheme, and
(e) an annuity purchased, or entered into, for the purpose of discharging liability in respect of a pension credit under section 29(1)(b) of the Welfare Reform and Pensions Act 1999 or under corresponding Northern Ireland legislation;

"personal pension scheme" has the same meaning as in the Pension Schemes Act 1993;
"prescribed" means prescribed by regulations;
"retirement annuity contract" means a contract or scheme approved under Chapter III of Part XIV of the Income and Corporation Taxes Act 1988;
"shareable state scheme rights" has the same meaning as in section 21A(1) above; and
"trustees or managers", in relation to an occupational pension scheme or a personal pension scheme, means –

(a) in the case of a scheme established under a trust, the trustees of the scheme, and
(b) in any other case, the managers of the scheme.

(4) In this section and sections 25B and 25C above, references to the person responsible for a pension arrangement are –

(a) in the case of an occupational pension scheme or a personal pension scheme, to the trustees or managers of the scheme,
(b) in the case of a retirement annuity contract or an annuity falling within paragraph (d) or (e) of the definition of "pension arrangement" above, the provider of the annuity, and
(c) in the case of an insurance policy falling within paragraph (d) of the definition of that expression, the insurer.

CHILDREN ACT 1989

SECTIONS 1, 2, 4, 8, 12

PART I

INTRODUCTORY

1 Welfare of the child

(1) When a court determines any question with respect to –

(a) the upbringing of a child; or
(b) the administration of a child's property or the application of any income arising from it,

the child's welfare shall be the court's paramount consideration.

(2) In any proceedings in which any question with respect to the upbringing of a child arises, the court shall have regard to the general principle that any delay in determining the question is likely to prejudice the welfare of the child.

(2A) A court, in the circumstances mentioned in subsection (4)(a) or (7), is as respects each parent within subsection (6)(a) to presume, unless the contrary is shown, that involvement of that parent in the life of the child concerned will further the child's welfare.

(2B) In subsection (2A) "involvement" means involvement of some kind, either direct or indirect, but not any particular division of a child's time.

(3) In the circumstances mentioned in subsection (4), a court shall have regard in particular to –

(a) the ascertainable wishes and feelings of the child concerned (considered in the light of his age and understanding);
(b) his physical, emotional and educational needs;
(c) the likely effect on him of any change in his circumstances;
(d) his age, sex, background and any characteristics of his which the court considers relevant;
(e) any harm which he has suffered or is at risk of suffering;
(f) how capable each of his parents, and any other person in relation to whom the court considers the question to be relevant, is of meeting his needs;
(g) the range of powers available to the court under this Act in the proceedings in question.

(4) The circumstances are that –

(a) the court is considering whether to make, vary or discharge a section 8 order, and the making, variation or discharge of the order is opposed by any party to the proceedings; or
(b) the court is considering whether to make, vary or discharge a special guardianship order or an order under Part IV.

(5) Where a court is considering whether or not to make one or more orders under this Act with respect to a child, it shall not make the order or any of the orders unless it considers that doing so would be better for the child than making no order at all.

(6) In subsection (2A) "parent" means parent of the child concerned; and, for the purposes of that subsection, a parent of the child concerned –

(a) is within this paragraph if that parent can be involved in the child's life in a way that does not put the child at risk of suffering harm; and
(b) is to be treated as being within paragraph (a) unless there is some evidence before the court in the particular proceedings to suggest that involvement of that parent in the child's life would put the child at risk of suffering harm whatever the form of the involvement.

(7) The circumstances referred to are that the court is considering whether to make an order under section 4(1)(c) or (2A) or 4ZA(1)(c) or (5) (parental responsibility of parent other than mother).

2 Parental responsibility for children

(1) Where a child's father and mother were married to each other at the time of his birth, they shall each have parental responsibility for the child.

(1A) Where a child –

(a) has a parent by virtue of section 42 of the Human Fertilisation and Embryology Act 2008; or
(b) has a parent by virtue of section 43 of that Act and is a person to whom section 1(3) of the Family Law Reform Act 1987 applies,

the child's mother and the other parent shall each have parental responsibility for the child.

(2) Where a child's father and mother were not married to each other at the time of his birth –

(a) the mother shall have parental responsibility for the child;
(b) the father shall have parental responsibility for the child if he has acquired it (and has not ceased to have it) in accordance with the provisions of this Act.

(2A) Where a child has a parent by virtue of section 43 of the Human Fertilisation and Embryology Act 2008 and is not a person to whom section 1(3) of the Family Law Reform Act 1987 applies –

(a) the mother shall have parental responsibility for the child;
(b) the other parent shall have parental responsibility for the child if she has acquired it (and has not ceased to have it) in accordance with the provisions of this Act.

(3) References in this Act to a child whose father and mother were, or (as the case may be) were not, married to each other at the time of his birth must be read with section 1 of the Family Law Reform Act 1987 (which extends their meaning).

(4) The rule of law that a father is the natural guardian of his legitimate child is abolished.

(5) More than one person may have parental responsibility for the same child at the same time.

(6) A person who has parental responsibility for a child at any time shall not cease to have that responsibility solely because some other person subsequently acquires parental responsibility for the child.

(7) Where more than one person has parental responsibility for a child, each of them may act alone and without the other (or others) in meeting that responsibility; but nothing in this Part shall be taken to affect the operation of any enactment which requires the consent of more than one person in a matter affecting the child.

(8) The fact that a person has parental responsibility for a child shall not entitle him to act in any way which would be incompatible with any order made with respect to the child under this Act.

(9) A person who has parental responsibility for a child may not surrender or transfer any part of that responsibility to another but may arrange for some or all of it to be met by one or more persons acting on his behalf.

(10) The person with whom any such arrangement is made may himself be a person who already has parental responsibility for the child concerned.

(11) The making of any such arrangement shall not affect any liability of the person making it which may arise from any failure to meet any part of his parental responsibility for the child concerned.

4 Acquisition of parental responsibility by father

(1) Where a child's father and mother were not married to each other at the time of his birth, the father shall acquire parental responsibility for the child if –

- (a) he becomes registered as the child's father under any of the enactments specified in subsection (1A);
- (b) he and the child's mother make an agreement (a "parental responsibility agreement") providing for him to have parental responsibility for the child; or
- (c) the court, on his application, orders that he shall have parental responsibility for the child.

(1A) The enactments referred to in subsection (1)(a) are –

- (a) paragraphs (a), (b) and (c) of section 10(1) and of section 10A(1) of the Births and Deaths Registration Act 1953;
- (b) paragraphs (a), (b)(i) and (c) of section 18(1), and sections 18(2)(b) and 20(1)(a) of the Registration of Births, Deaths and Marriages (Scotland) Act 1965; and
- (c) sub-paragraphs (a), (b) and (c) of Article 14(3) of the Births and Deaths Registration (Northern Ireland) Order 1976.

(1B) The Secretary of State may by order amend subsection (1A) so as to add further enactments to the list in that subsection.

(2) No parental responsibility agreement shall have effect for the purposes of this Act unless –

- (a) it is made in the form prescribed by regulations made by the Lord Chancellor; and
- (b) where regulations are made by the Lord Chancellor prescribing the manner in which such agreements must be recorded, it is recorded in the prescribed manner.

(2A) A person who has acquired parental responsibility under subsection (1) shall cease to have that responsibility only if the court so orders.

(3) The court may make an order under subsection (2A) on the application –

- (a) of any person who has parental responsibility for the child; or
- (b) with leave of the court, of the child himself,

subject, in the case of parental responsibility acquired under subsection (1)(c), to section 12(4).

(4) The court may only grant leave under subsection (3)(b) if it is satisfied that the child has sufficient understanding to make the proposed application.

PART II

ORDERS WITH RESPECT TO CHILDREN IN FAMILY PROCEEDINGS

General

8 Child arrangements orders and other orders with respect to children

(1) In this Act –

"child arrangements order" means an order regulating arrangements relating to any of the following –

(a) with whom a child is to live, spend time or otherwise have contact, and
(b) when a child is to live, spend time or otherwise have contact with any person;

...

"a prohibited steps order" means an order that no step which could be taken by a parent in meeting his parental responsibility for a child, and which is of a kind specified in the order, shall be taken by any person without the consent of the court;

... and

"a specific issue order" means an order giving directions for the purpose of determining a specific question which has arisen, or which may arise, in connection with any aspect of parental responsibility for a child.

(2) In this Act "a section 8 order" means any of the orders mentioned in subsection (1) and any order varying or discharging such an order.

(3) For the purposes of this Act "family proceedings" means any proceedings –

(a) under the inherent jurisdiction of the High Court in relation to children; and
(b) under the enactments mentioned in subsection (4),

but does not include proceedings on an application for leave under section 100(3).

(4) The enactments are –

(a) Parts I, II and IV of this Act;
(b) the Matrimonial Causes Act 1973;
(ba) Schedule 5 to the Civil Partnership Act 2004;
(c) *(repealed)*
(d) the Adoption Act and Children Act 2002;
(e) the Domestic Proceedings and Magistrates' Courts Act 1978;
(ea) Schedule 6 to the Civil Partnership Act 2004;
(f) *(repealed)*
(g) Part III of the Matrimonial and Family Proceedings Act 1984;
(h) the Family Law Act 1996.
(i) sections 11 and 12 of the Crime and Disorder Act 1998.

12 Child arrangements orders and parental responsibility

(1) Where –

(a) the court makes a child arrangements order with respect to a child,
(b) the father of the child, or a woman who is a parent of the child by virtue of section 43 of the Human Fertilisation and Embryology Act 2008, is named in the order as a person with whom the child is to live, and
(c) the father, or the woman, would not otherwise have parental responsibility for the child, the court must also make an order under section 4 giving the father, or under section 4ZA giving the woman, that responsibility.

(1A) Where –

(a) the court makes a child arrangements order with respect to a child,
(b) the father of the child, or a woman who is a parent of the child by virtue of section 43 of the Human Fertilisation and Embryology Act 2008, is named in the order as a person with whom the child is to spend time or otherwise have contact but is not named in the order as a person with whom the child is to live, and
(c) the father, or the woman, would not otherwise have parental responsibility for the child, the court must decide whether it would be appropriate, in view of the provision made in the order with respect to the father or the woman, for him or her to have parental responsibility for the child and, if it decides that it would be appropriate for the father or the woman to have that responsibility, must also make an order under section 4 giving him, or under section 4ZA giving her, that responsibility.

(2) Where the court makes a child arrangements order and a person who is not a parent or guardian of the child concerned is named in the order as a person with whom the child is to live, that person shall have parental responsibility for the child while the order remains in force so far as providing for the child to live with that person.

(2A) Where the court makes a child arrangements order and –

(a) a person who is not the parent or guardian of the child concerned is named in the order as a person with whom the child is to spend time or otherwise have contact, but
(b) the person is not named in the order as a person with whom the child is to live, the court may provide in the order for the person to have parental responsibility for the child while paragraphs (a) and (b) continue to be met in the person's case.

(3) Where a person has parental responsibility for a child as a result of subsection (2) or (2A), he shall not have the right –

(a) *(repealed)*
(b) to agree, or refuse to agree, to the making of an adoption order, or an order under section 84 of the Adoption and Children Act 2002, with respect to the child; or
(c) to appoint a guardian for the child.

(4) Where subsection (1) requires the court to make an order under section 4 or 4ZA in respect of a parent of a child, the court shall not bring that order to an end at any time while the child arrangements order concerned remains in force so far as providing for the child to live with that parent.

(5), (6) *(repealed)*

PRACTICE DIRECTION 27A

FAMILY PROCEEDINGS: COURT BUNDLES (UNIVERSAL PRACTICE TO BE APPLIED IN THE HIGH COURT AND FAMILY COURT)

This Practice Direction supplements FPR Part 27

1.1 The President of the Family Division has issued this practice direction to achieve consistency across the country in the Family Court and the Family Division of the High Court in the preparation of court bundles and in respect of other related matters.

Application of the practice direction

2.1 Except as specified in paragraph 2.4, and subject to specific directions given in any particular case, the following practice applies to:

(a) all hearings before a judge sitting in the Family Division of the High Court wherever the court may be sitting; and
(b) all hearings in the Family Court.

2.2 "Hearing" includes all appearances before the court, whether with or without notice to other parties and whether for directions or for substantive relief.

2.3 This practice direction applies whether a bundle is being lodged for the first time or is being re-lodged for a further hearing (see paragraph 9.2).

2.4 This practice direction does not apply to the hearing of any urgent application if and to the extent that it is impossible to comply with it.

Responsibility for the preparation of the bundle

3.1 A bundle for the use of the court at the hearing shall be provided by the party in the position of applicant at the hearing (or, if there are cross-applications, by the party whose application was first in time) or, if that person is a litigant in person, by the first listed respondent who is not a litigant in person. Where all the parties are litigants in person none of them shall, unless the court otherwise directs, be obliged to provide a bundle, but any bundle which they choose to lodge must be prepared and lodged so as to comply with this practice direction.

3.2 The party preparing the bundle shall paginate it using Arabic numbering throughout. If possible the contents of the bundle shall be agreed by all parties.

Contents of the bundle

4.1 The bundle shall contain copies of only those documents which are relevant to the hearing and which it is necessary for the court to read or which will actually be referred to during the hearing. In particular, copies of the following classes of documents must not be included in the bundle unless specifically directed by the court:

(a) correspondence (including letters of instruction to experts);
(b) medical records (including hospital, GP and health visitor records);
(c) bank and credit card statements and other financial records;
(d) notes of contact visits;
(e) foster carer logs;
(f) social services files (with the exception of any assessment being relied on by any of the parties);
(g) police disclosure.

This does not prevent the inclusion in the bundle of specific documents which it is necessary for the court to read or which will actually be referred to during the hearing.

4.2 The documents in the bundle shall be arranged in chronological order from the front of the bundle, paginated individually and consecutively (starting with page 1 and using Arabic numbering throughout), indexed and divided into separate sections (each section being separately paginated) as follows:

(a) preliminary documents (see paragraph 4.3) and any other case management documents required by any other practice direction;
(b) applications and orders;
(c) statements and affidavits (which must be dated in the top right corner of the front page) but without exhibiting or duplicating documents referred to in para 4.1;
(d) care plans (where appropriate);
(e) experts' reports and other reports (including those of a guardian, children's guardian or litigation friend); and
(f) other documents, divided into further sections as may be appropriate.

All statements, affidavits, care plans, experts' reports and other reports included in the bundle must be copies of originals which have been signed and dated.

4.3 At the commencement of the bundle there shall be inserted the following documents (the preliminary documents):

(a) an up to date case summary of the background to the hearing confined to those matters which are relevant to the hearing and the management of the case and limited, if practicable, to four A4 pages;
(b) a statement of the issue or issues to be determined (1) at that hearing and (2) at the final hearing;
(c) a position statement by each party including a summary of the order or directions sought by that party (1) at that hearing and (2) at the final hearing;
(d) an up to date chronology, if it is a final hearing or if the summary under (i) is insufficient;
(e) skeleton arguments, if appropriate;
(f) a list of essential reading for that hearing; and
(g) the time estimate (see paragraph 10.1).

Copies of all authorities relied on must be contained in a separate composite bundle agreed between the advocates.

4.4 Each of the preliminary documents shall be as short and succinct as possible and shall state on the front page immediately below the heading the date when it was prepared and the date of the hearing for which it was prepared. Where proceedings relating to a child are being heard by magistrates the summary of the background shall be prepared in anonymised form, omitting the names and identifying information of every person referred to other than the parties' legal representatives, and stating the number of pages contained in the bundle. Identifying information can be contained in all other preliminary documents.

4.5 The summary of the background, statement of issues, chronology, position statement and any skeleton arguments shall be cross-referenced to the relevant pages of the bundle.

4.6 The summary of the background, statement of issues, chronology and reading list shall in the case of a final hearing, and shall so far as practicable in the case of any other hearing, each consist of a single document in a form agreed by all parties. Where the parties disagree as to the content the fact of their disagreement and their differing contentions shall be set out at the appropriate places in the document.

4.7 Where the nature of the hearing is such that a complete bundle of all documents is unnecessary, the bundle (which need not be repaginated) may comprise only those documents necessary for the hearing, but

(a) the summary of the background must commence with a statement that the bundle is limited or incomplete; and
(b) the bundle shall if reasonably practicable be in a form agreed by all parties.

4.8 Where the bundle is re-lodged in accordance with paragraph 9.2, before it is re-lodged:

(a) the bundle shall be updated as appropriate; and
(b) all superseded documents (and in particular all outdated summaries, statements of issues, chronologies, skeleton arguments and similar documents) shall be removed from the bundle.

Format of the bundle

5.1 Unless the court has specifically directed otherwise, being satisfied that such direction is necessary to enable the proceedings to be disposed of justly, the bundle shall be contained in one A4 size ring binder or lever arch file limited to no more than 350 sheets of A4 paper and 350 sides of text.

5.2 All documents in the bundle shall (a) be copied on one side of paper only, unless the court has specifically directed otherwise, and (b) be typed or printed in a font no smaller than 12 point and with 1½ or double spacing.

5.3 The ring binder or lever arch file shall have clearly marked on the front and the spine:

(a) the title and number of the case;
(b) the place where the case has been listed;
(c) the hearing date and time;
(d) if known, the name of the judge hearing the case; and
(e) where in accordance with a direction of the court there is more than one ring binder or lever arch file, a distinguishing letter (A, B, C etc).

Timetable for preparing and lodging the bundle

6.1 The party preparing the bundle shall, whether or not the bundle has been agreed, provide a paginated index to all other parties not less than 4 working days before the hearing.

6.2 Where counsel is to be instructed at any hearing, a paginated bundle shall (if not already in counsel's possession) be delivered to counsel by the person instructing that counsel not less than 3 working days before the hearing.

6.3 The bundle (with the exception of the preliminary documents if and insofar as they are not then available) shall be lodged with the court not less than 2 working days before the hearing, or at such other time as may be specified by the court.

6.4 The preliminary documents shall be lodged with the court no later than 11 am on the day before the hearing and, where the hearing is before a judge of the High Court and the name of the judge is known, shall (with the exception of the authorities, which are to be lodged in hard copy and not sent by email) at the same time be sent by email to the judge's clerk.

Lodging the bundle

7.1 The bundle shall be lodged at the appropriate office. If the bundle is lodged in the wrong place the court may:

(a) treat the bundle as having not been lodged; and
(b) take the steps referred to in paragraph 12.

7.2 Unless the court has given some other direction as to where the bundle in any particular case is to be lodged (for example a direction that the bundle is to be lodged with the judge's clerk) the bundle shall be lodged:

(a) for hearings at the RCJ, in the office of the Clerk of the Rules, 1st Mezzanine (Rm 1M), Queen's Building, Royal Courts of Justice, Strand, London WC2A 2LL (DX 44450 Strand);
(b) for hearings at any other place, at such place as may be designated by the designated family judge responsible for that place and in default of any such designation at the court office for the place where the hearing is to take place.

7.3 Any bundle sent to the court by post, DX or courier shall be clearly addressed to the appropriate office and shall show the date and place of the hearing on the outside of any packaging as well as on the bundle itself.

7.4 Unless the court has given some other direction or paragraph 7.5 applies only one copy of the bundle shall be lodged with the court but the party who is responsible for lodging the bundle shall bring to court at each hearing at which oral evidence may be called a copy of the bundle for use by the witnesses.

7.5 In the case of a hearing listed before a bench of magistrates four copies of the bundle shall be lodged with the court.

7.6 In the case of hearings at the RCJ or at any other place where the designated family judge responsible for that place has directed that this paragraph shall apply, parties shall:

(a) if the bundle or preliminary documents are delivered personally, ensure that they obtain a receipt from the clerk accepting it or them; and
(b) if the bundle or preliminary documents are sent by post or DX, ensure that they obtain proof of posting or despatch.

The receipt (or proof of posting or despatch, as the case may be) shall be brought to court on the day of the hearing and must be produced to the court if requested. If the receipt (or proof of posting or despatch) cannot be produced to the court the judge may: (a) treat the bundle as having not been lodged; and (b) take the steps referred to in paragraph 12.

Lodging the bundle – additional requirements for Family Division or Family Court cases being heard at the RCJ

8.1 Bundles or preliminary documents delivered after 11 am on the day before the hearing may not be accepted by the Clerk of the Rules and if not shall be delivered:

(a) in a case where the hearing is before a judge of the High Court, directly to the clerk of the judge hearing the case;
(b) in a case where the hearing is before any other judge, to such place as may be specified by the Clerk of the Rules.

8.2 Upon learning before which judge a hearing is to take place, the clerk to counsel, or other advocate, representing the party in the position of applicant shall no later than 3 pm the day before the hearing:

(a) in a case where the hearing is before a judge of the High Court, telephone the clerk of the judge hearing the case;
(b) in a case where the hearing is before any other judge email the Clerk of the Rules at RCJ.familyhighcourt@hmcts.gsi.gov.uk;

to ascertain whether the judge has received the bundle (including the preliminary documents) and, if not, shall organise prompt delivery by the applicant's solicitor.

Removing and re-lodging the bundle

9.1 Unless either the court wishes to retain the bundle or specific alternative arrangements have been agreed with the court, the party responsible for the bundle shall, following completion of the hearing, retrieve the bundle from the court immediately or, if that is not practicable, collect it from the court within 5 working days. Bundles which are not collected in due time are liable to be destroyed without further notice.

9.2 The bundle shall be re-lodged for the next and any further hearings in accordance with the provisions of this practice direction and in a form which complies with para 4.7.

Time estimates

10.1 In every case a time estimate (which shall be inserted at the front of the bundle) shall be prepared which shall so far as practicable be agreed by all parties and shall:

(a) specify separately: (i) the time estimated to be required for judicial pre-reading; and (ii) the time required for hearing all evidence and submissions; and (iii) the time estimated to be required for preparing and delivering judgment;
(b) be prepared on the basis that before they give evidence all witnesses will have read all relevant filed statements and reports; and
(c) take appropriate account of any additional time likely to be incurred by the use of interpreters or intermediaries.

10.2 Once a case has been listed, any change in time estimates shall be notified immediately by telephone (and then immediately confirmed in writing):

(a) in the case of hearings in the RCJ, to the Clerk of the Rules; and
(b) in the case of hearings elsewhere, to the relevant listing officer.

Taking cases out of the list

11.1 As soon as it becomes known that a hearing will no longer be effective, whether as a result of the parties reaching agreement or for any other reason, the parties and their representatives shall immediately notify the court by telephone and email which shall be confirmed by letter. The letter, which shall wherever possible be a joint letter sent on behalf of all parties with their signatures applied or appended, shall include:

(a) a short background summary of the case;
(b) the written consent of each party who consents and, where a party does not consent, details of the steps which have been taken to obtain that party's consent and, where known, an explanation of why that consent has not been given;
(c) a draft of the order being sought; and
(d) enough information to enable the court to decide (i) whether to take the case out of the list and (ii) whether to make the proposed order.

Penalties for failure to comply with the practice direction

12.1 Failure to comply with any part of this practice direction may result in the judge removing the case from the list or putting the case further back in the list and may also result in a "wasted costs" order or some other adverse costs order.

Commencement of the practice direction and application of other practice directions

13.1 Subject to paragraph 13.2 this practice direction shall have effect from 22 April 2014.

13.2 Sub-paragraphs (a)–(c) and (e)–(g) of paragraph 4.1 and paragraphs 5.1 and 5.3(e) shall have effect from 31 July 2014. In the meantime paragraphs 5.1 and 5.3(e) shall have effect as if:

(a) paragraph 5.1 read "The bundle shall be contained in one or more A4 size ring binders or lever arch files (each lever arch file being limited to no more than 350 pages)."; and
(b) in paragraph 5.3(e) the words "in accordance with a direction of the court" were omitted.

14.1 This practice direction should where appropriate be read in conjunction with the Public Law Outline 2014 (PD 12A) and the Child Arrangements Programme 2014 (PD 12B). In particular, nothing in this practice direction is to be read as removing or altering any obligation to comply with the requirements of the Public Law Outline 2014 and the Child Arrangements Programme 2014.

PART III

LEADING CASES

KEY CASES: CATEGORISED BY TOPIC

APPLICATIONS FOR LEAVE

Re G; Re Z (Children: Sperm Donors: Leave to Apply for Children Act Orders) [2013] 1 FLR 1334

Re M (Care: Contact: Grandmother's Application for Leave) [1995] 2 FLR 86

Re S (Contact: Application by Sibling) [1998] 2 FLR 897

Re W (Care Proceedings: Leave to Apply) [2005] 2 FLR 468

APPLICATIONS FOR LEAVE ON NOTICE

Re F and R (Section 8 Order: Grandparent's Application) [1995] 1 FLR 524

Re M (Prohibited Steps Order: Application for Leave) [1993] 1 FLR 275

Re W (Contact Application: Procedure) [2000] 1 FLR 263

ARBITRATION

AI v MT (alternative dispute resolution) [2013] 2 FLR 371

S v S (Financial Remedies: Arbitral Award) [2014] 1 FLR 1257

BANKRUPTCY

Hill v Haines [2008] 1 FLR 1192

Paulin v Paulin [2009] 2 FLR 354, CA

CAPITALISATION AND VARIATION OF PERIODICAL PAYMENTS

Duxbury v Duxbury [1987] 1 FLR 7, CA

Hvorostovsky v Hvorostovsky [2009] 2 FLR 1574

Lauder [2007] 2 FLR 802

Pearce v Pearce [2003] 2 FLR 1144 (CA)

Vaughan v Vaughan [2010] 2 FLR 242

VB v JP [2008] 1 FLR 742

CHILD ARRANGEMENTS ORDERS (CONTACT)

Determining with whom a child lives

Re H (Contact: Adverse Finding of Fact) [2011] 2 FLR 1201

Domestic abuse

H (Contact: Domestic Violence) [2000] 2 FLR 334

Re H (Interim Contact: Domestic Violence Allegations) [2014] 1 FLR 41

Re L (Contact: Domestic Violence); Re v (Contact: Domestic Violence); Re M (Contact: Domestic Violence); Re H (Contact: Domestic Violence) [2000] 2 FLR 334

Re W (Children: Domestic Violence) [2014] 1 FLR 260

Duty on parents to work together

Re H-B (Contact) [2015] EWCA Civ 389

Re J and K [2015] 1 FLR 86

Re W (Contact: Permission to Appeal) [2013] 1 FLR 609

Re W (Direct Contact) [2013] 1 FLR 494

Grandparents

Re A (Section 8 *Order: Grandparent Application)* [1995] 2 FLR 153

Re W (Contact: Application by Grandparent) [1997] 1 FLR 793

Importance of biological parentage

Re A (A Child: Joint Residence: Parental Responsibility) [2008] 2 FLR 1593

A v B and C (Lesbian Co-parents: Role of Father) [2012] 2 FLR 607

Re B (A Child) [2010] 1 FLR 551

DB v AB and CB [2014] 2 FLR 1197

Re G (Shared Residence Order: Biological Mother of Donor Egg) [2014] 2 FLR 897

Re H (A Child) [2012] 2 FLR 627

H v S (Surrogacy Agreement) [2015] EWFC 36

Step-parents

Re H (A Minor) (Contact) [1994] 2 FLR 776)

CHILD ARRANGEMENTS ORDERS (LIVING ARRANGEMENTS)

Importance of biological parentage

Re E-R (A Child) [2015] EWCA Civ 405

Re B (A Child) [2010] 1 FLR 551

Re G (Children) [2006] 2 FLR 629, HL

Re G (Shared Residence Order: Biological Mother of Donor Egg) [2014] 2 FLR 897

H v S (Surrogacy Agreement) [2015] EWFC 36

COMPANIES – TREATMENT

A v A [2006] 2 FLR 115

R v R (Financial Relief: Company Valuation) [2005] 2 FLR 365

V v V (Financial Relief) [2005] 2 FLR 697

COMPANIES – VALUATION

Charman v Charman (No 2) [2007] 1 FLR 593

G v G (Financial Provision: Equal Division) [2002] 2 FLR 1143

H v H [2008] 2 FLR 2092

Irvine v Irvine [2006] EWHC 583 (Ch)

NA v MA [2007] 1 FLR 1760

P v P (Financial Relief: Illiquid Assets) [2005] 1 FLR 548

Re C (Divorce: Financial Relief) [2008] 1 FLR 625

Re Bird Precision Bellows Ltd [1984] 1 Ch 419, CA

COMPANIES – CORPORATE VEIL

Ben Hashem v Al Shayif [2009] 1 FLR 115

Gowers v Gowers [2012] 1 FLR 1040

M v M and Others [2014] 1 FLR 439

Prest v Petrodel Resources Ltd & Others [2013] 2 FLR 732

COMPENSATION

H v H [2014] 2 FLR 1338

Hvorostovsky v Hvorostovsky [2009] 2 FLR 1574

Lauder v Lauder [2007] 2 FLR 802

RP v RP [2007] 1 FLR 2105

CONDUCT

FZ v SZ and Others (Ancillary Relief: Conduct: Valuations) [2011] 1 FLR 64

H v H (Financial Relief: Attempted Murder as Conduct) [2006] 1 FLR 990

M v M (Third Party Subpoena: Financial Conduct) [2006] 2 FLR 1253

Miller v Miller; McFarlane v McFarlane [2006] 1 FLR 1186

S v S (Non-matrimonial Property: Conduct) [2007] 1 FLR 1496

WF v NF [2007] EWHC 3050 (Fam)

CONSENT ORDERS

Edgar v Edgar (1981) 2 FLR 19

Rose v Rose [2002] 1 FLR 978

TW v PL (Agreement) [2014] 2 FLR 106

X v X (Y and Z intervening) [2002] 1 FLR 508

Xydhias v Xydhias [1999] 1 FLR 683

CONTRIBUTIONS

Charman v Charman (No 4) [2007] 1 FLR 1246, CA

G v G (Financial Provision: Equal Division) [2002] 2 FLR 1143

H v H [2010] 1 FLR 1864

Lauder v Lauder [2007] 2 FLR 802 ,

Sorrell v Sorell [2006] 1 FLR 497

White v White [2000] 2 FLR 981

COSTS

Children proceedings

HH v BLW (Appeal: Cost: Proportionality) [2013] 1 FLR 420

Re G (Contact Proceedings: Cost) [2014] 1 FLR 517

MG and JG v JF [2015] EWHC 564 (Fam)

R v R (Costs: Child Case) [1997] 2 FLR 95

Financial

Baker v Rowe [2010] 1 FLR 761

Judge v Judge [2009] 1 FLR 1287

Joy v Joy-Morancho [2015] EWHC 2507 (Fam)

General

Calderbank v Calderbank (1975) FLR Rep 113, CA

Gojkovic v Gojkovic (No 2) [1991] 2 FLR 233

Sears Tooth (a firm) v Payne Hicks Beach (a firm) and others [1997] 2 FLR 116

COST ALLOWANCES – SCHEDULE 1, CHILDREN ACT 1989

CF v KM [2011] 1 FLR 208

Currey v Currey (No 2) [2007] 1 FLR 946

G v G (Child Maintenance: Interim Costs Provision) [2010] 2 FLR 1264

M-T v T [2007] 2 FLR 925

R v F (Schedule One: Child Maintenance: Mother's Costs of Contact Proceedings) [2011] 2 FLR 991

Re PG and TW (No 1) (Child: Financial Provision: Legal Funding) [2014] 1 FLR 508

COSTS ORDERS – SCHEDULE 1, CHILDREN ACT 1989

KS v ND (Schedule 1: Appeal: Costs) [2013] 2 FLR 698

DECLARATION OF MARITAL STATUS

Abbassi v Abbassi and Another [2006] 2 FLR 415

Galloway v Goldstein [2012] 1 FLR 1254

Solovyev v Solovyeva [2014] EWFC 1546

DEPARTURE FROM CAFCASS REPORT

Re J (Children) (Residence: Expert Evidence) [2001] 2 FCR 44

Re P (Custody of Children: Split Custody Order) [1991] 1 FLR 337

Re R (Residence Order) [2010] 1 FLR 509

Re V (Residence: Review) [1995] 2 FLR 1010

DISCLOSURE

Gohil v Gohil [2015] 1 FLR 178 (awaiting Supreme Court decision)

Imerman v Tchenguiz [2010] 2 FLR 814

S v S (Financial Remedies: Non-Disclosure: Materiality) [2014] 2 FLR 89 (awaiting Supreme Court decision)

Tchenguiz-Imerman v Imerman [2012] EWHC 4047 (Fam)

Young v Young [2013] EWHC 3637 (Fam)

DISCLOSURE – CHILDREN PROCEEDINGS

Re A and B (Minors) (No 2) [1995] 1 FLR 351

Re D (Minors) (Conciliation: Disclosure of Information) [1993] 1 FLR 932

DURATION OF THE MARRIAGE/CIVIL PARTNERSHIP

CO v CO (Ancillary Relief: Pre-marriage cohabitation) [2004] 1 FLR 1095

GW v RW (Financial Provision: Departure from Equality) [2003] 2 FLR 108

Miller v Miller; McFarlane v McFarlane [2006] 1 FLR 1186

ENFORCEMENT OF CHILD ARRANGEMENTS ORDERS

Re A (Intractable Contact Dispute: Human Rights Violations) [2014] 1 FLR 1185

Re L-W (Enforcement and Committal: Contact); CPL v CH-W and Others) [2011] 1 FLR 1095

EXPERT EVIDENCE

Re C (A Child) (Procedural Requirements of a Part 25 Application) [2015] EWCA CIV 539

Daniels v Walker (Practice Note) [2000] 1 WLR 1382

Re H-L [2013] 2 FLR 1434

EXPERT EVIDENCE – CHILDREN PROCEEDINGS

JG (A Child) v Legal Services Commission and Others [2013] 2 FLR 1174

Re H-L (Expert Evidence: Test for Permission) [2013] 2 FLR 1434

FACT FINDING

AA v NA and KAB [2010] 2 FLR 1173

Re H (Interim Contact: Domestic Violence Allegations) [2014] 1 FLR 41

Re R (Fact-Finding Hearing) [2009] 2 FLR 83

FINANCIAL COMPENSATION ORDER

Re L-W (Enforcement and Committal: Contact); CPL v CH-W and Others [2010] EWCA Civ 1253

HABITUAL RESIDENCE

Re A (Jurisdiction: Return of Child) [2014] 1 FLR 111

Mercredi v Chaffe [2011] 2 FLR 515

Re G (Abduction: Withdrawal of proceedings) [2008] 2 FLR 351

Re KL (A Child) [2014] 1 FLR 772

Re LC (Reunite: International Child Abduction Centre Intervening) [2014] 1 FLR 1486

HUMAN RIGHTS

Elsholz v Germany [2000] 2 FLR 486

Re C (Direct Contact: Suspension) [2011] 2 FLR 912

S and G v Italy [2000] 2 FLR 771

INJUNCTIONS

Finance

KY v DD (Injunctions) [2012] 2 FLR 200

Mareva Cia Naviera SA v International Bulk carriers SA [1980] 1 All ER 213, CA

ND v KP (Freezing Order: Ex Parte Application) [2011] 2 FLR 662

Shipman v Shipman [1991] 1 FLR 250

UL v BK (Freezing Orders: Safeguards: Standard Examples) [2013] EWHC 1735 (Fam)

Anti suit (*Hemain*)

Bloch v Bloch [2003] 1 FLR 1

Hemain v Hemain [1988] 2 FLR 388, CA

R v R (Divorce: Hemain Injunction) [2005] 1 FLR 386

S v S (Hemain Injunction) [2010] 2 FLR 502

T v T (Hemain Injunction) [2014] 1 FLR 96

INTRACTABLE CONTACT

Re A (Intractable Contact Dispute: Human Rights Violations) [2013] EWCA Civ 1104

Re G (Intractable Contact Dispute) [2014] Fam Law 23

Re H-B (Contact) [2015] EWCA Civ 389

Re M (Intractable Contact Dispute: Interim Care Order) [2003] 2 FLR 636

JURISDICTION – FORUM CONVENIENS

Chai v Peng (No 1) (Estoppel) [2014] EWHC 3519 (Fam) and *Chai v Peng (Jurisdiction) (No 2)* [2014] EWHC 3518 (Fam)

JKN v JCN (Divorce: Forum) [2011] 1 FLR 826

Mittal v Mittal [2014] 1 FLR 1514

Owusu v Jackson (Case C-281/02) [2005] QB 801

T v P (Jurisdiction: Lugano Convention and forum conveniens) [2013] 1 FLR 478

LEGAL SERVICES ORDERS

Chai v Peng (No 2) [2015] 1 FLR 637

AM v SS [2014] EWHC 4380 (Fam)

BN v MA [2013] EWHC 4250 (Fam)

Makarskaya v Korthagin [2013] EWHC 4393 (Fam)

MET v HAT (No 2) [2015] 1 FLR 576

Rubin v Rubin [2014] 2 FLR 1018

LIQUID V ILLIQUID ASSETS

P v P (Financial Relief: Illiquid Assets) [2005] 1 FLR 548

Wells v Wells [2002] 2 FLR 97, CA

LUMP SUMS

Banyard v Banyard [1984] FLR 643

Hamilton v Hamilton [2014] 1 FLR 55

Masefield v Alexander (Lump Sum: Extension of Time) [1995] 1 FLR 100

Milton v Milton [2009] 1 FLR 661, CA

MAINTENANCE PENDING SUIT AND INTERIM COSTS (ALSO SEE LEGAL SERVICE ORDERS ABOVE)

A v A (maintenance pending suit: payment of legal fees) [2001] 1 FLR 377

Chai v Peng [2014] 2 FLR 1189

M v M (Maintenance Pending Suit: Enforcement on Dismissal of Suit) [2009] 1 FLR 790

Moore v Moore [2010] 1 FLR 1413

TL v ML and others (Ancillary Relief: Claim against Assets of Extended Family) [2006] 1 FLR 1263

MARITAL AGREEMENTS

AH v PH (Scandinavian Marriage Settlement) [2014] 2 FLR 251

B v S (Financial Remedy: Marital Property Regime) [2012] 2 FLR 502

F v F (Pre-nuptial Agreement) [2010] 1 FLR 1743

Luckwell v Limata [2014] 2 FLR 168

Radmacher v Granatino [2010] 2 FLR 1900

V v V (Pre-Nuptial Agreement) [2012] 1 FLR 1315

Z v Z (No 2) (Financial Remedy: Marriage Contract) [2012] 1 FLR 1315

NON-MARRIAGE

Dukali v Lamrani [2012] 2 FLR 1099

Galloway v Goldstein [2012] 1 FLR 1254

Sharbatly v Shagroon [2013] 1 FLR 1493

NON-MOLESTATION & OCCUPATION ORDERS

C v C (Non-molestation Order: Jurisdiction) [1998] 1 FLR 554

Chalmers v Johns [1999] 1 FLR 392

JM v CZ [2015] 1 FLR 559

Johnson v Walton [1990] 1 FLR 350

M v W (Non-molestation order: Duration) [2000] 1 FLR 107

Re B-Q (A Child) [2008] EWCA Civ 586

Yemshaw v Hounslow London Borough Council [2011] 1 FLR 1614

PARENTAL RESPONSIBILITY

M v M (Parental Responsibility) [1999] 2 FLR 737

Re C and V (Minors) (Contact: Parental Responsibility Order) [1998] 1 FLR 392

Re D (Contact and parental responsibility: Lesbian mothers and known father) (No 2) [2006] EWHC 2 (Fam)

Re H (Parental Responsibility) [1998] 1 FLR 855, CA

Re M (Parental Responsibility Order) [2014] 1 FLR 339

Re S (Parental Responsibility) [1995] 2 FLR 648, CA

Re W (A Child) [2013] All ER (D) 243 (Feb)

PARENTAL RESPONSIBILITY – TERMINATION

P v D, X, Y, Z [2014] EWHC 2355 (Fam)

CW v SG [2013] 2 FLR 655

Re D (A Child) [2015] 1 FLR 166

Re P (Terminating Parental Responsibility) [1995] 1 FLR 1048

PART III MFPA 1984

Abuchian v Khojah [2015] 2 FLR 153

MA v SK [2015] EWHC 887 (Fam)

Agbaje v Agbaje [2010] 1 FLR 1813

M v W [2015] 1 FLR 465

Traversa v Freddi [2011] 2 FLR 272

Z v A [2012] 2 FLR 667

PENSIONS

Behzadi v Behzadi [2009] 2 FLR 649

H v H (Financial Relief: Pensions) [2010] 2 FLR 173

Martin Dye v Martin Dye [2006] 2 FLR 901, CA

Vaughan v Vaughan [2008] 1 FLR 1108, CA

PERIODICAL PAYMENTS – CHILD

T v T (Financial provision: Private Education) [2006] 1 FLR 903

PERIODICAL PAYMENTS – SPOUSAL

Wright v Wright [2015] EWCA Civ 201

SS v NS [2014] EWHC 4183 (Fam)

H v H [2014] EWCA Civ 1523

C v C (Financial Relief: Short Marriage) [1997] 2 FLR 26

Flavell v Flavell [1997] 1 FLR 353

G v G [2012] 2 FLR 48

Miller v Miller; McFarlane v McFarlane [2006] 1 FLR 1186, HL

POST-SEPARATION ACCRUALS

B v B (Ancillary Relief: Post-Separation Income) [2010] 2 FLR 1214

Evans v Evans [2013] 2 FLR 999

Gordon (formerly Stefanou) v Stefanou [2011] 1 FLR 1582

H v H [2010] 1 FLR 1864

H v W (Cap on Wife's Share of Bonus Payments) [2015] 1 FLR 75

H v W (Cap on Wife's Share of Bonus Payments) (No 2) [2015] 2 FLR 161

S v S (Ancillary Relief after Lengthy Separation) [2007] 1 FLR 2120

SK v WL (Ancillary Relief: Post-Separation Accrual) [2011] 1 FLR 1471

Cooper-Hohn v Hohn [2015] 1 FLR 745

POWER TO MAKE AN ORDER OF COURT'S OWN INITIATIVE

Gloucestershire County Council v P [1999] 2 FLR 61

Re C (Children) [2013] 1 FLR 1089

PRE-MARITAL/INHERITED WEALTH

C v C [2009] 1 FLR 8

Jones v Jones [2011] 1 FLR 1723

K v L (Non-Matrimonial Property: Special Contribution) [2011] 2 FLR 980

N v F (Financial Orders: Pre-Acquired Wealth) [2011] 2 FLR 533

S v S [2014] EWHC 4732 (Fam)

JL v SL [2015] EWHC 360 (Fam)

PROHIBITED STEPS ORDERS

Croydon London Borough Council v A (No 1) [1992] 2 FLR 341

F v R (Contact: Justices' Reasons) [1995] 1 FLR 227

R v Leicestershire Education Authority ex parte C [1991] Fam Law 302

Re H (Prohibited Steps Order) [1995] 1 FLR 638

Re L (A Child) [2013] 1 FLR 430

Re N (A Child: Religion: Jehovah's Witness) [2012] 2 FLR 917

Re PC (Change of Surname) [1997] 2 FLR 730

S v B and Newport City Council; Re K [2007] 1 FLR 1116

SH v MM and RM (Prohibited Steps Order: Abduction) [2012] 1 FLR 837

C v K [2014] EWHC 4125 (Fam)

PROPERTY ORDERS

Birch v Birch [2015] EWCA Civ 833

Curran v Collins [2015] EWCA Civ 404

Arif v Anwar and Rehan [2015] EWHC 124 (Fam)

Carson v Carson (1981) 2 FLR 352

Dinch v Dinch [1987] 2 FLR 162

Mesher v Mesher and Hall [1980] 1 All ER 126, CA

Prest v Petrodel Resources Ltd and Others [2013] 2 FLR 732

Sandford v Sandford [1986] 1 FLR 412

Wicks v Wicks [1998] 1 FLR 470

PUBLICITY

Birmingham City Council v Sarfraz Riaz and Others [2015] EWHC 1857 (Fam)

Re C (Publication of Judgment) [2015] EWCA Civ 500

City and County of Swansea v XZ and Others [2014] EWHC 212 (Fam)

Re J (A Child) [2014] 1 FLR 523

Re P (Enforced Caesarean: Reporting Restrictions) [2014] 2 FLR 410

Re S (Identification: Restrictions on Publication) [2005] 1 FLR 591

RELOCATION

Re R (A Child: Relocation) [2015] EWHC 456 (Fam)

H v F (Relocation) [2014] EWFC 11

K v K (Relocation: Shared Care Arrangement) [2012] 2 FLR 880

Payne v Payne [2001] EWCA Civ 166; [2001] 1 FLR 1052

SCHEDULE 1, CHILDREN ACT APPLICATIONS

Carer's allowance

Re PG and TW (No 2) (Child: Financial Provision) [2014] 1 FLR 923

Scope

Morgan v Hill [2007] 1 FLR 1480

N v C [2013] EWHC 399 (Fam)

PK v BC (Financial Remedies: Schedule 1) [2012] 2 FLR 1426

Re S (Child: Financial Provision) [2005] 2 FLR 94

Dickson v Rennie [2014] EWHC 4306 (Fam)

Re A (A Child) [2014] EWCA Civ 1577

Gap years

A v A (A minor: Financial Provision) [1994] 1 FLR 657

Phillips v Peace [1996] 2 FLR 230

Re N (Payments for Benefit of Child) [2009] 1 FLR 1442

Standard of living

F v G (Child: Financial Provision) [2005] 1 FLR 261

H v C [2009] 2 FLR 1540

J v C [1999] 1 FLR 152

MT v OT (Financial Provision: Costs) [2008] 2 FLR 1311

N v D [2008] 1 FLR 1629

Re P [2003] 2 FLR 865

Separate representation for child

Re S (Unmarried Parent: Financial Provision) [2006] 2 FLR 950

SEARCH ORDERS (ANTON PILLER)

Anton Piller KG v Manufacturing Processes Ltd [1976] Ch 55

Burgess v Burgess [1996] 2 FLR 34

Imerman v Tchenguiz [2010] 2 FLR 814

UL v BK (Freezing Orders: Safeguards: Standard Examples) [2013] EWHC 1735 (Fam)

SECTION 7 REPORTS

Re W (Welfare Reports) [1995] 2 FLR 142

SECTION 91(14) ORDERS

Re C (Litigant in Person: s 91(14) Order) [2009] 2 FLR 1461

Re M (Parental Responsibility Order) [2014] 1 FLR 339

Re P (Section 91(14) Guidelines) (Residence and Religious Heritage) [1999] 2 FLR 573

SHARED CARE (PRIOR TO CHILD ARRANGEMENTS ORDERS)

D v D (Shared Residence Order) [2001] 1 FLR 495

Re A (Joint Residence/Parental Responsibility) [2008] 2 FLR 1593

Re W (Shared Residence Order) [2009] 2 FLR 436

SPECIFIC ISSUE ORDERS

Dawson v Wearmouth [1997] 2 FLR 629

M v M (Specific Issue: Choice of School) [2007] 1 FLR 251

Re C (HIV Test) [1999] 2 FLR 1004

Re C (Welfare of Child: Immunisation) [2003] 2 FLR 1054

Re F (Internal Relocation) [2011] 1 FLR 1382

Re HG (Specific Issue Order: Sterilisation) [1993] 1 FLR 587

Re J (Specific Issue Orders: Child's Religious Upbringing and Circumcision) [2000] 1 FLR 571

Re PC (Change of Surname) [1997] 2 FLR 730

SPECIFIC ISSUE ORDERS – JURISDICTION

EY v RZ [2013] EWHC 4403 (Fam)

Re D (A Minor) (Child: Removal from Jurisdiction) [1992] 1 FLR 637

Re R (Children: Temporary Leave to Remove from Jurisdiction) [2014] 2 FLR 1402

STANDARD OF LIVING

G v G (Financial Remedies: Short Marriage: Trust Assets) [2012] 2 FLR 48

S v S [2008] 2 FLR 113

TIMETABLING

B v B (Minors) (Interviews and Listing Arrangements) [1994] 2 FLR 489, CA

Re A and B (Minors) (No 2) [1995] 1 FLR 351

Re H (Minors) (Welfare Reports) [1990] 2 FLR 172, CA

TOLATA 1996 APPLICATIONS

Jones v Kernott [2012] 1 FLR 45

Oxley v Hiscock [2004] 2 FLR 669

Smith v Bottomley [2014] 1 FLR 626

Stack v Dowden [2007] 1 FLR 1858

Thompson v Hurst [2014] 1 FLR 238

Bagum v Hafiz & Anor [2015] EWCA Civ 801

O'Kelly v Davies [2014] EWCA Civ 1606

TRANSFERRING RESIDENCE IN LIGHT OF REPEATED BREACHES OF ORDERS (PRIOR TO CHILD ARRANGEMENTS ORDERS)

Re A (Residence Order) [2010] 1 FLR 1083

Re C (Residence Order) [2008] 1 FLR 211

Re S (Transfer of Residence) [2011] 1 FLR 1789

TRUSTS

A v A [2007] 2 FLR 467

B v B (Ancillary Relief) [2010] 2 FLR 887

C v C (Ancillary Relief: Trust Fund) [2010] 1 FLR 337

De Bruyne v De Bruyne [2010] 2 FLR 1240

SR v CR (Ancillary Relief: Family Trusts) [2009] 2 FLR

Whaley v Whaley [2012] 1 FLR 735

WISHES AND FEELINGS

M v M (Removal from Jurisdiction) [1993] 1 FCR 5

R (A Child) [2009] EWCA Civ 445 [2010] 1 FLR 509

Re H (A Child) [2014] EWCA Civ 271

WITHOUT NOTICE APPLICATIONS

C (A Child) & Anor v KH [2014] 1 FLR 1239

Croydon LBC v A (No 3) [1992] 2 FLR 350

KY v DD [2012] 2 FLR 200

Re S (Ex Parte Orders) [2001] 1 FLR 308

Re W (Ex Parte Orders) [2000] 2 FLR 927

PART IV

2015–16 TABLES

INCOME TAX AND NATIONAL INSURANCE CONTRIBUTIONS

INCOME TAX ALLOWANCES 2015/16

Personal allowance for people born after 5 April 1948 (1)	£10,600
Income limit for personal allowance	£100,000
Personal allowance for people born between 6 April 1938 and 5 April 1948 (1)(2)	£10,600
Personal allowance for people born before 6 April 1938 (1)(2)	£10,660
Maximum amount of married couple's allowance (born before 6 April 1935) (2)(3)	£8,355
Income limit for the allowances for those born before 6 April 1948	£27,700
Minimum amount of married couple's allowance	£3,220
Blind person's allowance	£2,290

(1) The Personal Allowance reduces where the income is above £100,000 – by £1 for every £2 of income above the £100,000 limit.
(2) These allowances reduce where the income is above the income limit by £1 for every £2 of income above the limit.
(3) Tax relief for the Married Couple's Allowance is given at the rate of 10%.

INCOME TAX BANDS 2015/16

Starting rate for savings only	10%	£0 – 5,000
Basic rate	20%	£0 – £31,785
Higher rate	40%	£31,786 – £150,000
Additional rate	45% from 6 April 2013	Over £150,000

NATIONAL INSURANCE CONTRIBUTIONS: 2007–16

Limits	Year								
	15–16	14–15	13–14	12–13	11–12	10–11	09–10	08–09	07–08
Lower earnings limit, primary class 1	£112	£111	£109	£107	£102	£97	£95	£90	£87
Upper earnings limit, primary class 1	£815	£805	£797	£817	£817	£844	£844	£770	£670
Primary threshold	£155	£153	£149	£146	£139	£110	£110	£105	£100
Secondary threshold	£156	£153	£148	£144	£136	£110	£110	£105	£100
Employees' primary class 1 rate between primary threshold and upper earnings limit	12%	12%	12%	12%	12%	11%	11%	11%	11%

Limits	Year								
	15–16	14–15	13–14	12–13	11–12	10–11	09–10	08–09	07–08
Employees' primary class 1 rate above upper earnings limit	2%	2%	2%	2%	2%	1%	1%	1%	1%
Married women's reduced rate between primary threshold and upper earnings limit	5.85%	5.85%	5.85%	5.85%	5.85%	4.85%	4.85%	4.85%	4.85%
Married women's rate above upper earnings limit	2%	2%	2%	2%	2%	1%	1%	1%	1%
Employers' secondary class 1 rate above secondary threshold	13.8%	13.8%	13.8%	13.8%	13.8%	12.8%	12.8%	12.8%	12.8%
Class 2 rate	£2.80	£2.75	£2.70	£2.65	£2.50	£2.40	£2.40	£2.30	£2.20
Class 2 small earnings exception	Abolished	£5,885	£5,725	£5,595	£5,315	£5,075	£5,075	£4,825	£4,635
Class 2 small profits threshold	£5,965								
Class 3 rate	£14.10	£13.90	£13.55	£13.25	£12.60	£12.05	£12.05	£8.10	£7.80
Class 4 lower profits limit	£8,060	£7,956	£7,755	£7,605	£7,225	£5,715	£5,715	£5,435	£5,225
Class 4 upper profit limit	£42,385	£41,865	£41,450	£42,475	£42,475	£43,875	43,875	40,040	34,840
Class 4 rate between lower profit limit and upper profits limit	9%	9%	9%	9%	9%	8%	8%	8%	8%

GROSS TO NET INCOME CALCULATOR

Gross to net income calculator for employed persons

Gross income (£)	15–16	14–15	13–14	12–13	11–12	10–11	09–10	08–09
1,000	1,000	1,000	1,000	1,000	1,000	1,000	1,000	1,000
2,000	2,000	2,000	2,000	2,000	2,000	2,000	2,000	2,000
3,000	3,000	3,000	3,000	3,000	3,000	3,000	3,000	3,000
4,000	4,000	4,000	4,000	4,000	4,000	4,000	4,000	4,000
5,000	5,000	5,000	5,000	5,000	5,000	5,000	5,000	5,000
6,000	6,000	6,000	6,000	6,000	6,000	5,969	5,960	5,940
7,000	7,000	7,000	7,000	7,000	7,000	6,754	6,754	6,638
8,000	8,000	8,000	8,000	8,000	7,902	7,444	7,444	7,328
9,000	8,887	8,874	9,000	8,652	8,482	8,134	8,134	8,018
10,000	9,767	9,754	9,618	9,332	9,162	8,824	8,824	8,708
11,000	11,567	10,434	10,298	10,012	9,842	9,514	9,514	9,398
12,000	11,240	11,114	10,978	10,692	10,522	10,204	10,204	10,088
13,000	11,927	11,794	11,658	11,372	11,202	10,894	10,894	10,778
14,000	12,607	12,474	12,338	12,052	11,882	11,854	11,854	11,648
15,000	13,287	13,154	13,018	12,732	12,562	12,274	12,274	12,158
16,000	13,967	13,834	13,698	13,412	13,242	12,964	12,964	12,848
17,000	14,647	14,514	14,378	14,092	13,922	13,654	13,654	13,538
18,000	15,327	15,914	15,058	14,772	14,602	14,344	14,344	14,228
19,000	16,007	15,874	15,738	15,452	15,282	15,034	15,034	14,918

Gross income (£)	15–16	14–15	13–14	12–13	11–12	10–11	09–10	08–09
20,000	16,687	16,534	16,418	16,132	15,962	15,724	15,724	15,608
21,000	17,367	17,234	17,098	16,812	16,642	16,414	16,414	16,298
22,000	18,047	17,914	17,778	17,492	17,322	17,104	17,104	16,988
23,000	18,727	18,594	18,458	18,172	18,002	17,794	17,794	17,678
24,000	19,407	19,274	19,138	18,852	18,682	18,484	18,484	18,368
25,000	20,087	19,954	19,818	19,532	19,362	19,174	19,174	19,058
26,000	20,767	20,634	20,498	20,212	20,042	19,864	19,864	19,748
27,000	21,447	21,314	21,178	20,892	20,722	20,554	20,554	29,438
28,000	22,127	21,994	21,858	21,572	21,402	21,244	21,244	21,128
29,000	22,867	22,674	22,538	22,252	22,082	21,934	21,934	21,818
30,000	23,487	23,354	23,218	22,932	22,762	22,624	22,624	22,508
31,000	24,167	24,034	23,898	23,612	23,442	23,314	23,314	23,198
32,000	24,847	24,714	24,578	24,292	24,122	24,004	24,004	23,888
33,000	25,527	25,394	25,258	24,972	24,802	24,694	24,694	24,578
34,000	26,207	26,074	25,938	25,652	25,482	25,384	25,384	25,268
35,000	26,887	26,754	26,618	26,332	26,162	26,074	26,074	25,958
36,000	27,567	27,434	27,298	27,012	26,842	26,764	26,764	26,648
37,000	28,247	28,114	27,978	27,692	27,522	27,454	27,454	27,338
38,000	28,927	28,794	28,658	28,372	28,202	28,144	28,144	28,028
39,000	29,607	29,474	29,338	29,052	28,882	28,834	28,834	28,718
40,000	30,287	30,154	30,018	29,732	29,562	29,524	29,524	29,408
41,000	30,967	30,834	30,698	30,412	30,242	30,214	30,214	30,125
42,000	31,647	31,501	31,325	31,092	30,922	30,904	30,904	30,715
43,000	32,366	32,081	31,903	31,718	31,548	31,594	31,594	31,305
44,000	32,846	32,661	32,483	32,298	32,128	32,271	32,271	31,895
45,000	33,426	33,241	33,063	32,878	32,708	32,861	32,861	32,485
46,000	34,006	33,821	33,643	33,458	33,288	33,451	33,451	33,075
47,000	34,586	34,401	34,223	34,038	33,868	34,041	34,041	33,665
48,000	35,166	34,981	34,803	34,618	34,448	34,631	34,631	34,255
49,000	35,746	35,561	35,383	35,198	35,028	35,221	35,221	34,845
50,000	36,326	36,141	36,963	35,778	35,608	35,811	35,811	35,435
60,000	42,126	41,941	41,763	41,578	41,408	41,711	41,711	41,335
70,000	47,926	47,741	47,563	47,378	47,208	47,611	47,611	47,235
80,000	53,726	53,541	53,363	53,178	53,008	53,511	53,511	53,135
90,000	59,526	59,341	59,163	58,978	58,808	59,411	59,411	59,035
100,000	65,326	65,151	64,963	64,778	64,608	65,311	65,311	64,935
150,000	90,086	90,141	90,187	90,536	90,618	92,221	92,221	94,435
200,000	116,586	116,641	116,687	114,536	114,618	116,721	116,721	123,935
250,000	143,086	143,141	143,187	138,536	138,618	141,221	141,221	153,435
300,000	169,586	169,641	169,687	162,536	162,618	165,721	165,721	182,935

Gross to net income calculator for self-employed persons

Gross income (£)	15–16	14–15	13–14	12–13	11–12	10–11	09–10	08–09
1,000	1,000	1,000	1,000	1,000	1,000	1,000	1,000	1,000
2,000	2,000	2,000	2,000	2,000	2,000	2,000	2,000	2,000
3,000	3,000	3,000	3,000	3,000	3,000	3,000	3,000	3,000
4,000	4,000	4,000	4,000	4,000	4,000	4,000	4,000	4,000
5,000	5,000	5,000	5,000	5,000	5,000	5,000	4,875	4,880
6,000	5,854	5,857	5,860	5,862	5,870	5,852	5,875	5,835
7,000	6,854	6,857	6,860	6,862	6,718	6,667	6,770	6,562
8,000	7,854	7,853	7,838	7,757	7,695	7,387	7,570	7,282
9,000	8,770	8,763	8,748	8,509	8,405	8,107	8,370	8,002
10,000	9,680	9,673	9,546	9,219	9,115	8,827	9,170	8,722
11,000	10,150	10,383	10,256	9,929	9,825	9,547	9,970	9,442
12,000	11,220	11,093	10,966	10,639	10,535	10,267	10,770	10,162
13,000	11,930	11,803	11,676	11,349	11,245	10,987	11,570	10,882
14,000	12,640	12,513	12,386	12,059	11,955	11,707	12,370	11,602
15,000	13,350	13,223	13,096	12,769	12,665	12,427	13,170	12,322
16,000	14,060	13,933	13,806	13,479	13,375	13,147	13,970	13,042
17,000	14,770	14,643	14,516	14,189	14,085	13,867	14,770	13,762
18,000	15,480	15,353	15,226	14,899	14,795	14,587	15,570	14,482
19,000	16,190	16,063	15,936	15,609	15,505	15,307	16,370	15,202
20,000	16,900	16,773	16,646	16,319	16,215	16,027	17,170	15,922
21,000	17,610	17,483	17,356	17,029	16,925	16,747	17,970	16,642
22,000	18,320	18,193	18,066	17,739	17,635	17,467	18,770	17,362
23,000	19,030	18,903	18,726	18,449	18,345	18,187	19,570	18,082
24,000	19,740	19,613	19,486	19,159	19,055	18,907	20,370	18,802
25,000	20,450	20,323	20,196	19,869	19,765	19,627	21,170	19,522
26,000	21,160	21,033	20,906	20,579	20,475	20,347	21,970	20,242
27,000	21,870	21,743	21,616	21,289	21,185	21,067	22,770	20,962
28,000	22,580	22,453	22,326	21,999	21,895	21,787	23,570	21,682
29,000	23,290	23,163	23,036	22,709	22,605	22,507	24,370	22,402
30,000	24,000	23,873	23,746	23,419	23,315	23,227	25,170	23,122
31,000	24,583	24,583	24,456	24,129	24,025	23,947	25,970	23,842
32,000	25,420	25,293	25,166	24,839	24,735	24,667	26,770	24,562
33,000	26,130	26,003	25,876	25,549	25,445	25,387	27,570	25,282
34,000	26,840	26,713	26,586	26,259	26,155	26,107	28,370	26,002
35,000	27,550	27,423	27,296	26,843	26,865	26,827	29,170	26,722
36,000	28,260	28,133	28,005	27,353	27,375	27,547	29,970	27,442
37,000	28,970	28,843	28,715	27,863	27,885	28,267	30,770	28,162
38,000	29,680	29,553	29,425	28,373	28,395	28,987	31,450	28,882
39,000	30,390	30,263	30,135	28,883	28,905	29,707	32,050	29,602
40,000	31,100	30,973	30,845	29,393	29,415	30,427	32,650	30,322
41,000	31,810	31,683	31,556	29,903	29,925	31,217	33,250	31,076
42,000	32,520	32,337	32,156	30,413	30,435	31,867	33,850	31,666
43,000	33,150	32,956	32,774	30,960	30,982	32,457	34,450	32,256
44,000	33,730	33,536	33,354	31,540	31,562	33,047	35,050	32,846
45,000	34,310	34,116	33,934	32,120	32,142	33,881	35,639	33,436

Gross income (£)	15–16	14–15	13–14	12–13	11–12	10–11	09–10	08–09
46,000	34,890	34,696	34,514	32,700	32,722	34,471	36,229	34,026
47,000	35,470	35,276	35,094	33,280	33,302	35,061	36,819	34,616
48,000	36,050	35,856	35,674	33,860	33,882	35,651	37,209	35,206
49,000	36,630	36,436	36,254	34,440	34,462	36,241	37,559	35,796
50,000	37,210	37,016	36,834	35,020	35,042	36,831	38,589	36,386
60,000	43,010	42,816	42,634	40,820	40,842	42,731	44,489	42,286
70,000	48,810	48,616	48,434	46,620	46,642	48,631	50,389	48,186
80,000	54,610	54,416	54,234	52,420	52,442	54,531	56,289	54,086
90,000	60,410	60,216	60,034	58,220	58,242	60,431	62,189	59,986
100,000*	66,210	66,016	65,834	64,020	64,042	66,331	68,089	65,886
150,000	90,970	91,016	94,834	93,020	93,042	93,241	97,589	95,886
200,000	117,470	117,516	117,558	117,020	117,042	117,741	127,089	95,386
250,000	143,970	144,016	114,058	141,020	141,042	142,241	156,589	154,386
300,000	170,470	170,516	170,558	165,020	165,042	166,741	186,089	183,886

OTHER TAX RATES, LIMITS AND RELIEFS

CAPITAL GAINS TAX

Exempt assets

The following are wholly exempt from capital gains tax:

- wasting chattels (eg private motor cars, yachts etc);
- savings certificates and similar non-marketable securities;
- gilt-edged securities (eg Treasury stock);
- qualifying corporate bonds;
- cash (although foreign currency held as an investment is not exempt);
- pension and annuity rights.

Exempt disposals

Some gains arising from the disposal of certain assets are exempt from capital gains tax in particular circumstances; examples of assets which may qualify are:

- main residence;
- non-wasting chattels (valued at less than £6,000);
- debts (disposal by original creditor or his or her personal representative or legatee);
- policies of insurance/life assurance (if sold by original owner);
- SAYE terminal bonuses;
- compensation for personal injury.

Capital gains rate of tax 2015/16

Rates of tax	
Standard rate	18%
Higher rate	28%
Entrepreneurs' relief rate	10%

Capital gains annual allowance 2015/16

Individuals	£11,100
Trusts	£5,500

INHERITANCE TAX

Exempt gifts

Type of gift	Date given	Limits
Between husband & wife	Any time	None
To charity	Any time	None
Lump sum paid out by pension scheme	On death only	None
Annual exemption	Per tax year	£3,000 plus any unused balance from the previous tax year only.
Small gifts	Per tax year	Up to a total value of £250 per person, for any number of people.
Marriage gifts	On marriage	Parents can give £5,000 each, grandparents £2,500 each, others £1,000 each.
Regular gifts	During lifetime	Gift must be funded from income, not from savings.
Any gift to an individual not covered above	During lifetime	Exempt unless donor dies within 7 years of making the gift (see below). Gift must be made without 'strings attached'.

Inheritance tax rates

		2015/16
Nil band		£325,000
Death tax	40%	Excess
Lifetime tax	20%	Excess

Taper relief

Where tax is charged on death on any gift made within 7 years of death, taper relief may apply as follows:

Years before death	0–3	3–4	4–5	5–6	6–7
Percentage taxable on death	100	80	60	40	20

CORPORATION TAX RATES

The Corporation Tax rate for company profits from 1 April 2015 is 20%. It may be possible to obtain deductions or claim tax credits ('reliefs') on Corporation Tax – see further https://www.gov.uk/corporation-tax-rates/allowances-and-reliefs

The rate payable on profits prior to 1 April 2015 depends on the size of the profits (see below).

Rates for financial years starting on 1 April				
Rate	2011	2012	2013	2014
Small profits rate	20%	20%	20%	20%
Small profits rate can be claimed by qualifying companies with profits at a rate not exceeding	£300,000	£300,000	£300,000	£300,000
Marginal Relief Lower Limit	£300,000	£300,000	£300,000	£300,000
Marginal Relief Upper Limit	£1,500,000	£1,500,000	£1,500,000	£1,500,000
Standard fraction	3/200	1/100	3/400	1/400
Main rate of Corporation Tax	26%	24%	23%	21%

STAMP DUTY LAND TAX RATES AND THRESHOLDS

Stamp Duty Land Tax (SDLT) is charged on land and property transactions in the UK. The tax is charged at different rates and has different thresholds for different types of property and different values of transaction.

The tax rate and payment threshold can vary according to whether the property is residential or non-residential, and whether it is a freehold or leasehold. SDLT relief is available for certain kinds of property or transaction.

SDLT rates for residential property

The table below applies for all freehold residential purchases and transfers and the premium paid for a new lease or the assignment of an existing lease. (If the property will be used for both residential and non-residential purposes the rates differ).

New leases

If the transaction involves the purchase of a new lease with a substantial rent there may be an additional SDLT charge to that shown below, based on the rent. See the next section and further table 'SDLT on rent for new leasehold properties (residential)' for more detail.

Residential land or property SDLT rates and thresholds

Purchase price/lease premium or transfer value	SDLT rate
Up to £125,000	Zero
Over £125,000 to £250,000	2%
Over £250,000 to £925,000	5%

Over £925,000 to £1.5 million	10%
Over £1.5 million	12%

SDLT on rent – new residential leasehold purchase

When a new residential lease has a substantial annual rent, SDLT is payable on both of the following, which are calculated separately and then added together:

- the lease premium (purchase price) – see the table above
- the 'net present value' (NPV) of the rent payable

The NPV is based on the value of the total rent over the life of the lease and can be worked out using HMRC's online calculator.

SDLT on rent for new leasehold properties (residential)

Net present value of rent – residential	**SDLT rate**
£0–£150,000	Zero
Over £150,000	1% of the value that exceeds £150,000

FOSTERING ALLOWANCES

Minimum allowances for fostering are now set nationally by the Government. Current and historical figures are set out below.

Recommended fostering allowance per week

2015–2016: Minimum allowances rates

Weekly Rates	Babies	Pre-primary	Primary	11–15	16–17
London	£142	£145	£163	£184	£216
South East	£136	£140	£156	£177	£208
Rest of UK	£123	£126	£139	£159	£185

2014–2015: Minimum allowances rates

Weekly Rates	Babies	Pre-primary	Primary	11–15	16–17
London	£137	£140	£157	£178	£209
South East	£131	£135	£151	£171	£201
Rest of UK	£119	£122	£134	£154	£179

2013–2014: Minimum allowances rates

Weekly Rates	Babies	Pre-primary	Primary	11–15	16–17
London	£135	£140	£157	£178	£209
South East	£129	£133	£142	£167	£197
Rest of UK	£116	£119	£126	£151	£175

Tax-free earnings

A tax free exemption of up to £10,000 per year (less for a shorter period), shared equally among foster carers in the sane household, is available.

This means that you do not pay tax on first £10,000 you make from fostering.

Tax relief

In addition tax relief is available on earnings over £10,000:

Age of child	Tax relief
Under 11	£200 per child per week
Over 11	£250 per child per week

SOCIAL SECURITY BENEFITS

INTRODUCTION

The information below is intended to give a brief overview of the main benefits and tax credits in the state social security system, and to allow you to check benefit rates over the last five years.

Note the following provisos and points:

- Information on each benefit is meant as a simplified summary of the key qualifying conditions; the wording we use does not always correspond precisely to the legislative wording.
- You should be cautious about advising clients to make benefit claims, or lodge appeals, based on the information in this section and, if in doubt, check a reliable and current reference book such as Child Poverty Action Group's *Welfare Benefits and Tax Credits Handbook*, read the wording of the legislation, and preferably refer your client to a benefits specialist.
- It is in the nature of social security legislation that *nearly all* statements as to qualifying conditions have one or more exceptions; often there are exceptions to the exceptions as well – these are omitted here for the sake of brevity.
- All rates given are weekly amounts, except Tax Credits, which are annual figures, and Universal Credit which is monthly.
- For means-tested benefits and tax credits the weekly, monthly or annual rates of benefit are not the whole story: they should be used as part of the whole calculation which will often produce different results because of the effect of income on the final entitlement figures.
- The two new benefits introduced in 2013–2014, Personal Independence Payment and Universal Credit, are now in their third year. PIP replaces Disability Living Allowance for disabled claimants aged 16+ and under 65; no new DLA claims can be made except for children under 16, and existing 16+ DLA claimants are being invited to re-claim under PIP. UC is replacing Income Support, income-based Jobseeker's Allowance, income-related Employment and Support Allowance, Housing Benefit and Tax Credits. UC is being piloted in a number of areas for limited categories of claimant. For many claimants it is not a reality in 2015–16. The conversion of old Incapacity Benefit claims to Employment and Support Allowance is almost complete. However, claimants of both ESA and PIP are experiencing considerable upheaval in terms of proving their level of disability, with long delays a familiar part of the claim process.
- Council Tax Benefit was replaced from 1 April 2013 by local schemes designed and operated independently by each local authority, subject to national minimum standards.
- Since 13 March 2014 the definition of a couple who are not married or civil partners has changed in most social security law to '*living together as a married couple*'.
- The benefits cap operates for those on Housing Benefit or Universal Credit. It means that total benefit income (as defined) cannot exceed a given weekly amount (monthly amount in the case of UC).
- The term 'overlapping benefit' refers to a rule which prevents the duplication of certain benefits in cases where a claimant is on the face of it entitled to more than one. For example, it would not be possible to claim full Carer's Allowance at the same time as a full Widowed Parent's Allowance. Where one exceeds the other in value, then the excess value may be

added to the lower-value of the two available benefits. Note that further, more complex overlapping rules apply when a client has an entitlement to a war disablement pension or war widow's pension.

Disclaimer: this information is intended as a quick reference aid and should not be regarded as a substitute for proper reference books. Do look up the full details of any question that arises when advising about a real-life benefits situation. Most advisers will need to use CPAG's *Welfare Benefits & Tax Credits Handbook*. If there are mistakes, we apologise, and ask you to let us know, but we cannot accept any responsibility for the consequences of any such errors.

MEANS-TESTED BENEFITS

Universal Credit

A brand new flagship scheme to replace means-tested benefits and tax credits for those of working age. Its introduction is running very slowly at present. It is capped at £2167pcm for couples and those with children and £1517pcm for single people without children.

Standard allowances						
	2010–11	**2011–12**	**2012–13**	**2013–14 £ per month**	**2014–15 £ per month**	**2015–16 £ per month**
Single under 25				£246.81	£249.80	£251.77
Single 25+				£311.55	£314.67	£317.82
Couple both under 25				£387.42	£391.29	£395.90
Couple one or both 25+				£489.06	£493.95	£498.89
Elements						
First child				£272.08	£274.58	£277.08
Each other child				£226.67	£229.17	£231.67
Disabled child (lower rate)				£123.62	£124.86	£126.11
Disabled child (higher rate)				£352.92	£362.92	£367.92
Limited capability for work				£123.62	£124.86	£126.11
Limited capability for work-related activity				£303.66	£311.86	£315.60
Carer				£144.70	£148.61	£150.39
Childcare costs – 1 child				up to £532.29	up to £532.29	up to £532.29

Childcare costs – 2+ children				up to £912.50	up to £912.50	up to £912.50

contributory?	overlapping?	dependent additions?	means-tested?	counts as income for means-tested benefits?	counts as income for tax credits?
no	no	yes	yes	not applicable	not applicable

Who gets it?

People under pensionable age, on low incomes who are in or out of work, whether unemployed, carers, those with limited capability for work, single parents or others.

Only certain categories of claimant, and in pilot areas only, are so far able to claim

Other conditions and points

Maximum monthly amounts are offset by income (with some disregards) to produce a monthly entitlement.

Mortgage interest and rent are covered (within limits)

Income Support and income-based Jobseeker's Allowance

For people who have not yet reached the qualifying age for pension credit, in certain eligible groups such as lone parents with a child under five years and carers (Income Support), or those who are out of work and meeting the 'labour-market conditions' by signing on and looking for work (income-based Jobseeker's Allowance); they must also have a low enough income to qualify, and must not exceed the capital limits.

Personal allowances						
	2010–11	2011–12	2012–13	2013–14	2014–15	2015-16
16–24	£51.85	£53.45	£56.25	£56.80	£57.35	£57.90
25+	£65.45	£67.50	£71.00	£71.70	£72.40	£73.10
Lone parent under-18 normal rate	£51.85	£53.45	£56.25	£56.80	£57.35	£57.90
lone parent 18+	£65.45	£67.50	£71.00	£71.70	£72.40	£73.10
couple 18+	£102.75	£105.95	£111.45	£112.55	£113.70	£114.85
child under 20	£57.57*	£62.33*	£64.99*	£65.62*	£66.33*	£66.90*
* only in 'old scheme' Income Support claims – made before 6 April 2004, with no Child Tax Credit						
Premiums						
	2010–11	2011–12	2012–13	2013–14	2014–15	2015–16
Carer	£30.05	£31.00	£32.60	£33.30	£34.20	£34.60
Disability – single	£28.00**	£28.85**	£30.35**	£31.00**	£31.85**	£32.25**
Disability – couple	£39.85**	£41.10**	£43.25**	£44.20**	£45.40**	£45.95**
Enhanced Disability – single	£13.65	£14.05	£14.80	£15.15	£15.55	£15.75
Enhanced Disability – couple	£19.65	£20.25	£21.30	£21.75	£22.35	£22.60

Severe Disability – per qualifying person	£53.65	£55.30	£58.20	£59.50	£61.10	£61.85
Family	£17.40*	£17.40*	£17.40*	£17.40*	£17.45*	£17.45*
Disabled child	£52.08*	£53.62*	£56.63*	£57.89*	£59.50*	£60.06*
Enhanced Disability – child	£21.00*	£21.63*	£22.89*	£23.45*	£24.08*	£24.43*

* only in 'old scheme' Income Support claims – made before 6 April 2004, with no Child Tax Credit
** now largely superseded by Employment and Support Allowance except for claimants getting DLA but capable of work

contributory?	overlapping?	dependent additions?	means-tested?	counts as income for means-tested benefits?	counts as income for tax credits?
no	no	yes	yes	no	no

Who gets IS?

- lone parents with a child under 5
- carers
- a few other eligible groups

Who gets i-b-Jobseeker's Allowance?

- unemployed people who can show they are available for, and actively seeking, work

Other conditions and points

Applicable amounts are determined according to the above figures but must then be offset by amounts of income received by the claimant and any partner – as prescribed.

IS and i-b-JSA will be absorbed into UC

State pension credit

For people on a low enough income to qualify, who have reached the qualifying age – ie, for women: their pensionable age; and, for men: the pensionable age of a woman born the same day as he was.

	2010–11	2011–12	2012–13	2013–14	2014–15	2015-16
Standard minimum guarantee – single	£132.60	£137.35	£142.70	£145.40	£148.35	£151.20
Standard minimum guarantee – couple	£202.40	£209.70	£217.90	£222.05	£226.50	£230.85
Carer	£30.05	£31.00	£32.60	£33.30	£34.20	£34.60
Severe disability – per qualifying person	£53.65	£55.30	£58.20	£59.50	£61.10	£61.85
Savings Credit threshold – single	£98.40	£103.15	£111.80	£115.30	£120.35	£126.50
Savings Credit threshold – couple	£157.25	£164.55	£178.35	£183.90	£192.00	£201.80

Savings Credit maximum – single	£20.52	£20.52	£18.54	£18.06	£16.80	£14.82
Savings Credit maximum – couple	£27.09	£27.09	£23.73	£22.89	£20.70	£17.43

contributory?	**overlapping?**	**dependent additions?**	**means-tested?**	**counts as income for means-tested benefits?**	**counts as income for tax credits?**
no	no	yes	yes	no	No

Who gets it?

- those who have reached the qualifying age for pension credit can get the Guarantee Credit component
- those aged 65 or more (men or women) can also get the Savings Credit component

Other conditions and points

The above figures give weekly rates and maximums but the full calculation is too complex for inclusion here.

State Pension Credit will not be absorbed into UC

Housing Benefit

For people paying rent whose income is low enough for them to qualify. Council Tax Benefit was abolished from April 2013 and is replaced by variable local Council Tax reduction schemes. HB is capped where a person's total benefit income (with some exceptions) exceeds £500pw for couples and those with children and £350pw for single people without children. That may be reduced even further during 2015-2016.

Applicable Amounts

	2009–10	2011–12	2012–13	2013–14	2014–15	2015-16
	Weekly applicable amounts are largely aligned exactly with Income Support (or, for people with limited capability for work, income-related Employment and Support Allowance) – with some exceptions. Amounts in respect of children (ie child personal allowances, family premium, disabled child premium and enhanced disability premium for a child) are included in all relevant cases and unlike in Income Support are not just for pre-2004 old-scheme cases.					

contributory?	**overlapping?**	**dependent additions?**	**means-tested?**	**counts as income for income support?**	**counts as income for tax credits?**
no	no	yes	yes	no	no

Who gets it?

- HB: anyone paying rent on the property they occupy whose income is low enough for them to qualify

Other conditions and points

Those on Income Support, the Guarantee Credit part of State Pension Credit, income-related ESA or income-based Jobseeker's Allowance are passported onto maximum HB.

For others, the amounts payable are determined by measuring excess income above the relevant applicable amounts, and requiring the claimant to pay 65% of this excess towards the eligible rent; HB then meets the remainder of the cost up to limits as follows.

In both passported and non-passported cases, eligible rent in the private sector is usually restricted to what is considered a reasonable market rent, as determined by the Valuation Office Agency. This is called Local Housing Allowance. In the social housing sector the amount of HB is further reduced by a fixed proportion if there are too many bedrooms. This is widely called the bedroom tax.

HB will be absorbed into UC.

Tax Credits

For people who have children and/or are in full-time work, whose income is low enough for them to qualify.

Child tax credit and working tax credit						
		2011–12	2012–13	2013–14	2014–15	2015-16
		Annual figures				
Child tax credit	Family element	£545	£545	£545	£545	£545
	Family element (baby)	£545	*Abolished*			
	Child element	£2,555	£2,690	£2,720	£2,750	£2,780
	Disability element (child)	£2,800	£2,950	£3,015	£3,100	£3,140
	Severe disability element (child)	£1,130	£1,190	£1,220	£1,255	£1,275
Working tax credit	Basic element	£1,920	£1,920	£1,920	£1,940	£1,960
	Couple or lone parent element	£1,950	£1,950	£1,970	£1,990	£2,010
	30-hours element	£790	£790	£790	£800	£810
	Disabled worker element	£2,650	£2,790	£2,855	£2,935	£2,970
	Severe disability element	£1,130	£1,190	£1,220	£1,255	£1,275
	50+ years old element working 16–29 hours	£1,365	*Abolished*			
	50+ element working 30 hours or more	£2,030	*Abolished*			

Contributory?	Overlapping?	Dependent additions?	Means-tested?	Counts as income for income support?	Counts as income for tax credits?
no	no	yes	yes	no	No

Other conditions and points

- the amount of annual entitlement is determined by adding together the appropriate elements and reducing this total by 41% of excess income (if any) above the income threshold of £6,420 (all cases involving working tax credit) or £16,105 (cases involving child tax credit only).
- Tax credits will be absorbed into UC

BENEFITS FOR INCAPACITY OR LIMITED CAPABILITY FOR WORK

Statutory Sick Pay

For employees earning more than earnings threshold who are incapable of work for at least four days.

	2011–12	2012–13	2013–14	2014–15	2015-16
Weekly SSP	£81.60	£85.85	£86.70	£87.55	£88.45
Earnings threshold pw:	£102.00	£107.00	£109.00	£111.00	£112.00
contributory?	**overlapping?**	**dependent additions?**	**means-tested?**	**counts as income for income support?**	**counts as income for tax credits?**
no	no	no	no	yes	Yes

Who gets it?

- people who are in paid employment and
- are not in an 'excluded employees' group
- are off sick
- age 16+ and under qualifying age for pension credit
- for up to 28 weeks

Other conditions and points

Paid by and paid for by the employer.

Not available if an excluded employee.

Not for self-employed.

Example

Jim is a bar-worker at a large pub. He's worked there three years, full time. He goes off sick with a bad back, gets a doctor's note, and the brewery have to pay him SSP, even if his back problem lasts up to 28 weeks. His employer can ask him to keep supplying doctor's notes. He can't automatically be dismissed.

Typical client problems with this benefit

Very few problems.

Employers' reluctance to pay:

My employer just refuses to pay. He says I haven't been with him long enough and that there is a three-month qualifying period.

(Note that these objections to paying would not be correct.)

Employment and Support Allowance

Since October 2008, this replaces Incapacity Benefit and Income Support paid on grounds of disability. It has two versions, contributory and income-related. In either case, a claimant may be in the work-related activity group or the support group. That affects the components they receive and whether they have to do work-related activity.

	2010–11	2011–12	2012–13	2013–14	2014–15	2015-16
basic amounts	largely as for Income Support					
premiums	largely as for Income Support, except no disability premium					
work-related activity component	£25.95	£26.75	£28.15	£28.45	£28.75	£29.05
support component	£31.40	£32.35	£34.05	£34.80	£35.75	£36.20

contributory?	**overlapping?**	**dependent additions?**	**means-tested?**	**counts as income for income support?**	**counts as income for tax credits?**
yes (contributory version); **no** (income-related version)	**yes** (contributory version); **no** (income-related version)	yes	**no** (contributory version); **yes** (income-related version)	n/a	**yes** (contributory version); **no** (income-related version)

Who gets it?

- people who satisfy the Limited Capability for Work Assessment
- income-related Employment and Support Allowance will be absorbed into UC
- the contributory version of Employment and Support Allowance for those in the work-related activity group is only paid for one year

Other conditions and points

Subject to sometimes frequent medical examinations to apply the work capability assessment

May also be subject to attendance at work-focused interview and work-related activity

Typical client problems with this benefit

Employment and Support Allowance withdrawals:

'I had been on ESA happily for 2 years due to my lumbago, then I had to go to a medical. The nurse was hurried and not very sympathetic, and hardly asked any relevant questions. Now only days later I've had a letter saying I'm fit enough to work and I must go and sign on.'

Incapacity Benefit

No new claims: do not advise clients to claim this.

Previously paid to people incapable of work who had paid sufficient NI contributions. It was paid at short-term lower rate for the first 28 weeks, short-term higher rate weeks 29–52, long-term rate week 53 onward. Now abolished and replaced – for new claims – by Employment and Support Allowance from 27 October 2008. Existing claims should switch to ESA by 2015–16.

	2010–11	2011–12	2012–13	2013–14	2014–15	2015-16
short-term: lower	£68.95	£71.10	£74.80	£76.45	£78.50	£79.45
short-term: higher	£81.60	£84.15	£88.55	£90.50	£92.95	£94.05

long-term	£91.40	£94.25	£99.15	£101.35	£104.10	£105.35
Age additions						
to be added when the claimant's incapacity started at ages ...	2010–11	2011–12	2012–13	2013–14	2014–15	2015-16
under 35	£15.00	£13.80	£11.70	£10.70	£11.00	£11.15
35–44	£5.80	£5.60	£5.90	£6.00	£6.15	£6.20

contributory?	overlapping?	dependent additions?	Means-tested?	counts as income for income support?	counts as income for tax credits?
yes	yes	yes	No	yes	yes (except for short-term lower rate IB)

Who gets it?

- people who are incapable of work under the Personal Capability Assessment and
- who have paid sufficient NI contributions

Severe Disablement Allowance

No new claims: do not advise clients to claim this. It is unusual to find still-extant SDA claims.

For those who claimed before April 2001, who are incapable of work, at least 80% disabled, and did not pay enough National Insurance contributions to be entitled to Incapacity Benefit.

	2010–11	2011–12	2012–13	2013–14	2014–15	2015-16
Weekly SDA	£59.45	£62.95	£69.00	£71.80	£73.75	£74.65
Age additions						
to be added when the claimant's incapacity started at ages ...	2010–11	2011–12	2012–13	2013–14	2014–15	2015-16
under 40	£15.00	£13.80	£11.70	£10.70	£11.00	£11.15
40–49	£8.40	£7.10	£5.90	£6.00	£6.15	£6.20
50–59	£5.45	£5.60	£5.90	£6.00	£6.15	£6.20

contributory?	overlapping?	dependent additions?	means-tested?	counts as income for income support?	counts as income for tax credits?
no	yes	yes	yes	yes	No

Who gets it?

- those who were on SDA as of April 2001

Other conditions and points

Abolished for new claims from April 2001: now only payable to those already in receipt as of April 2001. Existing claims have mostly switched to ESA by now.

Typical client problems with this benefit

Few issues arise now, since its abolition.

BENEFITS FOR SEVERE DISABILITY AND CARERS

Personal Independence Payment: mobility component

For people 16+ and under 65 with disabilities, who have significant mobility problems.

				2013–14	2014–15	2015-16
enhanced rate				£55.25	£56.75	£57.45
standard rate				£21.00	£21.55	£21.80

contributory?	**overlapping?**	**dependent additions?**	**means-tested?**	**counts as income for income support?**	**counts as income for tax credits?**
no	no	no	no	no	No

Who gets it?

People aged 16+ and under 65 who score enough points on the schedule as to mobilising range and ability. You need 8+ points to get standard rate or 12+ points for enhanced rate. Points are scored for planning and following a journey and for standing and moving around.

Personal Independence Payment: daily living component

For people 16+ and under 65, who have significant care needs.

				2013–14	2014–15	2015-16
enhanced rate				£79.15	£81.30	£82.30
standard rate				£53.00	£54.45	£55.10

contributory?	**overlapping?**	**dependent additions?**	**means-tested?**	**counts as income for income support?**	**counts as income for tax credits?**
no	no	no	no	no	No

Who gets it?

People who can score enough points on the schedule of points for daily living activities. You need 8+ points to get standard rate or 12+ points for enhanced rate. Points are scored for things like washing, dressing, communicating, budgeting and engaging with other people.

Disability Living Allowance: mobility component

No new claims for those aged 16 or more: do not advise clients aged 16 or more to claim this.

	2010–11	2011–12	2012–13	2013–14	2014–15	2015-16
higher rate	£49.85	£51.40	£54.05	£55.25	£56.75	£57.45
lower rate	£18.95	£19.55	£20.55	£21.00	£21.55	£21.80

contributory?	**overlapping?**	**dependent additions?**	**means-tested?**	**counts as income for income support?**	**counts as income for tax credits?**
no	no	no	no	no	no

Who gets it?

- people aged 3+ (lower rate 5+) and under 65 who

Higher rate:

- are unable or virtually unable to walk, because of a physical problem, or

• the exertion of walking could endanger their health, or • have a severe visual impairment, or • are severely mentally impaired Lower rate: • can walk but ... ... need supervision or guidance in order to ... ... make progress ... ... out of doors ... ... in an unfamiliar place
Other conditions and points For lower rate children must need more supervision/guidance than normal. Three months pre-qualifying and six months post-qualifying periods. For higher rate based on inability or virtual inability to walk, disability must be a physical one.
Example Esther is 42 and has severe arthritis in all parts of her body. She can get about her flat, but only very slowly, with great pain mostly, and only holding onto things such as furniture as she goes. Out of doors she uses a walking frame, but can get 30m along the road on some days. This takes her about four–six minutes each way.
Typical client problems with this benefit Form too long and confusing. DWP underestimation of level of care needs. Clients' exaggeration of their abilities. Misunderstanding of distances. Is the problem physical or non-physical? Fluctuating conditions. The disabling role of pain/discomfort. *'I filled in the form with lots of detail about how far I can get, but it seems that because I was honest and said that some days I can make it to the post office they have penalised me and said I am able to walk. Yet most days I couldn't possibly manage that distance, and when I rarely do, it leaves me unable to do anything at all for a good 48 hours...'*

2015–16 Tables

Disability Living Allowance: care component

For people with disabilities aged under 65 when they first claim, who have significant care needs. No new claims for those aged 16 or more: do not advise clients aged 16 or more to claim this.

	2010–11	2011–12	2012–13	2013–14	2014–15	2015-16
highest rate	£71.40	£73.60	£77.45	£79.15	£81.30	£82.30
middle rate	£47.80	£49.30	£51.85	£53.00	£54.45	£55.10
lowest rate	£18.95	£19.55	£20.55	£21.00	£21.55	£21.80

contributory?	overlapping?	dependent additions?	means-tested?	counts as income for income support?	counts as income for tax credits?
no	no	no	no	no	no

Who gets it? Middle or highest rates: • people over three months and under 65 who • need frequent attention throughout the day, or

- prolonged or repeated attention at night, in connection with bodily functions; or
- who need continual daytime supervision to avoid danger
- or someone watching over them at night to avoid danger

Lowest rate:

- people unable to prepare a cooked main meal or
- who need attention in connection with bodily functions for a substantial portion of the day

Other conditions and points

Middle rate applies where care is needed night or day.

Highest rate applies where care needed night *and* day.

Typical client problems with this benefit

Does the care required have to be given by somebody else?

What is day and what is night?

What is a bodily function?

How frequent is frequent?

How dangerous is the danger?

What about mental health conditions?

Attendance Allowance

For people with disabilities aged 65 or more when they first claim, who have significant care needs.

	2010–11	2011–12	2012–13	2013–14	2014–15	2015-16
higher rate	£71.40	£73.60	£77.45	£79.15	£81.30	£82.30
lower rate	£47.80	£49.30	£51.85	£53.00	£54.45	£55.10

contributory?	overlapping?	dependent additions?	means-tested?	counts as income for income support?	counts as income for tax credits?
no	no	no	no	no	no

Who gets it?
people 65 or more who

- need frequent attention throughout the day, or
- prolonged or repeated attention at night, in connection with bodily functions; or
- who need continual daytime supervision to avoid danger,
- or someone watching over them at night to avoid danger

Other conditions and points

Lower rate applies where care is needed night or day.

Higher rate applies where care is needed night *and* day.

Six months pre-qualifying period.

No upper age limit.

Example

Violet is 89, suffers from severe short-term memory problems and lapses of awareness; and now needs someone around nearly all the time by day in her sheltered flat. This is in order to help her out of bed, get dressed, get washed, help her use the toilet, eat and take her pills; and also to make sure she is safe. At night she sleeps soundly and can call the warden with her emergency cord if necessary (she hardly ever has to).

Typical client problems with this benefit

See above under DLA Care Component.

'Why can't I get anything for mobility problems just because I'm so old?'

Carer's Allowance

For carers of someone getting PIP Daily Living Component (either rate), DLA Care Component (middle or highest rates), or Attendance Allowance, who do not work full time and who give regular and substantial amounts of caring.

	2010–11	2011–12	2012–13	2013–14	2014–15	2015-16
Weekly rate	£53.90	£55.55	£58.45	£59.75	£61.35	£62.10

contributory?	overlapping?	dependent additions?	means-tested?	counts as income for income support?	counts as income for tax credits?
no	yes	yes	no	yes	yes

Who gets it?

- people aged 16+
- looking after someone getting DLA Care Component Highest/Middle rate, PIP Daily Living Component or Attendance Allowance,
- giving 35 hours a week care, and
- not earning more than the earnings threshold (currently £102pw) and
- not in full-time education

Other conditions and points

Breaks in caring of up to four weeks in any six-month period are allowed.

Example

Janet Tregear is 58 and spends most days looking after her elderly mother, Violet. Some days she shares the caring responsibility with her brother Derek. Janet does not do any paid work, though her husband Rod does.

Typical client problems with this benefit

Impact of the earnings rule.

Disabled person comes off PIP (DL component), DLA Care or AA, or DLA Care goes down to lowest rate: CA ends.

Disabled person dies: CA ends after 8 weeks

Two carers both doing at least 35 hours' care pw for one person and both wanting to claim CA (only one of them may).

'My earnings in a shop went over the limit for about 2 months during the Christmas period when work was very busy. I didn't tell the DWP and now they have found out. They want to go back over my last 5 years' wageslips to see if there were other times I should have told them. I'm really worried it's going to land me with a bill for thousands of pounds'

OTHER BENEFITS

Industrial Injuries Disablement Benefit

For those who have a disablement of at least 14% through an industrial injury or disease.

depending on percentage disablement sliding scale up to	2010–11	2011–12	2012–13	2013–14	2014–15	2015-16
lowest level (14% disablement)	£29.16	£30.06	£31.62	£32.32	£33.20	£33.60
highest level (100% disablement)	£145.80	£150.30	£158.10	£161.60	£166.00	£168.00

contributory?	overlapping?	dependent additions?	means-tested?	counts as income for income support?	counts as income for tax credits?
no	no	no	no	yes	no

Who gets it?

- people with an industrial injury or
- prescribed industrial disease
- with long-term disablement of at least 14%

Other conditions and points

There are a number of obsolete additions to IIDB, such as reduced earnings allowance, which some people still get due to transitional protection.

You must have been an employed earner.

If an industrial disease it must correspond with the prescribed list; so must the job that the claimant was in when disease was contracted.

Under-18s get lower rates.

Example

Serkan worked in a financial organisation inputting data into a computer using a keyboard. Because of the way staff workstations were set up, Serkan ended up with severe repetition strain injuries in both his wrists. As his loss of faculty is classed as 19%, he is entitled to the minimum £33.20 rate of IIDB.

Typical client problems with this benefit

Too low a percentage assessment: '*I have been assessed as 13% disabled by my industrial hearing loss. This means I don't qualify for IIDB at all. What can I do about this?*'

Wrong job: '*I incurred hearing loss after working 20 years on oil rig engines. The DWP say this doesn't count as a "ship's engine room" so they won't pay me IIDB.*'

Contribution-based Jobseeker's Allowance

For people who become unemployed having recently paid National Insurance contributions.

aged	2010–11	2011–12	2012–13	2013–14	2014–15	2015-16
under 25	£51.85	£53.45	£56.25	£56.80	£57.35	£57.90
25+	£65.45	£67.50	£71.00	£71.70	£72.40	£73.10

contributory?	overlapping?	dependent additions?	means-tested?	counts as income for income support?	counts as income for tax credits?
yes	yes	no	no	yes	yes

Who gets it?
people who are

- unemployed
- available for work and
- actively seeking work, and
- who have paid enough National Insurance contributions

Other conditions and points

Amount received is less any part-time earnings, and pensions.

Paid for 6 months only.

Example

Lou Shook Ching is a solicitor who has just been made redundant. She is unemployed to start with, following her loss of work. She has worked full time for the last seven years at the same firm. She should get 26 weeks' JSA.

Typical client problems with this benefit
Failure to take up a job offer, or to job seek sufficiently – leading to very heavy sanctions.
Satisfying the labour market conditions.
Jobcentre imposes over-stringent jobseeking requirements.
Low take-up among well-off groups.
Additional DWP pressure to find work after 13 weeks' unemployment.
'There's no way I can afford a season ticket to get to Chippenham every day out of the wages I'm being offered, yet the Jobcentre Plus say that if I don't take the job they'll sanction me ***and*** *prevent me getting benefit on a fresh claim as well.'*

Child Benefit

For people who have children with whom they live and for whom they are responsible.

	2010–11	2011–12	2012–13	2013–14	2014–15	2015-16
first child	£20.30	£20.30	£20.30	£20.30	£20.50	£20.70
each other child	£13.40	£13.40	£13.40	£13.40	£13.55	£13.70

contributory?	**overlapping?**	**dependent additions?**	**means-tested?**	**counts as income for income support?**	**counts as income for tax credits?**
no	No	no	no	no (in 'new scheme' Income Support); yes (for 'old-scheme' IS)	no

Example
Leslie and Pete have two children. They get one higher rate award and one lower rate award of Child Benefit, payable to Leslie. Later they split up; the children both live with Leslie, so she carries on receiving both lots of Child Benefit

Typical client problems with this benefit
Competing claims: '*Since my wife and I split up our children spend half the time with her and half the time with me. But she still gets the child benefit for both of them. This isn't fair because it stops me getting income support as a lone parent.'*
Coming from abroad: *'as we're subject to immigration control they say I can't get any Child Benefit yet.'*
For people with income of £50,000 or more in a tax year, although CB is paid as normal, income tax is adjusted so as to reduce or eliminate the value of the CB as income rises to £60,000.

Statutory Maternity Pay, Statutory Paternity Pay and Statutory Adoption Pay

For women employees on at least £111 per week who are in the SMP-payable maternity period (39 weeks), men in the paternity period (two weeks and further extended period after mother returns to work), or those who are adopting.

	2010–11	2011–12	2012–13	2013–14	2014–15	2015-16
SMP for 6 weeks	90% earnings	90% earnings	90% earnings	90% earnings	90% earnings	90% earnings
then SMP for 33 weeks	£124.88	£128.73	£135.45	£136.78	£138.18	£139.58

SPP SAP	£124.88	£128.73	£135.45	£136.78	£138.18	£139.58
contributory?	**overlapping?**	**dependent additions?**	**means-tested?**	**counts as income for income support?**	**counts as income for tax credits?**
no	no	no	no	yes	yes – excess over £100pw

Who gets SMP?

- women expecting a baby in the next 11 weeks or who have given birth and are still within an overall 39-week maternity period
- who worked in their present job for at least 26 weeks ending in the 15th week before the due date
- earning more than earnings threshold (£112pw)

Who gets SPP?

- those whose spouse, civil partner or partner recently gave birth or adopted
- available for 2 weeks
- additional SPP also now available for fathers taking time off when mother goes back to work within the maternity period

Who gets SAP?

those adopting a child

available for 26 weeks

Other conditions and points

Paid by the employer.

Example
Amina worked in her present job for the last 2 years. Now she is pregnant; her baby is due in three months' time. Once the expected week of birth is 11 weeks away, she can take maternity leave and claim SMP.

Typical client problems with this benefit
Not many problems.
Employer reluctance to pay: '*My employer says he isn't obliged to pay me SMP, and that he'll dismiss me if I take the matter further.*'

Maternity Allowance

For women during the maternity period who cannot get Statutory Maternity Pay.

	2010–11	2011–12	2012–13	2013–14	2014–15	2015-16
standard rate	£124.88	£128.73	£135.45	£136.78	£138.18	£139.58

contributory?	**overlapping?**	**dependent additions?**	**means-tested?**	**counts as income for income support?**	**counts as income for tax credits?**
no	yes	yes	no	yes	No

Who gets it?
women with 11 weeks or less to go before the birth

- who worked for at least 26 weeks ...
- for at least £30pw in 13 of those weeks ...
- during the 66 weeks before the due date
- and who are not working during maternity period

Other conditions and points

Stays in payment for 39 weeks.

Example Baljit has worked part time, earning between £50 and £150 pw, for the last three years, often changing jobs every few months. Now she is pregnant; her expected date of delivery is in 10 weeks' time. Baljit's current employer says she cannot get SMP from her because the job has only lasted three weeks so far.
Typical client problems with this benefit Few problems arise. Occasional difficulties working out qualifying work weeks: just use a calendar!

Bereavement Payment

A single payment for those who have been widowed.

	2010–11	2011–12	2012–13	2013–14	2014–15	2015-16
	£2,000	£2,000	£2,000	£2,000	£2,000	£2,000

contributory?	overlapping?	dependent additions?	means-tested?	counts as capital for income support?	counts as income-generating capital for tax credits?
yes	no	no	no	yes	yes

Who gets it? • those widowed whilst under 60 • whose late spouse or civil partner paid enough National Insurance contributions • available for survivors in same-sex marriages just as in opposite-sex ones
Other conditions and points NI conditions very easy to meet Must be claimed within 12 months of the death.
Example Soniya's wife Jayne dies. Soniya has one year in which to claim her bereavement payment. Jayne was 32 when she died, and had worked full time continuously since she left school at age 18. She paid sufficient contributions in at least one tax year, so satisfies the NI condition for BP, so Soniya gets her payment.
Typical client problems with this benefit Occasional failure to claim in time (now better, with longer claim period) – no solution to this problem. Client may need NI conditions explained.

Bereavement Allowance

For those who have been widowed, are still single, and whose late spouse or civil partner paid enough National Insurance.

	2010–11	2011–12	2012–13	2013–14	2014–15	2015-16
maximum rate, with sliding age-related reductions if under 55	£97.65	£100.70	£105.95	£108.30	£111.20	£112.55

contributory?	overlapping?	dependent additions?	means-tested?	counts as income for income support?	counts as income for tax credits?
yes	yes	yes	no	yes	yes

2015–16 Tables

Who gets it?

- those widowed between age 45 and pensionable age
- and still under pensionable age
- whose late spouse/civil partner paid enough National Insurance contributions
- and who is still single
- available for survivors in same-sex marriages just as in opposite-sex ones

Other conditions and points

Lasts for 52 weeks from death of spouse/civil partner.

Unmarried partners don't qualify.

NI conditions waived if spouse/civil partner died from industrial injury or disease.

Ends if you remarry or re-civil-partner.

Suspended if you re-partner (not married or civil partners).

Example
Lucas' wife Marta died in May, from cancer. She was 56; he's 54. She'd worked full-time as a nurse in the UK since she was 36. Since she only worked 18 of the 36 requisite years out of her working life of 40 years, Lucas is entitled to a 50% rate of Bereavement Allowance

Typical client problems with this benefit

Few problems.

Clients may need NI conditions worked out and explained.

Sometimes non-entitlement due to re-partnering is an issue, especially if client hasn't re-married but cohabitation is alleged.

Widowed Parent's Allowance

For those who have been widowed, have children, are still single, and whose late spouse/civil partner paid enough National Insurance.

	2010–11	2011–12	2012–13	2013–14	2014–15	2015-16
	£97.65	£100.70	£105.95	£108.30	£111.20	£112.55

contributory?	overlapping?	dependent additions?	means-tested?	counts as income for income support?	counts as income for tax credits?
yes	yes	yes	no	yes	yes

Who gets it?

- those under pensionable age
- widowed whilst
- entitled to Child Benefit for, and living with, one or more children, or
- pregnant by late husband or
- living with spouse at time of death and pregnant by artificial insemination, and
- whose late spouse/civil partner paid enough National Insurance contributions
- available for survivors in same-sex marriages just as in opposite-sex ones

Other conditions and points

Ends if you remarry or enter a civil partnership.

Suspended if you re-partner other than marriage or civil partnership.

Example
Lisa's husband Will dies in April. They have two children. Will was 32 when he died, and had worked full time continuously since he left school at age 18. His working life was 16 years (from 16 to age at death); to get a full record he must have contributed sufficiently in 14 of those years. He satisfies this condition, so Lisa gets WPA.

Typical client problems with this benefit

As for Bereavement Allowance.

Some complexity with definition of qualifying child – but problems rare.

Retirement Pension

For those who have reached pensionable age and paid enough National Insurance during their working life.

	2010–11	2011–12	2012–13	2013–14	2014–15	2015–16
main category A rate; category B for surviving spouse or civil partner	£97.65	£102.15	£107.45	£110.15	£113.10	£115.95
category B for spouses and civil partners; category D for over-80s	£58.50	£61.20	£64.40	£66.00	£67.80	£69.50

contributory?	overlapping?	dependent additions?	means-tested?	counts as income for income support?	counts as income for tax credits?
yes	yes	yes	no	yes	yes

Who gets it?

Category A:

- men and women who have reached pensionable age
- who paid sufficient National Insurance contributions

Category B:

- married person or civil partner who has reached pensionable age
- whose spouse or civil partner is over pensionable age

Category B also for some widows, widowers and surviving civil partners

Other conditions and points

Can be deferred in return for increase in its value or a lump sum.

Entitlement is regardless of whether working or not.

Pensionable age is 60 for women born before 6 April 1950, rising for those born after that; 65 for men.

Note that major reforms creating a single-rate State Retirement Pension will affect those reaching pensionable age from April 2016.

Example

Albert worked from age 20 to age 65, then waited a year before claiming retirement pension. He has a full NI record, having worked more than the 30 requisite years. As he has deferred for a year his weekly entitlement is enhanced with an extra amount for life.

Typical client problems with this benefit: very few problems arise.

Clients may need advice about deferring (don't advise yes or no, just give them the facts).

'What pension will I get if I divorce?'

'I'm a 56-year-old woman: do I need to carry on paying NI in order to get a full pension?'

'How do I claim my pension?'

'Can I claim in advance?'

RETAIL PRICE INDEX AND CONSUMER PRICE INDEX

RETAIL PRICE INDEX

Year	Jan	Feb	Mar	Apr	May	Jun	Jul	Aug	Sep	Oct	Nov	Dec
1967	15.7	15.7	15.7	15.8	15.8	15.9	15.85	15.7	15.7	15.8	15.9	16.0
1968	16.1	16.2	16.2	16.5	16.5	16.6	16.6	16.6	16.6	16.7	16.8	17.0
1969	17.1	17.2	17.2	17.4	17.4	17.5	17.5	17.4	17.8	17.6	17.6	17.8
1970	17.9	18.0	18.1	18.4	18.4	18.5	18.6	18.6	18.7	18.9	19.0	19.2
1971	19.4	19.5	19.7	20.1	20.2	20.4	20.5	20.5	20.6	20.7	20.8	20.9
1972	21.0	21.1	21.2	21.3	21.5	21.6	21.7	21.9	22.0	22.3	22.4	22.5
1973	22.7	22.8	23.0	23.4	23.6	23.6	23.8	23.8	24.0	24.6	24.7	24.9
1974	25.6	25.8	26.0	26.9	27.3	27.6	27.8	27.8	28.1	28.7	29.2	29.7
1975	30.4	30.9	31.5	32.7	34.1	34.8	35.1	35.1	35.6	36.1	36.6	37.1
1976	37.5	38.0	38.2	38.9	39.3	39.5	39.6	40.1	40.7	41.4	42.0	42.6
1977	43.7	44.1	44.6	45.7	46.1	46.5	46.6	46.8	47.1	47.3	47.5	47.8
1978	48.0	48.3	48.6	49.3	49.6	50.0	50.2	50.6	50.8	51.0	51.3	51.8
1979	52.5	53.0	53.4	54.3	54.7	55.7	58.1	58.5	59.1	59.7	60.3	60.7
1980	62.2	63.1	63.9	66.1	66.7	67.3	67.9	68.1	68.5	68.9	69.5	69.9
1981	70.3	70.9	72.0	74.1	74.6	75.0	75.3	75.9	76.3	77.0	77.8	78.3
1982	78.7	78.8	79.4	81.0	81.6	81.9	81.9	81.9	81.9	82.3	82.7	82.5
1983	82.6	83.0	83.1	84.3	84.6	84.8	85.3	85.7	86.1	86.4	86.7	86.9
1984	86.8	87.2	87.5	88.6	89.0	89.2	89.1	89.9	90.1	90.7	91.0	90.9
1985	91.2	91.9	92.8	94.8	95.2	95.4	95.2	95.5	95.4	95.6	95.9	96.1
1986	96.3	96.6	96.7	97.7	97.9	97.8	97.5	97.8	98.3	98.5	99.3	99.6
1987	100.0	100.4	100.6	101.8	101.9	101.9	108.7	102.1	102.4	102.9	103.4	103.3
1988	103.3	103.7	104.1	105.8	106.2	106.6	106.7	107.9	108.4	109.5	110.0	110.3
1989	111.0	111.8	112.3	114.3	115.0	115.4	115.5	115.8	116.6	117.5	118.5	118.8
1990	119.5	120.2	121.4	125.1	126.2	126.7	126.8	128.1	129.3	130.3	130.0	129.9
1991	130.2	130.9	131.4	133.1	133.5	134.1	133.8	134.1	134.6	135.1	135.6	135.7
1992	135.6	136.3	136.7	138.8	139.3	139.3	138.8	138.9	139.4	139.9	139.7	139.2
1993	137.9	138.8	139.3	140.6	141.1	141.0	140.7	141.3	141.9	141.8	141.6	141.9
1994	141.3	142.1	142.5	144.2	144.7	144.7	144.0	144.7	145.0	145.2	145.3	146.0
1995	146.0	146.9	147.5	149.0	149.6	149.8	149.1	149.9	150.6	149.8	149.8	150.7
1996	150.2	150.9	151.5	152.6	152.9	153.0	152.4	153.1	153.8	153.8	153.9	154.4
1997	154.4	155.0	155.4	156.3	156.9	157.5	157.5	158.5	159.3	159.5	159.6	160.0
1998	159.5	160.3	160.8	162.6	163.5	163.4	163.0	163.7	164.4	164.5	164.4	164.4
1999	163.4	163.7	164.1	165.2	165.6	165.6	165.1	165.5	166.2	166.5	166.7	167.3
2000	166.6	167.5	168.4	170.1	170.7	171.1	170.5	170.5	171.7	171.6	172.1	172.2
2001	171.1	172.0	172.2	173.1	174.2	174.4	173.3	184.0	174.6	174.3	173.6	173.4
2002	173.3	173.8	174.5	175.7	176.2	176.2	175.9	176.4	177.6	177.9	178.2	178.5
2003	178.4	179.3	179.9	181.2	181.5	181.3	181.3	181.6	182.5	182.6	182.7	183.5
2004	183.1	183.8	184.6	185.7	186.5	186.8	186.8	187.4	188.1	188.6	189.0	189.9
2005	188.9	189.6	190.5	191.6	192.0	192.2	192.2	192.6	193.1	193.3	193.6	194.1

Year	Jan	Feb	Mar	Apr	May	Jun	Jul	Aug	Sep	Oct	Nov	Dec
2006	193.4	194.2	195	196.5	197.7	198.5	198.5	199.2	200.1	200.4	201.1	202.7
2007	201.6	203.1	204.4	205.4	206.2	207.3	206.1	207.3	208.0	208.9	209.7	210.9
2008	209.8	211.4	212.1	214.0	215.1	216.8	216.5	217.2	218.4	217.7	216.0	212.9
2009	210.1	211.4	211.3	211.5	212.8	213.4	213.4	214.4	215.3	216	216.6	218
2010	217.9	219.2	220.7	222.8	223.6	224.1	223.6	224.5	225.3	225.8	226.8	228.4
2011	229.0	231.3	232.5	234.4	235.2	235.5	234.7	236.1	237.9	238.0	238.5	239.4
2012	238.0	239.9	240.8	242.5	242.4	241.8	242.1	243.0	244.2	245.6	245.6	246.8
2013	245.8	247.6	248.7	249.5	250	249.7	249.7	251	251.9	251.9	252.1	253.4
2014	252.6	254.2	254.8	255.7	255.9	256.3	256.0	257.0	257.6	252.7	257.1	257.5
2015	255.4	256.7	257.1	258.0	258.5	258.9	258.6	259.8				

CONSUMER PRICE INDEX

Year	Jan	Feb	Mar	Apr	May	Jun	Jul	Aug	Sep	Oct	Nov	Dec	Ann
2015	127.1	127.4	127.6	128.0	128.2	128.2	128.0	128.4					
2014	126.7	127.3	127.7	128.1	128	128.3	127.8	128.3	128.4	128.5	128.2	128.2	127.9
2013	124.4	125.2	125.6	125.9	126.1	125.9	125.8	126.3	126.8	126.9	127	127.5	126.1
2012	121.1	121.8	122.2	122.9	122.8	122.3	122.5	123.1	123.5	124.2	124.4	125	123
2011	116.9	117.8	118.1	119.3	119.5	119.4	119.4	120.1	120.9	121	121.2	121.7	119.6
2010	112.4	112.9	113.5	114.2	114.4	114.6	114.3	114.9	114.9	115.2	115.6	116.8	114.4
2009	108.7	109.6	109.8	110.1	110.7	111	110.9	111.4	111.5	111.7	112	112.6	110.8
2008	105.5	106.3	106.7	107.6	108.3	109	109	109.7	110.3	110	109.9	109.5	108.4
2007	103.2	103.7	104.2	104.5	104.8	105	104.4	104.7	104.8	105.3	105.6	106.2	104.7
2006	100.5	100.9	101.1	101.7	102.2	102.5	102.5	102.9	103	103.2	103.4	104	102.3
2005	98.6	98.8	99.3	99.7	100	100	100.1	100.4	100.6	100.7	100.7	101	99.9
2004	97	97.2	97.4	97.8	98.1	98.1	97.8	98.1	98.2	98.4	98.6	99.1	97.9

HOUSE PRICE INDEX

Reproduced below is the Halifax House Price Index, which has been published annually since 1984. There are many house price indices available including those produced by the Royal Institute of Chartered Surveyors, the *Financial Times*, Nationwide Building Society and the Land Registry.

Halifax House Price Index: all houses 1983 onwards

Year	Region	Index	% Change	Std Price
1983	North	100.0	.	25,232
1983	Yorks&Humb	100.0	.	23,090
1983	N.West	100.0	.	25,578
1983	E.Mids	100.0	.	26,138
1983	W.Mids	100.0	.	28,223
1983	E.Ang	100.0	.	30,086
1983	Wales	100.0	.	25,878
1983	S.West	100.0	.	33,064
1983	S.East	100.0	.	40,590
1983	Gr.Lon	100.0	.	39,818
1983	N.Ire	100.0	.	25,715
1983	Scot	100.0	.	28,927
1983	U.K.	100.0	.	30,898
1984	North	104.8	4.8	26,432
1984	Yorks&Humb	106.1	6.1	24,491
1984	N.West	103.9	3.9	26,580
1984	E.Mids	106.9	6.9	27,941
1984	W.Mids	103.9	3.9	29,319
1984	E.Ang	108.4	8.4	32,612
1984	Wales	104.5	4.5	27,034
1984	S.West	106.3	6.3	35,151
1984	S.East	109.7	9.7	44,532
1984	Gr.Lon	111.6	11.6	44,446
1984	N.Ire	107.9	7.9	27,755
1984	Scot	109.1	9.1	31,545
1984	U.K.	107.2	7.2	33,117
1985	North	109.6	4.6	27,659
1985	Yorks&Humb	112.0	5.6	25,856
1985	N.West	110.1	6.0	28,165
1985	E.Mids	116.6	9.1	30,476
1985	W.Mids	109.7	5.6	30,957
1985	E.Ang	121.2	11.8	36,476
1985	Wales	111.1	6.3	28,738
1985	S.West	117.7	10.7	38,904
1985	S.East	123.9	13.0	50,302
1985	Gr.Lon	131.2	17.6	52,253

Year	Region	Index	% Change	Std Price
1985	N.Ire	114.1	5.7	29,350
1985	Scot	115.9	6.3	33,523
1985	U.K.	117.0	9.1	36,145
1986	North	114.5	4.5	28,890
1986	Yorks&Humb	119.6	6.8	27,624
1986	N.West	118.9	8.0	30,415
1986	E.Mids	126.8	8.7	33,133
1986	W.Mids	119.4	8.9	33,704
1986	E.Ang	138.9	14.6	41,796
1986	Wales	118.3	6.6	30,625
1986	S.West	131.6	11.8	43,505
1986	S.East	144.3	16.5	58,578
1986	Gr.Lon	159.6	21.6	63,562
1986	N.Ire	121.4	6.4	31,230
1986	Scot	119.9	3.4	34,672
1986	U.K.	129.9	11.0	40,126
1987	North	122.0	6.5	30,779
1987	Yorks&Humb	130.5	9.1	30,130
1987	N.West	127.9	7.6	32,717
1987	E.Mids	145.2	14.6	37,958
1987	W.Mids	136.9	14.6	38,638
1987	E.Ang	174.1	25.3	52,370
1987	Wales	130.4	10.2	33,741
1987	S.West	158.1	20.2	52,281
1987	S.East	181.0	25.4	73,475
1987	Gr.Lon	200.6	25.7	79,878
1987	N.Ire	121.5	0.1	31,255
1987	Scot	126.8	5.8	36,666
1987	U.K.	149.9	15.4	46,315
1988	North	136.7	12.1	34,492
1988	Yorks&Humb	155.0	18.8	35,791
1988	N.West	149.0	16.5	38,119
1988	E.Mids	187.0	28.8	48,886
1988	W.Mids	185.8	35.7	52,427
1988	E.Ang	248.9	43.0	74,889
1988	Wales	162.3	24.5	42,001
1988	S.West	217.6	37.6	71,959
1988	S.East	232.4	28.4	94,337
1988	Gr.Lon	245.3	22.3	97,683
1988	N.Ire	126.7	4.2	32,578
1988	Scot	139.7	10.2	40,410
1988	U.K.	184.8	23.3	57,087
1989	North	182.8	33.7	46,119
1989	Yorks&Humb	222.7	43.6	51,414
1989	N.West	202.0	35.5	51,667
1989	E.Mids	243.2	30.0	63,564
1989	W.Mids	240.7	29.6	67,930
1989	E.Ang	255.5	2.6	76,855
1989	Wales	215.5	32.8	55,766
1989	S.West	242.7	11.5	80,234
1989	S.East	244.3	5.1	99,148

Year	Region	Index	% Change	Std Price
1989	Gr.Lon	251.1	2.3	99,976
1989	N.Ire	130.6	3.1	33,596
1989	Scot	165.0	18.1	47,737
1989	U.K.	223.1	20.8	68,946
1990	North	207.7	13.6	52,408
1990	Yorks&Humb	237.5	6.6	54,832
1990	N.West	227.4	12.6	58,175
1990	E.Mids	234.4	-3.6	61,271
1990	W.Mids	238.0	-1.1	67,160
1990	E.Ang	225.8	-12.0	67,919
1990	Wales	219.6	1.9	56,827
1990	S.West	221.8	-8.6	73,332
1990	S.East	224.5	-8.1	91,134
1990	Gr.Lon	236.6	-5.8	94,204
1990	N.Ire	132.1	1.1	33,975
1990	Scot	182.1	10.4	52,686
1990	U.K.	223.2	0.0	68,950
1991	North	213.5	2.8	53,866
1991	Yorks&Humb	240.4	1.2	55,513
1991	N.West	236.3	3.9	60,451
1991	E.Mids	227.9	-2.8	59,571
1991	W.Mids	240.4	1.0	67,840
1991	E.Ang	214.4	-5.0	64,509
1991	Wales	217.1	-1.1	56,188
1991	S.West	210.4	-5.1	69,557
1991	S.East	210.8	-6.1	85,569
1991	Gr.Lon	222.9	-5.8	88,737
1991	N.Ire	146.9	11.2	37,776
1991	Scot	192.8	5.9	55,785
1991	U.K.	220.5	-1.2	68,130
1992	North	210.1	-1.6	53,001
1992	Yorks&Humb	231.9	-3.6	53,541
1992	N.West	226.1	-4.3	57,828
1992	E.Mids	214.4	-5.9	56,034
1992	W.Mids	229.4	-4.6	64,735
1992	E.Ang	198.5	-7.4	59,725
1992	Wales	207.7	-4.3	53,758
1992	S.West	193.9	-7.8	64,106
1992	S.East	192.8	-8.5	78,257
1992	Gr.Lon	202.0	-9.4	80,430
1992	N.Ire	145.5	-1.0	37,416
1992	Scot	193.2	0.2	55,883
1992	U.K.	208.1	-5.6	64,309
1993	North	206.3	-1.8	52,063
1993	Yorks&Humb	228.3	-1.6	52,706
1993	N.West	219.3	-3.0	56,104
1993	E.Mids	208.3	-2.8	54,451
1993	W.Mids	219.1	-4.5	61,850
1993	E.Ang	193.2	-2.7	58,132
1993	Wales	204.5	-1.6	52,908
1993	S.West	185.9	-4.1	61,472

Year	Region	Index	% Change	Std Price
1993	S.East	186.4	-3.3	75,653
1993	Gr.Lon	192.0	-4.9	76,459
1993	N.Ire	151.7	4.3	39,009
1993	Scot	196.4	1.6	56,801
1993	U.K.	202.1	-2.9	62,455
1994	North	203.6	-1.3	51,382
1994	Yorks&Humb	226.3	-0.9	52,253
1994	N.West	215.8	-1.6	55,205
1994	E.Mids	209.1	0.4	54,653
1994	W.Mids	218.3	-0.4	61,618
1994	E.Ang	195.8	1.3	58,906
1994	Wales	201.9	-1.2	52,255
1994	S.West	188.6	1.5	62,367
1994	S.East	189.8	1.8	77,027
1994	Gr.Lon	195.5	1.8	77,863
1994	N.Ire	162.1	6.9	41,692
1994	Scot	199.4	1.6	57,681
1994	U.K.	203.1	0.5	62,750
1995	North	195.9	-3.8	49,419
1995	Yorks&Humb	219.2	-3.1	50,617
1995	N.West	207.8	-3.7	53,147
1995	E.Mids	203.9	-2.5	53,293
1995	W.Mids	215.6	-1.2	60,853
1995	E.Ang	193.5	-1.1	58,229
1995	Wales	194.2	-3.8	50,250
1995	S.West	186.1	-1.3	61,548
1995	S.East	190.3	0.3	77,248
1995	Gr.Lon	194.9	-0.4	77,590
1995	N.Ire	172.8	6.6	44,444
1995	Scot	199.4	0.0	57,684
1995	U.K.	199.6	-1.7	61,666
1996	North	201.9	3.1	50,936
1996	Yorks&Humb	224.5	2.4	51,828
1996	N.West	210.7	1.4	53,892
1996	E.Mids	209.4	2.7	54,727
1996	W.Mids	224.6	4.2	63,387
1996	E.Ang	197.7	2.1	59,473
1996	Wales	205.5	5.9	53,192
1996	S.West	195.1	4.8	64,499
1996	S.East	199.9	5.0	81,120
1996	Gr.Lon	212.4	9.0	84,554
1996	N.Ire	204.5	18.3	52,577
1996	Scot	204.9	2.8	59,272
1996	U.K.	208.6	4.5	64,441
1997	North	206.5	2.3	52,113
1997	Yorks&Humb	228.5	1.8	52,764
1997	N.West	216.7	2.9	55,433
1997	E.Mids	221.5	5.8	57,887
1997	W.Mids	237.3	5.6	66,960
1997	E.Ang	211.0	6.7	63,472
1997	Wales	212.0	3.1	54,868

Year	Region	Index	% Change	Std Price
1997	S.West	209.7	7.5	69,335
1997	S.East	221.2	10.7	89,793
1997	Gr.Lon	246.3	16.0	98,075
1997	N.Ire	210.6	3.0	54,153
1997	Scot	204.7	-0.1	59,212
1997	U.K.	221.7	6.3	68,504
1998	North	211.2	2.3	53,300
1998	Yorks&Humb	229.8	0.5	53,051
1998	N.West	220.4	1.7	56,378
1998	E.Mids	229.9	3.8	60,086
1998	W.Mids	250.0	5.4	70,568
1998	E.Ang	224.4	6.4	67,512
1998	Wales	220.2	3.8	56,971
1998	S.West	226.4	8.0	74,848
1998	S.East	244.2	10.4	99,114
1998	Gr.Lon	272.3	10.5	108,407
1998	N.Ire	235.6	11.9	60,574
1998	Scot	209.8	2.5	60,681
1998	U.K.	233.7	5.4	72,196
1999	North	220.1	4.2	55,536
1999	Yorks&Humb	236.5	2.9	54,600
1999	N.West	231.0	4.8	59,079
1999	E.Mids	244.8	6.5	63,995
1999	W.Mids	254.7	1.9	71,883
1999	E.Ang	241.1	7.5	72,549
1999	Wales	232.3	5.5	60,114
1999	S.West	248.8	9.9	82,278
1999	S.East	271.2	11.0	110,061
1999	Gr.Lon	317.9	16.8	126,584
1999	N.Ire	248.8	5.6	63,978
1999	Scot	212.8	1.4	61,546
1999	U.K.	250.5	7.2	77,405
2000	North	221.9	0.8	55,998
2000	Yorks&Humb	243.9	3.2	56,322
2000	N.West	242.6	5.0	62,051
2000	E.Mids	265.0	8.2	69,258
2000	W.Mids	282.2	10.8	79,647
2000	E.Ang	279.7	16.0	84,135
2000	Wales	245.0	5.5	63,407
2000	S.West	291.0	17.0	96,226
2000	S.East	318.3	17.4	129,191
2000	Gr.Lon	373.6	17.5	148,753
2000	N.Ire	264.4	6.3	67,996
2000	Scot	214.2	0.7	61,964
2000	U.K.	275.1	9.8	85,005
2001	North	234.0	5.5	59,054
2001	Yorks&Humb	257.5	5.6	59,452
2001	N.West	255.7	5.4	65,396
2001	E.Mids	287.3	8.4	75,085
2001	W.Mids	301.5	6.8	85,084
2001	E.Ang	322.6	15.4	97,071

Year	Region	Index	% Change	Std Price
2001	Wales	263.8	7.7	68,267
2001	S.West	327.8	12.6	108,392
2001	S.East	354.7	11.4	143,960
2001	Gr.Lon	428.3	14.7	170,551
2001	N.Ire	296.8	12.2	76,322
2001	Scot	220.0	2.7	63,628
2001	U.K.	298.6	8.5	92,256
2002	North	271.4	16.0	68,485
2002	Yorks&Humb	297.7	15.6	68,736
2002	N.West	292.8	14.5	74,891
2002	E.Mids	361.7	25.9	94,551
2002	W.Mids	363.7	20.7	102,656
2002	E.Ang	386.0	19.6	116,133
2002	Wales	299.8	13.6	77,576
2002	S.West	403.4	23.0	133,367
2002	S.East	413.7	16.6	167,916
2002	Gr.Lon	499.4	16.6	198,834
2002	N.Ire	307.4	3.6	79,050
2002	Scot	238.5	8.4	68,988
2002	U.K.	350.6	17.4	108,342
2003	North	370.6	36.5	93,508
2003	Yorks&Humb	395.6	32.9	91,345
2003	N.West	366.3	25.1	93,705
2003	E.Mids	457.5	26.5	119,578
2003	W.Mids	460.7	26.7	130,015
2003	E.Ang	465.0	20.5	139,911
2003	Wales	397.2	32.5	102,796
2003	S.West	477.7	18.4	157,957
2003	S.East	483.8	17.0	196,384
2003	Gr.Lon	563.3	12.8	224,305
2003	N.Ire	340.3	10.7	87,507
2003	Scot	274.5	15.1	79,401
2003	U.K.	429.1	22.4	132,589
2004	North	490.3	32.3	123,704
2004	Yorks&Humb	495.0	25.1	114,299
2004	N.West	472.8	29.1	120,941
2004	E.Mids	541.4	18.3	141,510
2004	W.Mids	540.5	17.3	152,552
2004	E.Ang	522.3	12.3	157,134
2004	Wales	516.3	30.0	133,610
2004	S.West	545.4	14.2	180,340
2004	S.East	528.8	9.3	214,638
2004	Gr.Lon	608.5	8.0	242,296
2004	N.Ire	397.9	16.9	102,327
2004	Scot	330.6	20.4	95,637
2004	U.K.	507.6	18.3	156,831
2005	North	533.3	8.8	134,555
2005	Yorks&Humb	549.3	11.0	126,824
2005	N.West	523.7	10.8	133,949
2005	E.Mids	564.9	4.3	147,654
2005	W.Mids	565.4	4.6	159,568

Year	Region	Index	% Change	Std Price
2005	E.Ang	536.0	2.6	161,269
2005	Wales	553.7	7.3	143,298
2005	S.West	552.6	1.3	182,709
2005	S.East	537.0	1.5	217,963
2005	Gr.Lon	621.4	2.1	247,419
2005	N.Ire	486.0	22.1	124,965
2005	Scot	375.7	13.6	108,671
2005	U.K.	536.6	5.7	165,807
2006	North	567.3	6.4	143,148
2006	Yorks&Humb	602.4	9.7	139,099
2006	N.West	565.1	7.9	144,540
2006	E.Mids	599.4	6.1	156,676
2006	W.Mids	602.8	6.6	170,130
2006	E.Ang	581.1	8.4	174,816
2006	Wales	589.7	6.5	152,606
2006	S.West	587.5	6.3	194,244
2006	S.East	571.2	6.4	231,847
2006	Gr.Lon	680.9	9.6	271,127
2006	N.Ire	644.4	32.6	165,716
2006	Scot	421.7	12.2	121,974
2006	U.K.	581.3	8.3	179,601
2007	North	601.8	6.1	151,898
2007	Yorks&Humb	640.5	6.3	149,695
2007	N.West	596.8	5.6	152,650
2007	E.Mids	632.4	5.6	168,046
2007	W.Mids	640.7	6.2	179,048
2007	E.Ang	637.3	9.7	194,627
2007	Wales	640.7	8.7	165,472
2007	S.West	641.9	9.3	212,400
2007	S.East	636.9	11.5	265,117
2007	Gr.Lon	776.6	14.2	320,847
2007	N.Ire	844.5	31.1	221,004
2007	Scot	488.2	15.8	141,158
2007	U.K.	635.9	9.4	198,898
2008	North	547.2	-9.1	138,067
2008	Yorks&Humb	580.0	-9.4	133,920
2008	N.West	558.3	-6.5	142,793
2008	E.Mids	582.4	-8.0	152,118
2008	W.Mids	591.9	-7.6	167,055
2008	E.Ang	600.8	-5.7	180,746
2008	Wales	579.4	-9.6	149,935
2008	S.West	583.2	-9.1	192,825
2008	S.East	588.6	-7.6	238,923
2008	Gr.Lon	705.3	-9.3	280,833
2008	N.Ire	679.2	-19.6	174,658
2008	Scot	478.2	-2.1	138,312
2008	U.K.	585.9	-7.9	181,032
2009	North	500.2	-8.6	126,212
2009	Yorks&Humb	526.3	-9.3	121,532
2009	N.West	492.8	-11.7	126,061
2009	E.Mids	518.2	-11.0	135,459

Year	Region	Index	% Change	Std Price
2009	W.Mids	534.1	-9.8	150,728
2009	E.Ang	520.2	-13.4	156,512
2009	Wales	512.0	–11.6	132,501
2009	S.West	540.0	-7.4	178,552
2009	S.East	532.1	-9.6	215,968
2009	Gr.Lon	622.0	-11.8	247,648
2009	N.Ire	563.7	-17.0	144,968
2009	Scot	426.6	-10.8	123,398
2009	U.K.	524.6	-10.5	162,085
2010	North	511.5	2.3	129,069
2010	Yorks&Humb	538.2	2.3	124,274
2010	N.West	486.7	-1.3	124,483
2010	E.Mids	541.7	4.5	141,580
2010	W.Mids	549.5	2.9	155,095
2010	E.Ang	540.9	4.0	162,737
2010	Wales	530.3	3.6	137,233
2010	S.West	568.5	5.3	187,965
2010	S.East	561.4	5.5	227,857
2010	Gr.Lon	659.9	6.1	262,741
2010	N.Ire	506.2	-10.2	130,183
2010	Scot	421.4	-1.2	166,739
2010	U.K.	539.6	2.9	166,739
2011	North	483.1	-5.6	121,897
2011	Yorks&Humb	513.2	-4.6	118,511
2011	N.West	485.0	-0.4	124,043
2011	E.Mids	517.9	-4.4	135,380
2011	W.Mids	530.9	-3.4	149,845
2011	E.Ang	544.1	0.6	163,693
2011	Wales	521.5	-1.7	134,952
2011	S.West	547.3	-3.7	180,946
2011	S.East	553.1	-1.5	224,489
2011	Gr.Lon	659.6	0.0	262,633
2011	N.Ire	444.1	-12.3	114,202
2011	Scot	406.8	-3.5	117,675
2011	U.K.	525.4	-2.6	162,322
2012	North	478.1	-1.0	120,635
2012	Yorks&Humb	509.1	-0.8	117,544
2012	N.West	468.6	-3.4	119,851
2012	E.Mids	523.1	1.0	136,716
2012	W.Mids	528.8	-0.4	149,235
2012	E.Ang	540.7	-0.6	162,675
2012	Wales	505.6	-3.0	130,836
2012	S.West	553.1	1.1	182,894
2012	S.East	558.8	1.0	226,832
2012	Gr.Lon	674.4	2.2	268,539
2012	N.Ire	405.4	-8.7	104,248
2012	Scot	384.3	-5.5	111,162
2012	UK	522.1	-0.6	161,308
2013	North	496.8	3.92	125,363
2013	Yorks&Humb	527.3	3.59	121,766
2013	N.West	501.9	7.11	128,367

Year	Region	Index	% Change	Std Price
2013	E.Mids	539.2	3.08	140,925
2013	W.Mids	540.7	2.26	152,613
2013	E.Ang	551.1	1.93	165,810
2013	Wales	557.3	10.23	144,216
2013	S.West	565.8	2.28	187,064
2013	S.East	591.0	5.76	239,892
2013	Gr.Lon	737.2	9.31	293,527
2013	N.Ire	368.9	-9.00	94,861
2013	Scot	400.5	4.21	115,842
2013	UK	547.0	4.77	169,003
2014	North	507.7	2.2	128,099
2014	Yorks&Humb	562.1	6.6	129,799
2014	N.West	540.4	7.7	138,234
2014	E.Mids	584.3	8.4	152,730
2014	W.Mids	574.3	6.2	162,071
2014	E.Ang	601.2	9.1	180,878
2014	Wales	572.8	2.8	148,236
2014	S.West	610.5	7.9	201,845
2014	S.East	654.6	10.8	265,698
2014	Gr.Lon	855.2	16.0	340,532
2014	N.Ire	430.8	16.8	110,790
2014	Scot	430.2	7.4	124,451
2014	UK	593.5	8.5	183,391
2015 Q1	North	524.1	3.6	132,235
2015 Q1	Yorks&Humb	595.8	5.8	137,572
2015 Q1	N.West	567.9	3.5	145,269
2015 Q1	E.Mids	609.6	1.4	159,334
2015 Q1	W.Mids	615.8	1.5	173,792
2015 Q1	E.Ang	612.5	0.8	184,275
2015 Q1	Wales	585.2	-0.8	151,438
2015 Q1	S.West	632.6	4.2	209,177
2015 Q1	S.East	690.7	1.1	280,354
2015 Q1	Gr.Lon	930.1	4.1	370,352
2015 Q1	N.Ire	401.3	-8.2	103,198
2015 Q1	Scot	439.8	-2.8	127,213
2015 Q1	U.K.	622.5	2.7	192,327
2015 Q2	North	534.0	1.9	134,746
2015 Q2	Yorks&Humb	623.2	4.6	143,892
2015 Q2	N.West	580.7	2.3	148,537
2015 Q2	E.Mids	628.4	3.1	164,248
2015 Q2	W.Mids	629.0	2.2	177,535
2015 Q2	E.Ang	678.0	10.7	203,967
2015 Q2	Wales	578.9	-1.1	149,813
2015 Q2	S.West	640.1	1.2	211,634
2015 Q2	S.East	715.5	3.6	290,435
2015 Q2	Gr.Lon	981.9	5.6	390,960
2015 Q2	N.Ire	441.2	9.9	113,453
2015 Q2	Scot	477.1	8.5	138,003
2015 Q2	U.K.	643.2	3.3	198,722

INTEREST RATES

BANK OF ENGLAND BASE RATES 1999–PRESENT

Date	Rate
7 Jan 99	6.00%
4 Feb 99	5.50%
3 Mar 99	5.50%
8 April 99	5.25%
6 May 99	5.25%
10 Jun 99	5.00%
8 Jul 99	5.00%
5 Aug 99	5.00%
8 Sep 99	5.25%
7 Oct 99	5.25%
4 Nov 99	5.50%
9 Dec 99	5.50%
13 Jan 00	5.75%
10 Feb 00	6.00%
9 Mar 00	6.00%
6 Apr 00	6.00%
4 May 00	6.00%
7 Jun 00	6.00%
6 Jul 00	6.00%
3 Aug 00	6.00%
7 Sept 00	6.00%
5 Oct 00	6.00%
9 Nov 00	6.00%
7 Dec 00	6.00%
11 Jan 01	6.00%
8 Feb 01	5.75%
8 Mar 01	5.75%
5 Apr 01	5.50%
10 May 01	5.25%
6 Jun 01	5.25%
5 Jul 01	5.25%
2 Aug 01	5.00%
6 Sep 01	5.00%
18 Sep 01	4.75%
4 Oct 01	4.50%
7 Nov 01	4.00%

Date	Rate
5 Dec 01	4.00%
10 Jan 02	4.00%
7 Feb 02	4.00%
7 Mar 02	4.00%
4 Apr 02	4.00%
9 May 02	4.00%
21 Dec 02	4.50%
6 Jun 02	4.00%
4 Jul 02	4.00%
1 Aug 02	4.00%
5 Sep 02	4.00%
10 Oct 02	4.00%
7 Nov 02	4.00%
5 Dec 02	4.00%
9 Jan 03	4.00%
6 Feb 03	3.75%
6 Mar 03	3.75%
10 Apr 03	3.75%
8 May 03	3.75%
5 Jun 03	3.75%
10 Jul 03	3.50%
7 Aug 03	3.50%
4 Sep 03	3.50%
9 Oct 03	3.50%
6 Nov 03	3.75%
4 Dec 03	3.75%
8 Jan 04	3.75%
5 Feb 04	4.00%
4 Mar 04	4.00%
8 Apr 04	4.00%
6 May 04	4.25%
10 Jun 04	4.50%
8 Jul 04	4.50%
5 Aug 04	4.75%
9 Sep 04	4.75%
7 Oct 04	4.75%
4 Nov 04	4.75%
9 Dec 04	4.75%
13 Jan 05	4.75%
10 Feb 05	4.75%
10 Mar 05	4.75%
7 Apr 05	4.75%
9 May 05	4.75%
9 Jun 05	4.75%
7 Jul 05	4.75%

Date	Rate
4 Aug 05	4.50%
8 Sep 05	4.50%
6 Oct 05	4.50%
10 Nov 05	4.50%
8 Dec 05	4.50%
12 Jan 06	4.50%
9 Feb 06	4.5%
9 Mar 06	4.5%
6 Apr 06	4.5%
4 May 06	4.5%
4 Jun 06	4.5%
6 Jul 06	4.5%
3 Aug 06	4.75%
7 Sep 06	4.75%
5 Oct 06	4.75%
9 Nov 06	5.00%
7 Dec 06	5.00%
11 Jan 07	5.25%
8 Feb 07	5.25%
8 Mar 07	5.25%
5 Apr 07	5.25%
10 May 07	5.5%
7 Jun 07	5.5%
5 Jul 07	5.75%
2 Aug 07	5.75%
6 Sep 07	5.75%
4 Oct 07	5.75%
8 Nov 07	5.75%
6 Dec 07	5.5%
10 Jan 08	5.5%
07 Feb 08	5.25%
06 Mar 08	5.25%
10 Apr 08	5.00%
8 May 08	5.00%
5 Jun 08	5.00%
10 Jul 08	5.00%
7 Aug 08	5.00%
4 Sep 08	5.00%
8 Oct 08	4.50%
6 Nov 08	3.00%
14 Dec 08	2.00%
8 Jan 09	1.50%
5 Feb 09	1.00%
5 Mar 09	0.50%
9 Apr 09	0.50%

Date	Rate
7 May 09	0.50%
4 Jun 09	0.50%
9 Jul 09	0.50%
6 Aug 09	0.50%
10 Sep 09	0.50%
8 Oct 09	0.50%
5 Nov 09	0.50%
10 Dec 09	0.50%
7 Jan 10	0.50%
4 Feb 10	0.50%
4 Mar 10	0.50%
8 Apr 10	0.50%
10 May 10	0.50%
10 Jun 10	0.50%
08 Jul 10	0.50%
05 Aug 10	0.50%
09 Sep 10	0.50%
07 Oct 10	0.50%
04 Nov 10	0.50%
09 Dec 10	0.50%
13 Jan 11	0.50%
10 Feb 11	0.50%
10 Mar 11	0.50%
7 Apr 11	0.50%
5 May 11	0.50%
9 Jun 11	0.50%
7 Jul 11	0.50%
4 Aug 11	0.50%
8 Sep 11	0.50%
6 Oct 11	0.50%
10 Nov 11	0.50%
8 Dec 11	0.50%
12 Jan 12	0.50%
9 Feb 12	0.50%
8 Mar 12	0.50%
5 Apr 12	0.50%
10 May 12	0.50%
7 Jun 12	0.50%
5 Jul 12	0.50%
2 Aug 12	0.50%
5 Jul 12	0.50%
2 Aug 12	0.50%
6 Sep 12	0.50%
4 Oct 12	0.50%
8 Nov 12	0.50%

Date	Rate
6 Dec 12	0.50%
10 Jan 13	0.50%
7 Feb 13	0.50%
7 Mar 13	0.50%
4 Apr 13	0.50%
9 May 13	0.50%
13 Jun 13	0.50%
13 Jul 13	0.50%
13 Aug 13	0.50%
5 Sept 13	0.50%
10 Oct 13	0.50%
7 Nov 13	0.50%
5 Dec 13	0.50%
9 Jan 14	0.50%
6 Feb 14	0.50%
6 Mar 14	0.50%
10 Apr 14	0.50%
8 May 14	0.50%
5 Jun 14	0.50%
10 Jul 14	0.50%
7 Aug 14	0.50%
4 Sept 14	0.50%
9 Oct 14	0.50%
6 Nov 14	0.50%
4 Dec 14	0.50%
8 Jan 15	0.50%
5 Feb 15	0.50%
5 Mar 15	0.50%
9 April 15	0.50%
11 May 15	0.50%
4 Jun 15	0.50%
9 Jul 15	0.50%
6 Aug 15	0.50%
10 Sept 15	0.50%